SHAKKAI

S·H·A·K·K·A·I

Woman of the Sacred Garden

LYNN V. ANDREWS

HarperPerennial
A Division of HarperCollinsPublishers

A hardcover edition of this book was published in 1992 by HarperCollins Publishers.

HarperCollins books may be purchased for educational, business, or sales promotional use. For information please write: Special Markets Department, HarperCollins Publishers, Inc., 10 East 53rd Street, New York, NY 10022.

First HarperPerennial edition published 1993.

Designed by Jessica Shatan
Illustrations by Ginny Joyner

The Library of Congress has catalogued the hardcover edition as follows:
Andrews, Lynn V.
  Shakkai : woman of the sacred garden / Lynn V. Andrews. — 1st ed.
  p.   cm.
  ISBN 0-06-016711-4 (cloth)
  1. Andrews, Lynn V. 2. Gardens, Japanese—Miscellanea.
3. Nature—Religious aspects. 4. Women—Religious life. I. Title.
BP610.A54158 1992   91-58368
299'.93—dc20

ISBN 0-06-092179-X (pbk.)

93 94 95 96 97 ❖/HC 10 9 8 7 6 5 4 3 2 1

I dedicate this book to Shakkai, my teacher,
who is the mother of peace within my heart.

But with no less love and respect, I would like to acknowledge Kathy Duckworth for her tireless hours at the computer; Janet Goldstein, my editor at HarperCollins; Al Lowman, my agent and friend; Cyrena Kopcha for her wisdom and insight; Caroline Kulhanek for her friendship; and Anita, my gatekeeper and secretary; and all of you who are very gracious and loving friends of the Sisterhood of the Shields. Without every one of you, this work would not be the same.

Some of the names and places in this book have been changed to protect the privacy of those involved.

◆

The world has a beginning
that is the mother of the world.
Once you've found the mother,
thereby you know the child.
Once you know the child,
you return to keep the mother,
not perishing though the body dies.
Close your eyes, shut your doors,
and you do not toil all your life.
Open your eyes, carry out your affairs,
and you are not saved all your life.
Seeing the small *is called clarity,*
keeping flexible is called strength.
Using the shining radiance,
you return again to the light,
not leaving anything to harm yourself.
This is called entering the eternal.

—LAO-TZU,
TAO TE CHING

◆

Contents

Prologue

All I could hear was the sound of wind at high speed. The whistle was so piercing and intense that it hurt my ears. I saw nothing but the white flower. The samurai stood before me, in his position of power, his sword raised to strike. I did not see it move. My eyes fixed on the lotus blossom; I saw it lift almost imperceptibly into the air and then settle back down onto its stalk. It was cleanly severed. I had not blinked. I had not seen the blade move through the air, it had been so swift. The samurai's movements had been impeccable, faster than a cobra's strike.

The cool morning glow of the sun shone down through the branches of the bamboo trees that surrounded the pond next to where we stood. The snow-covered cone of Mount Fuji glistened in poised reflection and power. I knew that all existence was perfect, that this lifetime was about to end, like the life of the lotus blossom. The flowering of my youth was gone, but the fragrance of my life force continued. Soon I would be like that magnificent flower, my head severed from my body and yet still resting on the stalk as if nothing had happened, as if everything was as it had been.

I looked toward the samurai, knowing that our hearts beat as one. There was no space between us. There was no difference, man or woman. It did not matter that no one understood our bond. The mysteries that we had shared together were ours alone. I was holding my sacred *hu*, my gourd that represented the *shakkai*, the captured landscape of our lives together. Everything was represented there—the sacred mountain, the powerful spirit that loomed over our life and permeated our beings with sacredness every moment that we had been alive. Represented in this tiny garden was a reflection pond that mirrored the light of the mountain spirits, just as the pond beside us reflected the magnificence of Fuji. Too tiny was the garden to step into with anything but our spirit feet, and we would walk there for all time, knowing the blending of our souls and the history of our work on this earth.

There were no words between the samurai and me. We knelt down facing each other on the tatami mat spread with sacred white cloth. I placed the *hu* between us. We had created a magic that would live on beyond our years. I bowed before my samurai as he raised his sword. I looked again at the lotus blossom shimmering in the sunlight. It was still moist with the morning dew, each droplet reflecting a tiny picture of our sacred mountain, just as every one of us reflects the light of the Great Spirit. In moments I would be like the lotus blossom, forever gone to this reality and yet reflecting its magical light into the universe. The last thing I heard was the swish of the blade. It sounded like the freedom of the wind that I so dearly loved. How fitting that it was my last awareness. Our sacrifice was the offering of life to the highest dream.

SHAKKAI

Introduction

This book is like a series of clouds drifting high above in the trade winds. Each cloud, each chapter, is like a dream, like a shadow between our earthly life and the brilliance of the sun in eternity. This shadow is not a darkness, but a brilliant reality that is usually hidden from view. I call it a shadow because it is partially transparent and lives in a state of vulnerability and clarity that is usually unknown to our physical existence.

A long time ago, I brought a radio to relatives of one of my aboriginal teachers in central Australia. These beautiful people had never been spoiled by civilized society. They had lived according to their traditional ways for centuries. Their lives were simple and complete, and I wanted to give them a great gift of enjoyment, something that would make them laugh and tell them a little about another world. I set the radio down on the ground in their hut, and I spoke about music and the sounds on the invisible airwaves. They looked at me as if I were mad, laughing and poking fun at me. Then I brought in my shaman sister and we related this radio to a sacred ceremony, a ceremony that they had, indeed, just taken part in. They had gone into the sacred Dreamtime through the rainbow gateway in a crystal, and they had met guardians of the other worlds. I told them that this radio was not sacred like their crystals, but that it had a purpose nevertheless, and if they would keep in mind their ceremony and how they had moved into another reality while still lying on the ground around the central fire, then perhaps they would understand what I was trying to say.

I turned the radio on and said, "It is just as if you were tuning your own instrument, your own magnificent body, to be able to accept other levels of consciousness. That is how I want you to see this radio." I flipped the dial and Beethoven's Fifth Symphony

filled the hut with all of its beautiful harmonics and levels of
sound. They sat around the radio in wonderment, and we talked
late into the night about what energies float on the airwaves and
how, when you tune in to a radio station, the signal doesn't mix
with those of other stations. Our bodies and our consciousness
tune in to a specific vibration, a certain energy flow that is all our
own; we are all made of energy, and our thoughts help to create
that energy and our state of health or disease. We, as unique
beings, do not all vibrate at the same level. When you are thinking
a certain way in your life, your energy field and the electromagnetic field around your body vibrate at a certain pitch, just as a
radio selects a given frequency among all the different bands. Very
simplistically speaking, because of that, other lifetimes do not mix
with this one.

We spent many days talking about enlightenment and past and
future lives, and finally the elders of the village decided that
though they honored my gift and it had been a fascinating experience, they would like me to take the radio with me when I left.
They feared it would become an addiction and take them away
from the sacred center of their own spirit, that it would remove
them from the powers of their ceremonies, though the experience
had lent scope to their knowledge of the outside world. They felt
they already knew in a different way about our world of civiliza-
tion.

The teachings in *Shakkai* are about this miracle of other dimensions existing right along with this one. In thinking of a future life
or a past one, remember that you are not going up or down a lad-
der in a linear fashion. Perhaps it is best to think of this phe-
nomenon as being like the layers of a cake, all part of the greater
whole, each level of filling and cake, one layer upon another, until
you experience the cake as a total reality, which, indeed, gives
you the frosting on the cake, the eternal life that we are all searching for.

Each chapter of this book, for the most part, is a journey into a
different level of spirit that, as my teachers have told me, exists at
the same time as our current physical existence. I learned that a

future lifetime is a great teacher, and that to become centered in the reality of this present life, to become enlightened in this lifetime, to move toward evolvement in a more positive way, one needs to experience a past lifetime and a future lifetime.

This book is about a future life that balances the energy and the lessons that I learned with the Woman of Wyrrd in a past life, which was my first experience with moving from one radio band, or energy level, to another. This process is called "double dreaming," and is a technique that can be learned through the teachings of shamanism. Through it, you can develop your capabilities so that you are able to dream within the dream and actually project yourself or your double into a time span of experience different from your present reality. In terms of the logical mind, this concept might seem illogical, but in fact, as obscure as it sounds, double dreaming is possible, as I can attest from my own experience. The process takes a great deal of careful practice and work, and you must have a powerful teacher to guide you. Once you have learned how to tune your instrument, a whole new world of mystery and possibilities can be explored. But it is not to be played with, because it is a sacred process meant to further you on your path of enlightenment.

I have written about my past life journey with the Woman of Wyrrd in sixteenth-century England to help give you courage to trace your own spiritual heritage. *Shakkai, Woman of the Sacred Garden* was written to open doors in your heart and give you strength to redefine your own feelings about life, death, and your sacred path of evolvement. Because *Shakkai* is about a future life, the experience challenged my own traditional ideas about life and death. I felt a sense of timelessness, as if the life with Shakkai could have taken place in ancient history or in the future. We were living in a rural mountain setting, so, in a way, we were out of time. Certain events were mentioned, however, by Shakkai having to do with explorations on the planet Venus, wars that had come and gone, and earthquakes in Asia, that made me realize that we were definitely living beyond the year 2000. I was instructed not to write about these things, because this is not a book of prophecy. The exact date in the future was not given to me, because in a sense, this life with Shakkai would imply my death in my present lifetime and would not be concurrent with the way of learning in the Sisterhood of the Shields.

The portrayal of time frame was one difficulty I had, and the use of Japanese words was another. We have so few words in English to describe the transformation into the spiritual experience. We use clichés like *vibration* and *levels,* but to invent or use a special vocabulary would make these teachings more obscure than they already are. I decided to use familiar words to convey the meaning and the truth that I want to share with you.

Now I will tell you the story from the Woman of Shakkai, who lives within the compound of her sacred garden near the foot of Mount Fuji in Japan. Her name is Shakkai, which literally means "the captured landscape." She is the mistress of her own magical spirit, and chose to live out the remainder of her years hidden away within her exquisite garden wilderness. She created a *shakkai,* a garden temple of several acres, in which to worship her inner mirror of flowers, the sacred Tao. Every moment of her life is spent in serenity and peace within her private and mysterious universe of jade gourds, eternal fires, and the Isles of the Immortals. Shakkai is my teacher in my future life in Japan.

A Calling from the Dreamtime

♦

"CLEAR EVENING AFTER RAIN"

The sun sinks towards the horizon.
The light clouds are blown away.
A rainbow shines on the river.
The last raindrops spatter the rocks.
Cranes and herons soar in the sky.
Fat bears feed along the banks.
I wait here for the west wind.
And enjoy the crescent moon
Shining through misty bamboos.

— TU FU

♦

Something happened in the summer of 1990 that changed my life forever. It seemed such an ordinary thing to do—plant bamboo around my house so that the wind could murmur through the leaves. The rustling sound and the dancing light comforted me and reminded me of my long summers in the north of Canada with my teachers Agnes Whistling Elk and Ruby Plenty Chiefs. As the sun shone through the delicately quaking leaves, I was reminded of days long gone, their memory washing over me like the cool spring waters at Estavan Falls in Manitoba.

In the heart of the thriving metropolis of Los Angeles, the city's chaotic surge whirling around me, I found myself waking up from an hour-long meditation. I was sitting on the ground in my backyard, looking up at the bamboo and the light penetrating through its branches. On the periphery of my consciousness there was a knocking, a shadowy memory awaiting admittance, an invitation to enter, but I could not find the door, the gateway through which to let it in. Then my mind relaxed and my heart opened with a flood of intense emotion. So often in my work with Agnes and Ruby I have been at this stage, at a singular moment like this, when suddenly everything is outside of time and space, where there is no movement, but only pure being. I can count such moments on the fingers of one hand. They have such a profound meaning for me. They are like the opening of an eye, looking out into the world and seeing reality for one moment, and then the eye closes and the vision is lost. Only the memory is left. That memory takes many forms, but it is always surrounded by light, as pure and bright as the glow filtering through the stalks of bamboo.

On this day Agnes came up behind me in my dreaming. She placed her spirit hands on my shoulders, gently but firmly. "It is time, my daughter," she said, her voice like the rushing sound in the wind. "It is time to hold a ceremony to bring in the powers of the west, of rebirth and transformation. We will meet by the new moon in my cabin in the far north, and we will hold hands across this illusion of time that separates us. I will make your future journey known to you. You see, my daughter, the bamboo is an invitation to you. As the dolphins led your way to Australia, the bamboo is like a chimera. It reminds you of something, but you know not what. It stirs a memory within you, and you feel a longing. *Do not get lost in your longing.* There will be a time to understand this feeling, but it is not now.

"You have been through a test of wills. You have moved through a darkness like the shadows that surround a dying person. You had to move through the darkness of your pain alone, so that you could emerge on the other side through the effort of your own individual will. From your extraordinary isolation of will, you feel the first taste of true achievement. This achievement looks like understanding, like a knowing in the silence of the night, but the day of wisdom will come and the sun will rise, and there is a meaning to all the pain and to all the joy. You have healed from the meeting with the Woman of Wyrrd. You had quite a tussle with your past lifetime, and now to recalibrate the balance of your lifetimes, your future lifetime, which you soon will experience, is stalking you just as a story stalks you. It circles you in the light of day through the voice of the stalks of bamboo. At night it comes in your dreams, and it is the meaning of the hooded figure you see before dawn."

As I awoke from the dream, I heard a sharp crack behind me. My head swiveled around. A beautiful barn owl swept its wings, furled them beneath its feathered neck, and settled into an acacia tree. Her eyes were watching me, glowing amber, as the sun set behind her over the hills to the west. To me the owl is the sign of the Sacred Clown. She represents my teacher, Agnes Whistling Elk. I knew I had only a few days before the new moon and my journey to the north.

· 2 ·

Big Medicine Country

◆

We live on earth to celebrate our life in unison with the universe.

— NATIVE AMERICAN SHAMAN

◆

The big medicine sky of Manitoba seemed to stretch for hundreds of miles in all directions. I sniffed the late spring air that floated in through the open car window as I sped down the blacktop road toward Agnes Whistling Elk's cabin. It seemed that I had been driving this road for lifetimes, and each time it appeared different. I saw different colors, different birds. The formation of the clouds seemed to have changed to such a degree that the sky was new to me and filled me with excitement and awe. Going to see my teachers is forever thrilling, but the excitement is not always of a peaceful nature. There's usually a tinge of fear at the back of my throat, and my stomach is often tied in knots by the time I get there. I never know what to expect and I always know that the person who arrives there is going to be very changed when she leaves.

I thought back to a woman standing before me at a book signing not long ago. She was lovely and wanted to know what path I was studying and what I had learned from my teachers. I had scrambled through my mind for the proper words to express the deep nature of their teachings and how they encompass a whole world of truth. I laughed to myself as I thought of how I had mumbled something to her about the fact that even though Agnes and Ruby were Native American, they did not teach me traditional Native American medicine. They were teaching me a process of shamanism that was not Native American in origin and was very ancient. The look in the woman's eyes was blank. She obviously did not understand what I was trying to tell her. I spoke about finding the self-wound within and healing our emotional nature and taking our power as women in the 1990s and learning how to communicate better with our families. Then there was a spark of understanding and we began to converse.

I remembered the time, years ago, when I had first started working with Agnes, and how she would never rely on words to describe something to me or to answer a question. She would always grab me and take me outside and put me through something experiential so that I could form an answer to my own question. I smiled when I thought of how difficult that would be in a bookstore in Pittsburgh. I could not take someone outside into the wilderness. I would get so frustrated because I could not give them the proper answers, or explain in a few minutes a process of enlightenment nearly as old as the earth itself. How do you make your own personal experience and dream part of someone else's reality? After all these years, I now realize what Agnes and Ruby had faced when trying to teach me, a fledgling in this sacred world. How difficult it must have been for them, having to struggle with the differences in language and the differences in our cultural backgrounds. What a feat it had been to bring me to the point where I could teach and work with people as they had once worked with me.

As these thoughts montaged through my mind, a large bird that had been working on a roadkill on the shoulder of the road suddenly loomed up over the hood of my car. Its wingspan was at least as broad as my car. I caught my breath and cried aloud, "Grandfather eagle, forgive me for almost killing you." I screeched to a stop, skidding my car halfway across the road. Taking some tobacco from the beaded pouch that was tied to my belt, I left it on the wind as an offering to the spirit of the bird. I looked nervously for traffic in either direction. There was none. Stepping out of the car, I turned in all directions, looking for the eagle, but he was nowhere to be seen. I couldn't believe he had disappeared so quickly. I had never seen an eagle take a roadkill. He should have been circling in the updrafts high above me. Then I heard what I thought was laughter off to the left side of the road, behind a stand of chokecherry bushes. I peered into them, but saw nothing. Then more laughter came from the right side of the road, from behind some rocks. A thrill of fear went up my spine. I sensed that I was in danger, but I couldn't imagine where it was coming from. Then a man's figure slowly began to emerge from behind the chokecherry bushes, wearing a dark shirt, black pants, and a black hat. The figure was tall and thin. At first I didn't recognize him.

"Well, it looks like you haven't learned much since the last time I saw you," the man said. And I realized it was Ben.

My mouth dropped open in stunned surprise. Then I heard a voice from behind the rocks. I spun around to see Drum stand up, heavier than he was the last time I had seen him, wearing a Pendleton shirt and jeans, with his hair tied back in a long ponytail, his dark Native American face even darker than before. He was wearing yellow sunglasses.

"We told you you'd never learn anything with Agnes Whistling Elk or Ruby Plenty Chiefs."

I looked over at Ben and then at Drum, and something bubbled up inside me. Instead of feeling fear, I found myself laughing so hard that I had to sit down in the center of the deserted highway. Tears were running down my cheeks, and then I realized that I couldn't stop laughing. Ben and Drum were standing on either side of the road, legs spread, Ben slowly shaking a rattle and Drum making movements in the air with his fingers, his eyes shut, his head back. A voice inside me said: This is nuts. You don't believe in this sorcery stuff. And I remembered Agnes's words in Nepal when I had been so frightened by a healer in the foothills of the Himalayas. "Sorcerers never kill you," she had said. "They make you kill yourself." And I thought: Yes, you give away your power because of your own terror and your own fear.

Suddenly I stopped laughing and stood up, wiping the tears off my cheeks, and smiled at Ben and Drum, who, surprised at my sudden movements, decided to stop playing their games. They came over to me, shook my hand, and said hello for the first time in many years. I got back in my car and pulled off to the side of the road, where I offered Ben and Drum a sandwich and a couple of bottles of Coca-Cola. We sat down by the side of the road and talked for some time. Ben and Drum had been the apprentices of Red Dog, the sorcerer who had been my adversary for so many years. He had taught me how to identify evil and understand the dark side. I had learned how to fight, and I had learned how to be a good enemy. That was all past now, because Red Dog had gone on to the other side two years ago. No one had known what had happened to Ben and Drum. I had not seen them in years, or heard anything about them.

"Where have you been?" I finally asked.

Ben and Drum looked at each other and laughed, as though sharing a very private joke. Even though they had great disdain for women and certainly did not like my teachers and were afraid of them, there was a certain bond between us. We had been involved in many experiences over the years, even if we had been at opposite ends of a coup stick. They had definitely not fared well in pitting themselves against the Sisterhood of the Shields.

"Well, in answer to your question," Ben said, "we have been living in Red Dog's cabin for several years now. We have traveled a lot and we have learned many things."

"That's good," I said.

"What happened when you swerved your car back there?" Drum asked, squinting his eyes at me.

"A big bird, it looked like an eagle, was feeding on that roadkill. It came up over the top of my car. I wanted to make sure I didn't hit him."

They both laughed hysterically, slapping their knees.

"We sure didn't see any eagle," Drum and Ben said in unison and laughed some more. "We just thought you'd lost control of your car."

"Very funny," I said. "I suppose you want me to think you did sorcery on me. Aren't we past all that by now?"

Both of them became very still and serious. Drum looked at me and said, "Power is the only game in town. You have your way of personal power. We have ours."

Then Ben said, "You are part of the Sisterhood of the Shields. What you do has nothing to do with us. I am Native American, and we follow the old ways as they are taught to us."

"Could have fooled me," I said. Then I started to laugh, and they laughed with me, their high cheekbones and black hair shining in the afternoon light.

Ben and Drum stood up abruptly. "Say hello to Agnes and Ruby for us," Drum said as they turned on their heels and walked straight out into the field, away from the road and any visible trail.

Ben called over his shoulder, "Don't take any wooden nickels." And they disappeared over a hill as quickly as they had appeared.

That afternoon, Agnes Whistling Elk and I sat around the potbellied stove in the center of her cabin. A blustering south wind beat against the old boards on the outside of the cabin, and they groaned and strained against the pressure. The branches of the big pine tree rubbed against the tin roof of the cabin, making ghostly noises. Agnes was darning a pair of socks as she spoke to me. In the firelight from the gas lanterns, I could see her salt-and-pepper hair pulled back and caught at the nape of her neck. She wore a red sweater and a faded blue skirt. A red beaded shield hung around her neck. I noticed she was wearing the silver earrings that Ani had given her in Nepal. They reflected the dancing light from the fire, and I could see the ancient Nepali design carved into their surface. My heart brimmed with love for this grandmotherly woman who had taught me so much. Agnes is often called "the One Who Knows How," because she travels the magical trails of the universe and knows the truth. She is a consummate woman of power.

Agnes looked up from the work she was doing and slowly turned her gaze toward me. Her deep brown eyes were tinged with the amber glow of the wood fire, giving them the yellow intensity of a mountain lion, until she moved her head and softened her expression. Then she had a quizzical look on her face. She said nothing for several moments, and then we both burst out laughing.

"You think you've come a very long way, don't you?" she finally asked, taking one last stitch with her needle and tying a knot with her calloused brown fingers.

"Yes, I feel I have," I answered.

"For as far as you have come," Agnes said, "there is still that length to go, and even farther. I do not say these words to make you feel tired or sad or as if you need to give up."

There was silence between us for several minutes, then I said, "There is something inside me, Agnes, that makes me not ever want to stop learning. Somehow, to come to the end of my apprenticeship makes me think of death, makes me feel like there's an end to life's magic in some way. It frightens me."

Agnes took a sip of tea with a floating grace in her fingers and a youthful twist to her wrist. She sniffed the steam rising from the cup. "That is why so many people enjoy living on the edge. They dwell in the world of becoming, and never completely accomplish, not really. They never truly *become*. They are afraid to own what they have accomplished, because somehow that would mean that they are finished. In actuality, becoming is only the beginning. Perhaps that is what you need to see, my daughter. That is part of your next teaching."

As I watched Agnes speak in her animated way, she appeared to become younger and more girlish in some imperceptible way. I observed her and listened in fascination.

"It is part of what we must learn together," she continued. "There will come a time when we will have learned all we can from each other. From each other, I say, because when a teacher has an apprentice, that teaching always extends in both directions. If it does not, then the teaching is not appropriate. I have learned much from you, Little Wolf," Agnes said, smiling almost to herself in a way that never ceased to make me a bit uncomfortable.

"I cannot imagine my life without you, Agnes."

"But you see, it is not as it appears," Agnes said. She tapped the top of the table with her knuckles. "Nothing is as it seems. You must remember this and never forget it. When you are no longer an apprentice, then you will be a true teacher. Then your apprenticeship is to someone different. It is to the Great Spirit. It is to the great deities that live on the other side. It is only then that you will learn what true apprenticeship really means."

Agnes stood and opened the window above her kitchen sink. A warm breeze blew through the curtains, making the daisy print dance like a field of wildflowers in the wind. Crow, the giant crow that was Agnes's longtime friend, lit on the sill and cawed loudly, demanding dinner. Agnes placed a large crust of bread into his open beak, and he flew away, sure to return moments later. Agnes walked across the room and sat in front of me. She looked at me questioningly because I was staring at her.

"What?" she finally asked.

"Agnes, there is a serenity about you that I have not seen in a very long time," I said.

"That's because you haven't been here in a long time," Ruby said, suddenly throwing open the door and joining us. She wore a denim skirt and a bright yellow ribbon shirt. Her face was dark from the sun, her blind eyes like blue shields set in a deeply furrowed expression of intensity. I was so happy to see Ruby, the tears were streaming down my cheeks. I got up and gave her a big hug, obviously ruffling her feathers, as she hugged me and then gently pushed me away. She smelled of cedar and the north wind.

"Come, come, now, Little Wolf. It hasn't been that long." Lovingly she pinched my cheek and slid into the chair on the other side of me.

Ruby is blind, but it is my experience that she has developed her senses to a point where she can see better than any of us. She is a woman of great abilities. They often call her "She Who Walks Last and Picks Up the Trail." That is the position of power.

Now I was sitting between them. In the past, this had always been a position of confrontation for me. First of all, I am much more comfortable when someone sits across the table from me. I rarely feel comfortable with someone sitting by my side. Now I had two women of power sitting on either side, toying with me. When this happened, I knew that my teaching had begun, but what teaching, I knew not. There was a long silence, and then suddenly both women started to laugh, casting their eyes toward the rafters, which were hung with herbs, blankets, and drums. Their laughter was so outrageous and silly that I couldn't help but join in the merriment with them, even though I was not sure what we were laughing about. But I knew it was something I had or hadn't done.

Ruby reached out, poked me in the ribs, and said, "Little Wolf, you're getting too fat. We have to make you work harder."

"I am not too fat. I'm in wonderful shape," I said indignantly. "Besides, Ruby, you can't even see me."

The old blind Native American woman, her hair pulled to the sides of her face in two gray braids reaching to her waist, shook her head and smiled. Her milky blue eyes appeared to have the vision of an eagle, even though I knew they were blind. She rubbed her hands together and blew the spirit of her breath across her flattened palms.

"Your energy field feels very big to me," Ruby said, holding her hands about two feet away from my body. "I don't want you to grow your body out to meet this big aura you're creating." She winked at me and then at Agnes, and the two of them started to laugh again.

"Ruby, what are you getting at? You know very well that I'm thin."

"All fat cats look alike," she said.

"Are you calling me a fat cat?" I asked.

"No, certainly not. You're a black wolf," Ruby said, now squinting at me.

"If you will excuse me for interrupting you two," Agnes said, arching her eyebrows and leaning forward. "You have gained great power, Lynn, from your journey with the Woman of Wyrrd. Ruby is commenting on your aura, which has grown and become much more powerful. What often happens is that when you grow a big aura, your body grows to fit that aura." She patted me on the shoulder. "Your hoops of energy are developing just fine."

"You know, Agnes, I think I can explain myself without your help," Ruby retorted with a sniff.

"Looked to me like you were having trouble. Sorry."

I was so happy to be with my two teachers, it wouldn't have made any difference what they said to me. I was just basking in their presence and energy, so beautifully contagious. Again Crow landed on the sill of the window, cawing for more food. Agnes chattered to him in her native tongue and fed him more crusts of bread. She picked up a red-tailed hawk's feather and stroked the top of his head with it, which he liked immensely. He almost responded like a cat being stroked, twisting his body this way and that, preening himself with his long, pointed beak.

Yet, no matter how good I felt with these two women, Ruby always put me ill at ease. It was not because I didn't love her, or because she didn't love me. It wasn't a matter of love. It was a matter of my own personal power and evolvement and the various stages in which I found myself along my path. Ruby always seemed to appear in my life when I thought I had accomplished something, when I felt some sort of ego satisfaction. I knew it was important for me to feel good about what I had accomplished so that I would have the energy to continue my work, but Ruby always made it very clear to me that I needed to learn more—that, in a sense, I was only at the beginning. It was Ruby who could arouse my anger and put the energy that resulted from that anger into my power center, right around my navel. One of the first lessons I learned in shamanism was that anger and even fear can infuse you with needed energy and power at times, perhaps when you are most depleted. Those lessons are hard ones, and Ruby was always the initiator of that knowledge. Agnes and Ruby always played off each other. As is often the case in shaman teaching, the apprentice stands between two extraordinary forms of energy and power and is bounced around like a ball until the lesson is learned.

Ruby often teaches with humor and by behaving like a child or an eccentric old woman. She performs antics that you would think not even a madwoman would attempt. Years ago, when she first began these antics, I was shocked and totally at a loss as to what to do. I find myself still at a loss today. She always turns me in on myself, providing a mirror that I cannot avoid. In a sense, she does not teach me, but forces me to teach myself and find the shaman woman of power within myself to consult. It is as if Ruby, through words and behavior, paints an exquisite picture with just the right colors, the exact representation and imagination for what I need to know.

It also takes timing, and often Agnes will interrupt at just the right moment to move my mind in another direction. Then Ruby will react with some absurdity that pulls me in another direction, so that pretty soon my mind gets confused and drops away, and I shift my consciousness then into my body-mind. I begin to perceive with my intuition and my true vision of power. Only then is the lesson learned.

Ruby was now sitting next to me, cocking her head to one side, not unlike Crow, who was still hopping up and down on the sill. Her eyes were partially shut and she was perceiving me from the left side of her body. Suddenly she stood up and said, "Come, Lynn. Let's go for a walk."

I followed her outside, looking back at Agnes and shrugging my shoulders. Agnes waved good-bye like a mother to her daughter. I was not sure whether the smile on Agnes's face was ominous or simply a smile. It was very subtle. But I had no time to figure it out, because Ruby was pulling at my sleeve and moving quickly down the path toward Dead Man's Creek.

"Where are we going?" I asked.

"I would like to walk over to the Dreamlodge with you. It is time that we talked about your next journey."

"Doesn't Agnes need to come with us?" I said.

"Agnes will come soon enough, but this journey is between us," Ruby said.

"Oh, that's wonderful," I said, not at all sure I meant it. Fear was beginning to work its way up my spine. My muscles began to tighten between my shoulder blades.

Again Ruby giggled as she put her arm around my shoulders. "Lynn, after all these years, are you still afraid of me—an old, blind Native American woman? Come now, this can't really be so."

Her blue eyes shone like two moons in the glittering sunlight flickering through the poplar trees. If she was trying to scare me, she was succeeding. It's difficult to explain why her countenance is frightening. Ruby is a woman of consummate power and strength; I have seen her look at the strongest man or woman who was an adversary to her and watched them wither before my eyes. Red Dog and his apprentices were terrified of her. It was not that she ever did anything to hurt anyone. It is simply that she is made of power, like lightning, and there is no way you can avoid seeing it and experiencing that vortex of energy that is her. For some reason, when you do not live in that much power yourself, it begins to burn next to you like a flame, and you wonder if that flame is going to consume you or give you life.

"Ruby, you're right, you do scare me, and I don't even know why, but I love you, and I don't want to hurt your feelings by the fact that I'm nervous sometimes."

"Don't worry, Little Wolf. You can't hurt me, and we are going to have some fun."

I gulped down my next words of complaint and nodded, managing a smile, as we walked through the poplar trees until the

Dreamlodge came into view. I hadn't seen it since my last journey there. I felt in some inexplicable way like I was going home. Tears stung my eyelids as Ruby let me go ahead. Suddenly I was no longer worried about Ruby. Instead, I was filled with anticipation and excitement as I approached my Dreamlodge, which had obviously been tended to and cared for in a very sacred and careful way. Everything was clean around the structure. The stones were laid perfectly, one next to another. Smoke was drifting in tendrils above the smoke hole in the center of the lodge. The Hudson Bay blankets that hung over the doorway beckoned to me as they flapped gently in the breeze, their reds and yellows shining brilliantly in the sunlight. I walked around the lodge four times and said prayers to the four directions as I went. Ruby followed me, chanting quietly as we walked. This was not a traditional Native American dreamlodge, but one that had been built by my teachers for the shaman technique of double dreaming. It was built specifically for me—an Anglo woman and their apprentice.

I parted the blankets and entered the lodge, and caught my breath as I saw the small fire that had been built in the center. Everything was as I had left it. The beautiful amulet necklace hung over my altar, the tiny, diamondlike mirror reflecting a rainbow across the interior of the lodge. It was beautiful, and it inspired me to the very depths of my being. Thoughts of Windhorse flashed through my mind, montages of my previous life as Catherine, and visions of the Woman of Wyrrd. Tears of joy and sadness rolled down my cheeks, as I thought of Grandmother, the Lady of the Mist, and her beautiful peregrine falcon. I had not thought of Grandmother for some time; it had taken so much energy out of me to move back in time to a past life. But Windhorse had become even more a part of my life. I had mated with my spirit husband in my meetings with him in the fifteenth century. It was Windhorse who was my consort in this lifetime on the spiritual plane. It was he who helped me make decisions in my spiritual life. It was he who gave me encouragement when I felt the most alone. And it was he who gave me courage to continue on my path.

I went before my altar, and I offered sweetgrass, tobacco, and *pajo,* or corn pollen, to the spirits, and made prayers to the Great Spirit, to the powers of the four directions, to my ancestors, to my power animals, and to my sacred teachers and all those who love me. I made special prayers to my family, to my mother and those who had passed on, praying for their light and for their continued enlightenment and happiness. It was only then that I became aware of a sense of imbalance. Though I was feeling unsure where this feeling was coming from, I knew that it had nothing to do with my current physical life.

It was then, as if Ruby were answering the questions in my mind, that she entered my Dreamlodge and sat down on the other side of the fire.

·3·

Journey into the Future

We are alone with everything we love.

— NOVALIS
(FRIEDRICH VON HARDENBERG)

It is time, my daughter," Ruby said, looking at me from across the fire. "You have healed from your journey into your past life, and now it is time to bring balance back within you. I must begin to teach you about your journey into the future, into your future lifetime. It is now that our teaching must begin. We had to wait until you felt it in your body, and you would only feel that imbalance when you had healed and gathered your power once again for a new journey.

"Watch carefully." Ruby picked up a prayer stick and balanced it on her gnarled brown finger. "I want you to imagine that my finger represents your life as you experience it today. This prayer stick represents your succession of lifetimes, your karma, from the beginning into all time." She squinted at me and went someplace within herself that I could not experience.

Then she poked one end of the prayer stick and said, "Little Wolf, this, if you can imagine, was your lifetime with the Woman of Wyrrd." As she poked the stick on the left-hand side, it fell off her finger. "You see, this is like the imbalance that you are feeling within yourself. You are feeling that something is not quite right. Am I correct?" She looked toward me.

"Yes," I said. "I became aware of it, really, for the first time, when I was sitting before my altar. I realized that my energy flow was different and that I needed to learn something new to bring it back into balance again. That is the only way I can explain it."

Ruby nodded her head. "Yes, Little Wolf, you perceive correctly. As I said, that is the sign I was waiting for."

She picked the prayer stick up and placed it on her finger again. It balanced perfectly. "Now I'll put weight on one end of the stick, and as I do this you reach over and put weight on the other end of the stick, so that this time it does not fall from my finger." I did so, applying equal pressure, and the stick balanced and stayed where it was.

"Now, your new pressure," Ruby said, "represents your future lifetime, the one that you are about to journey into. The process is very similar to moving into a past lifetime. You arouse your inner fire, but this time you move more totally into your blood, because it is the blood that carries the karma, not only of past lifetimes, but of future ones. In actuality it is all the same."

"I don't understand," I said, looking at Ruby and still keeping my finger on the stick.

"Time is only a process of your ego and your mind. Time is a coyote, a trickster. It circles us and keeps us in form in this relative world. It is part of karma; it is part of what we have to let go of, but it should not be let go of until you are truly ready. You will understand much more when you move into this new lifetime. It will be hard for you, and you have some training to do to get your body in even better shape than it is in, because it has to be as strong physically as you are spiritually to move into this mysterious world."

"I don't know how to do this. Are you going to teach me?"

"Yes, Little Wolf, I am going to teach you. Not only will I teach you, but I will, in a sense, take you there. I will mark your trail. Never fear." Ruby picked the prayer stick off her finger and placed it back into the earth next to the fire. "Agnes tells me that you had an invitation from the bamboo at your home in Los Angeles."

I stared at Ruby, considering her use of the word *invitation*. I thought for several minutes about my hours spent lying under the bamboo leaves and watching the light parade in splendid shades of green and yellow, leaving pools of waving white light on the ground.

"It is true, Ruby, I was transfixed by the bamboo. It was a calling, almost. I became obsessed by simply watching the leaves and listening to the wind talk to me through them."

I watched Ruby move subtly into a Buddhalike posture. Her eyes closed and a faint smile appeared at the corners of her lips. She sat in perfect stillness, her hands folded in her lap. She had often sat with me thus, but I had never noticed the profound quality of stillness before. Perhaps she was different now. Ruby picked up a medium-sized gourd rattle that had tiny points of turquoise embedded in it, representing the Pleiades.

"This rattle holds dream crystals," she said, listening to the sound it made—so soft and gentle, almost like a small waterfall. "You see, my daughter, a story is stalking you once again. I want you to sit in meditation with me now for a time. The fire tells me that you are ready sooner than I thought."

Ruby had never used the word *meditation* with me before. I was stunned to hear it, but knew better than to question her. I simply closed my eyes and sat in a comfortable lotus position, as the fire crackled and plumes of smoke lifted up and out through the smoke hole above us. I began to relax and move into my breathing. The scent of cedar and sweetgrass filled my senses. At first I found it difficult to quiet my mind; there were so many things I wanted to ask Ruby. I was excited at being in my lodge once again, and wanted to look at everything and touch my sacred things.

Then Ruby stood and, shaking the rattle, circled my head with the sound many times. "Let the Star Rattle bring you to the center of your circle," she whispered over and over.

At last the chatter in my mind quieted down. We worked a long time doing "small death" breathing—taking air in for a count of twelve seconds, holding for twelve seconds, and exhaling for twelve seconds and holding again. Then I felt a pulling at my solar plexus, almost as if an umbilical cord had been reattached at my bellybutton. Energetically, I began to follow the tugging and let myself imagine an umbilical cord stretching out. I imagined my hands touching the cord. It felt warm and pulsating with blood and life force in my hands. It felt like a mother cord leading to the uterus of all life, as if the Great Mother were giving forth abundance and birth. I sensed Ruby coming up behind me, and then I felt her hit me once, hard, on my back. I heard a cracking sound inside me, like a branch breaking away from a tree. For a moment I was spinning. I felt myself falling for a long time through a star-filled space. I heard strange languages in my head. Then I was floating in a cocoonlike enclosure, the softness of silk against my cheeks, the warmth of pink and golden light, and the drumlike sound of a heartbeat lulling me into pleasant sleep in a surreal

existence outside of time and space and the Dreamlodge in
Manitoba. I floated there like a cloud in the sky, feeling supported
as if by the great hands of the Goddess Mother. I felt what could
only be her womb encircling me, holding me, and yet letting me
go; giving me life, and yet keeping me from it. Then I realized I
must not yet have been born. I knew I was somehow incubating. I
was floating in some kind of giant egg, the shell of which protected me from all evil. I began to turn ever so slowly in a spiraling
fashion in this sacred dream, in a long night in space, the stars
shining around me. The seven sister stars of the Pleiades related
themselves to me. I knew that in some way I was made from the
stars, and that one day I would return to the stars from whence I
had come. Inside me was a hidden knowledge of them, an intrinsic
feeling that they were part of my protection and that for some reason I had been sent by the stars to perform some sort of ceremony
out here in time.

Again I became aware of the gentle beat of the drumlike heart
close to my ears. I was aware of the pulsation of blood and the
growth of part of me. Something was taking form, and as I took
form, I was beginning to lose my relationship with the cocoon
around me. There was a pulling away, a sense of remembering and
then forgetting. I had thought I represented a whole large, marvelous piece of life, part of a mosaic of something larger and more
sacred, and yet it was part of me, and there was no separation, no
duality, no darkness and light, but only the constant throbbing
and the gentle protection of this silken cocoon.

Then suddenly I knew that my form was complete. I didn't
know what I looked like, but I knew that I was getting too large,
that somehow I needed to emerge from the safety and pleasure of
my fluidity into a new and strangely mysterious environment.
Something inside me said I was ready, that it was time, and I felt a
wrenching squeeze in part of me. I squirmed and turned and tried
to swim, but that didn't seem appropriate. More contractions, and
then I felt as if I were about to die. I could no longer find suste-
nance; somehow it had been cut off. The throbbing beat of life in
my ears became louder and faster. After a seemingly interminable
time, I burst into a flood of light, and I was real and separate and
definitive and in form. I held karma between my teeth and life

force within my blood. I was born—a girl child, Japanese, with a tiny fringe of black hair on my head. I screamed out against the pain and the shock and the light that blinded me and hurt my eyes. I came out fighting to regain my peace, never to lose that instinctual longing for the rest of my life. I yearned for the softness, the cocoon, the safety, the certainty of life, the lullaby of the drumbeat, my mother's heart, the first musical instrument that I ever heard. The drum became sacred to me. I could not bear the isolation. I wanted to return, but there was no way. I had to discover another path to find my way home. Only magic could take me back to the primal experience of existence that lived in my soul. I felt captured and controlled.

Suddenly the cord was cut and the umbilical snapped back and struck my imagination and my dreaming and shocked me back into my Dreamlodge. I became aware of Ruby shaking my shoulders. She was speaking urgently in my ear, saying, "Lynn, you have gone too far. Come back, come back now. Lynn, hear me."

As always, when I move too quickly out of my body and come back with such sharpness, I became sick to my stomach. Ruby held my shoulders and helped me outside, where I vomited and regained my composure.

We sat next to the creek and made cups out of our hands and drank the cool water that was rushing by. We said nothing for a long time. I needed to assimilate what I had seen. It had been a sudden and shocking experience, and I realized that the birth I had experienced was not my birth in this lifetime. Ruby was nodding at me as I sat there with my thoughts tumbling through my mind.

"Ruby, help me." I reached out and she held my hand. I needed to feel something that grounded me. I dug the fingers of my other hand into the earth, searching for a feeling of security. Finally finding it, I took a deep breath and began to tell Ruby about my experience.

As I finished, I asked her, "Is this child—am I—going to be a young woman, a woman in Japan?"

"You tell me," she said. "You certainly don't waste any time jumping into an experience!"

"That was the impression I was given. I felt Japanese and born in a different time in a very familiar yet strange land, with blue-tiled pagodas, high bamboo trees swaying in the wind, and black-haired women in silk kimonos."

"This land is familiar to you, little one, because it is at a similar latitude to where you were born in this lifetime, Seattle. The atmosphere is not unfamiliar to you."

"I see," I said. Ruby rubbed my tummy in a spiraling fashion with her right hand, soothing my stomach. "It is almost as if I can feel that umbilical cord," I said to her. "This experience was so powerful, I'm not sure I can bear it. It's very disrupting to my sense of balance, and yet, through your explanation to me earlier, I see it is necessary. I see that there is a weight that is created through experiencing something in the future. The only way I can explain it is that there is a weight, and even more than that, there is a fragrance and a sound to it, just as there was with the Woman of Wyrrd. But it is very different and its weight balances. I see why you used that stick as an example. I see already why this is important, and, truly, Ruby, I haven't the faintest idea how to explain it to anyone."

Ruby cocked her head to one side and pulled on her earlobe. "You know, there are times when things are best left unexplained. As I have often told you, Little Wolf, when you feel the presence of great truth, when you have an opening of light, like an eye seeing something that it has never seen before, it is, perhaps, a glimpse of perfection and beauty. And then the eye closes and that vision is extinguished. You cannot describe that vision, because to describe it exactly is to destroy it, to destroy its power and to lose it. When you describe such a magnificent happening, you must circle it, just as a story that is stalking you circles you. You must describe it in a circular fashion, because all life is a circle, and to reach truth, we must move within that sacred circle. When you move in such a way, you create an atmosphere for truth to live. You create a mirror that people can look into if they choose. Perhaps they will not see exactly the same truth that you saw, but they will find a truth that relates to their own evolving selves. Do you understand?"

"Yes, but, Ruby, this is almost like science fiction to me. There is a quality to it that scares me—that is so unknown. I see what you're saying, but I don't understand it rationally; I understand it from my gut, from my shaman center. I know that what you say is true, because of the work I have done with people. I know that to describe what you tell me exactly is to lose the power of it. I have to describe the circumstance in which I was immersed to define whatever you're trying to teach me. I thank you for the opportunity to experience this, Ruby. I know this is going to be a very great teaching. I feel the need now to be alone. I need to walk upstream and assimilate the feelings I have just had. They were beautiful and extraordinary and very disturbing, and I need to give myself time."

I put my arms around Ruby and gave her a hug. She kissed me on the forehead and placed a small bag of *pajo* in my left hand. I turned and walked upstream. I felt the need to be near water. If there had been a bathtub nearby, I would have immersed myself in its warmth. There was something so extraordinarily beckoning about the womb experience. I realized that, in a sense, I had always wanted to go back to the womb. I had always wanted to hide, to find a way to be anonymous. I had always wanted to just float in ecstasy. How different my life had become since the womb and what seemed to be the origin of my truth. It was fascinating to me that the search for truth had brought me so far away from my beginnings, and yet so close to them.

· 4 ·

Mirror of Truth

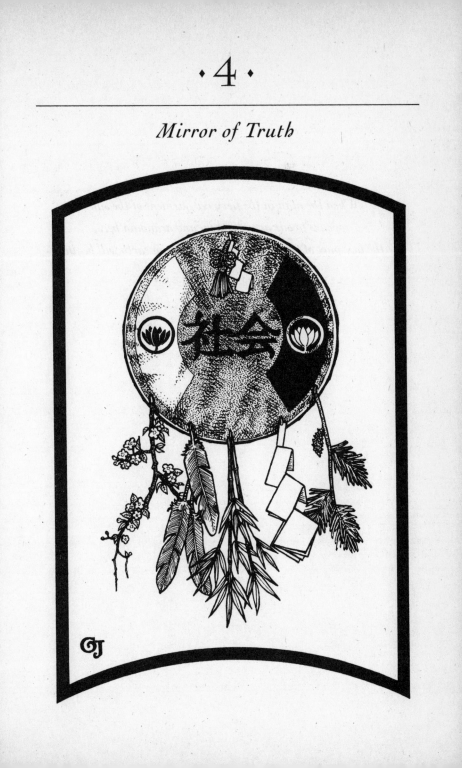

When the man in the fiery red garment of the sun
appears to our grandfathers and grandmothers,
the last part of the Great Change of life on earth will begin.

— HOPI PROPHECY

The next afternoon, when Ruby had left to go back to her own cabin, Agnes and I sat together in the one room, her drums, rattles, beadwork, feathered fans, and sacred bundles hanging in a gaiety of texture and color from every corner. We sat together talking until very late. I told her about my journey—my process of rebirth. The dream was still rolling around in my mind as one of the most startling events that had ever happened to me. At one point we both stopped talking and just enjoyed the fire in the pot-bellied stove and the silence. Finally I said, "Agnes, these have been two of the most difficult years I have ever lived through, and I think it has been difficult for all my friends as well. In fact, there has been so much stress that I wonder sometimes how I can give my work with you every part of my being, as I always have."

Agnes placed her hand over the top of her tea mug, feeling the steam as she so often did with her fingers, and laughed a little to herself, her shoulders jiggling. "Little Wolf," she said, "you try too hard, sometimes, in your work. It is part of what you need to learn in this earthwalk, to relax and trust in the Great Spirit that everything you are doing and feeling is correct for the time." She looked at me for several moments, as I stared back at her, the etched furrows around her eyes deepening with a kindly smile.

"I know you have said this before, Agnes, but I feel right now that I am struggling every moment of the day and night just to maintain my equilibrium."

"But you're maintaining it very well," she answered. "You don't give yourself enough credit. That has always been a difficulty for you. You are very critical of yourself. You need to be easier on Lynn. You are doing a lot in the world, and because of your child-hood struggles, you still don't believe you have accomplished much. It would help you if you would relax a little, within your own heart, and accept the fact that everything is going to be okay."

"But, Agnes, there is a part of me that can't accept that, that can't relax. I don't know that everything is going to be all right. Even with all I know, even with all the work and all the journeying, there is still, every once in a while, a time when I doubt."

"I don't think *doubt* is the word," Agnes said, "if I may rephrase your statement. I think the word is *fear*. You are afraid, and it is no wonder. You had a very difficult beginning as a child, full of fear every moment you were awake, and even while you slept, you feared for your life. So it is no wonder that it extends into your adult life. How do you feel now?"

"Well, actually, I feel great joy in my heart. I feel even close to tears. I feel happy, and actually quite at ease."

Agnes threw back her head and laughed and slapped her thigh. "See? That's what I mean. You live in your body, in your shaman center, and it is at ease. The only part of you that is in terror any longer is your little girl that lives forever inside your heart, needing, needing, and needing. When that little papoose becomes frightened, she grabs hold of your mind and puts you into the weirds."

"What do you mean, 'the weirds'?" I asked.

"It is what we call a state of discomfort, when you feel desperately off center, when you feel frightened, when you don't know whether you're coming or going, when the words of other people hit you like arrows in the heart and you feel sad, and you don't know the trail home any longer. Remember, long ago, when you had the weirds? I told you to take a bath in Epsom salts or in sea salt. Remember?"

"Oh yes, Agnes, I do remember. It helped a great deal. Gee, that was a long time ago."

"You see, Little Wolf, your problem is that you always want to be the apprentice, because you don't want to be abandoned. You do not want to be deserted by your teachers. It is a great fear of yours, isn't it?"

I thought for several moments, not wanting Agnes to know what my fear was, because to teach me, she might produce it in my life. But slowly I nodded and said, "Yes, it is true. You are my

family. I have lost many in my family now, so you are more important to me than ever, Agnes. You can't be mad at me for that?"

"No, wolf girl, I am not angry at you for that, but remember
what our relationship is about. It is about illumination. It is about
finding your way home. Our relationship is like a tiny turquoise
bead along this trail. It is just a signpost. It is just a piece of the
love, the greater love, that you will be immersed in later on in your
lifetimes."

Agnes piled several small stones—beautiful, smooth river stones
that she had sitting on her table—one on top of another. As she
piled them she looked at me, under heavy lids and eyes that shone
like silvery mirrors in the firelight.

"The path of illumination is the path of balance, the path of balance with one foot in the material world and one foot securely
rooted in the spiritual world. Many people today who are on this
path, the path of spirit, are filled with anger from their child-
hoods. They never deal with that anger, and they throw away the
physical life out of a need to reject the pain of their earlier life, and
they call themselves spiritual. But they sabotage themselves at
every turn. They hold up a spirit shield, but their feet are not
planted on bedrock. Their feet are planted in quicksand, and spiritual power will eventually overwhelm them. Then one day they
will have to hear the voice of the great teachers, and that voice will
tell them that they need to go back and learn to walk in balance.
For everything you do spiritually, you need to strengthen your
body as well, and you have learned that, Little Wolf. You understand that, and that is what you teach well."

Then Agnes touched the stones that were carefully balanced,
and they tumbled onto the table.

"The moment you move off your center, little pup, your insides,
your emotions, come tumbling down like this small mountain of
rocks, and you cannot function. That is not you. You are stacked
up real good at this point," she laughed, poking my shoulder.
"You must stay centered, always living in your center, looking out
from that place of your sacred witness into the world." Agnes
tilted her head, squinting one eye. "You have one difficulty."

"What is that?" I asked.

"You're often not at ease. You care too much," she said.

"But if I didn't care about this earth and the people on it, I could not do what I do. I could not have given up my life as I have, to write and teach and be with you."

"But there are many kinds of caring," Agnes said, gathering up the stones and placing them in a circle. "Just like alcohol or drugs or addictive relationships, you can be addicted to caring to the point that it pulls you off center. Caring is important, but it is only part of the whole of who you are. You cannot care so much that it becomes an obsession. You must see the totality of things and realize where your caring, like everything else, fits into the perspective of your life. Emotions are important; all of what you feel and think is important, because these things make you who you are. Negative ideas are parts of you that need to be honored, so that they can then be healed and brought back into balance. To judge yourself is simply being hard on yourself unnecessarily."

"But I don't know how not to do that, Agnes. It is definitely a big problem for me."

"Remember when we sat in the cow pasture, Lynn, when I first knew you, and I had you pick up a stone for everything you believed in?"

"Yes, I sure do, Agnes," I said, taking a bite out of a nice red apple.

"Well, many people carry around a bagful of stones, a whole bagful of conceptions, that weights them down, that limits their growth and puts a fence around their consciousness so that they cannot see beyond that fence. It is important to have ideas and feelings, because with those ideas and feelings you create mirrors, and those mirrors are great teachers for you. But when you are full of ideas, those ideas give you what you think is the right to pass judgment on what other people do. That is one of the greatest wasting processes of life that I know. Your people do a lot of that, and so do mine, and that is a tragedy, because they get lost in their judgments. They get lost in their criticism, and they forget where they're going, why they're alive, and what their purpose on earth is. They will tell you what their purpose is, but in reality they have lost their way, and they are frightened."

"It's so easy to criticize isn't it, Agnes? Because when you criticize, you are simply putting something down that someone else has done, that perhaps you're jealous of, because they've made a commitment, an effort, which you have been unable to do. But to talk constructively about a work of art, something in the world that has been done well, takes creativity. It takes some talent to express that."

"Yes, it is true. When you move into this future life, you are going to be working on not only letting go of belief structures, but also on the state of ease that you so dearly need in your life. Through learning that yourself, I think you will be able to give that teaching to other people. It is what we need as a civilized society today. The stress that people are under is inhuman. It should not ever be as it is today, and yet we cannot go back to the old ways, at least not now. So one of the great teachings of this particular time in history is to learn how to live one life with the stress of three or four lives all at once and still maintain your center and your ease and your joy—a very, very difficult thing to do. But it is like a problem in logic, like a mathematical equation using trade beads. It can be done, but the right symbolism has to be learned. The right thoughts must be written for the outcome to be beautiful."

Agnes stood up, walked over to her bed, and picked up a beautiful chief's blanket that had been given to her. She took it off the bed and brought it to me, then, sitting down, she spread it on the table before me. I ran my fingers across its beautiful texture, its beautiful design in horizontal lines across the blanket in black on red. The threads had all been colored with natural dyes.

"This is very old, isn't it?" I said.

"Yes, it was given to me by a relative. I have always cherished this blanket. It has meant a great deal to me."

"Why is that, Agnes?"

"Because it was woven by a great teacher. You have never met her. She taught through her weaving. Do you see these strong vertical threads?" she asked, pulling the fibers apart with her fingers.

I said, "Yes."

"Touch them," she said.

I did. The fibers felt taut and strong.

"Do you feel how strong they are?"

"Yes," I answered.

"Those are the vertical threads, the threads that are first cast on the loom. They are the warp. They are the fibers that all the rest of the blanket is built upon. If that warp is not strong and perfect, the blanket will be imperfect. Correct?"

"Yes," I said, nodding and taking a sip of tea.

"But you see, that is like life, isn't it?" Agnes said, running her hand over the crown of her head and pulling a wisp of gray hair out of her eyes. "You see, for you to move into a future life, your warp must be very, very strong. You must be secure in your knowledge of the physical and the spiritual, the emotional and mental hoops of power. As a teacher, you cannot take people into a future life, into the process of double dreaming, without preparing them properly, as you would prepare a loom. Once those vertical threads are prepared, once you are carefully taught so that you are strong, then, and only then, can you bring in the higher spiritual life, the other dimensions of reality. On a loom they are represented by the woof or the weft, the cross-fibers that are then woven into the warp."

"So you could say," I said, "that the vertical threads, the warp, are like your physical life, and the horizontal threads, the weft, are your spiritual life. Is that true?" I asked.

"Yes, my daughter. That is correct. The cross fibers add the color, the texture, and the grace to your work of art, to your life. So your understanding of your spirituality, your ability to thrive and to work with the good spirits and the light, is what gives your tapestry, your blanket, its character and its integrity. Now that you are moving into a future life, you are adding integrity to your tapestry of life, to the tapestry, to the blanket that is, indeed, your sacred skill in this lifetime."

"Agnes, how does that relate to the spirit shield that is imprinted from one lifetime to another?"

"It is another teaching, my daughter. It is the teaching of your soul. This is a way of seeing different aspects of a similar concept. In other words, when you work with an apprentice, you need to approach an idea or a problem from as many different angles as you know. You are a very visual person, so I always show you in visual ways. I help you to see things because you want to see them. I have you touch them, feel them, smell them, taste them. It helps you to understand, whereas another apprentice might perceive things on a more intuitive or sensational level. Not that you don't have your share or need of sensation!" Agnes laughed and winked at me. "But, Lynn, what I want you to see is that your future lifetime experience is going to add a whole other depth of color. There is a true fragrance, as you said when you explained your first journey of rebirth. And that fragrance is very subtle, is it not?"

"Yes," I answered.

"As you weave this tapestry of yours, this magnificent blanket, you're adding still another color, a thread of silver or gold, something very, very precious to your weaving. Perhaps it is the central design balanced by your past life experience. So, if you were thinking of a shield, you would place symbolism in the center of your shield or toward the north or on either side. This would be symbolism representing the past and the future lives. Most likely, if you were working with shields, you would do a past-life shield with symbolism from the Woman of Wyrrd, and you would do a future-life shield for the future, and that would be a beautiful thing to do. And they would stand on either side of your self shield. You see, the spirit shield imprints and also contains symbolism from the other two shields. It is another way of seeing, explaining, and understanding tangibly what is very intangible in your mind and in your heart. Sometimes, if we can see something in a tangible way, with a weaving, with a shield, we then become very clear about what we need to work on, what is needed to improve the overall design of our life."

Agnes carefully folded up the beautiful blanket and placed it again at the foot of her bed. She took a leaf of sage and placed it on the blanket and patted it gently with the palms of her hands. Then she turned to me and said, "Little Wolf, I think it is time for us to sleep."

I could always stay up with Agnes or Ruby and talk day and night. I was fascinated with Agnes's words and with the way she expressed herself, and with the knowledge that she was so kind to impart to me. We cleaned the table, put the cups away, and within minutes after splashing water on our faces, we were in bed and sound asleep.

Becoming Ronin

◆

Blessed are the poor in spirit,
for theirs is the kingdom of heaven.

— JESUS CHRIST

◆

Before my next journey in the Dreamlodge, I spent two days fasting. Then, after hours of sweat lodge ceremonies and meditation, and with the help of Ruby's celestial rattle, I moved more easily into the sacred dream. I felt a deep yearning to experience this future life. I found myself as a Japanese woman in her thirties, sitting with my teacher, Shakkai, in a room of a paper-screened house with a deeply thatched roof. One whole wall slid aside and opened the room to the outside. I could see that the house sat like a beautiful island surrounded by rectangular lanterns in a remote forest near Mount Fuji, with a placid lake fed by rushing streams that vaulted through the craggy rock landscape above us. The house was simple, but displayed the extraordinary refinement and taste of its owner. It was situated in an exquisite garden, surrounded by a seemingly deep wilderness. Ginkgo trees with thick yellow foliage separated the whitewashed walls of the compound from the house, nestled into a grove of bamboo. Through the open partition I could see out to a stand of red dwarf maples and clumps of purple and white irises bowing to the spring winds. The sparkling, crystal clear water of a spring-fed stream trickled by in the distance, reminding me of the impermanence of my earthly life. I realized that the garden encompassed several acres of land. The artful simplicity of polished wood and woven wicker screens implied the perfection of Shakkai's quiet vision. The world and its crush of endeavors and conflict seemed light years away.

We were sitting on *zabuton* cushions placed on tatami mats, diagonally across from each other, a small square table called a *kotatsu* placed between us, and Shakkai was serving us tea in the most ceremonious and refined way. We were in the *chaseki* room of her house, reserved for serving tea. I could see through to another room where musical instruments—a set of eight or ten bells hanging on a stem, slapping sticks for percussion, reed and bamboo flutes and small drums—were set in order. She handed me a cup of steaming hot liquid, as if she were handing me an extension of her own body, as if that cup were an extension of her own arms and fingers. I took the cup with the same reverence, as if I were taking her hand in mine. I turned the smooth cup in my hands, feeling it.

For a moment I was jolted by my own reflection on the surface of the tea. My eyes were dark and almond-shaped, and my mouth full beneath a small nose. My black hair, parted in the middle, hung long on either side of a roundish face with high cheekbones. I laughed at my shock, as if I hadn't recognized my own face.

Covering up my second of confusion, I said, "Everyone knows that my father is like a madman."

Shakkai watched my shift in thinking and then giggled.

"Ah, yes, and some of the holiest people of the land are madmen," she said with a questioning look at me.

"And how do you mean that, Shakkai?"

The old woman bowed her head to me in respect for my family. Her gray hair was shiny and perfectly tethered in a small bun at the top of her head. Red silk ties hung down, matching the red flowers on her white kimono.

"I mean that people become mad because they have become so focused on something that they move into a state of imbalance. Your father did just that. He was the last of his dynasty. He found it desperately important to maintain a certain image, a certain quality of life, and that required enormous effort. So, my daughter, if I may call you that, you must understand him, and I hope that in our work together you will forgive him, because all that he did was part of his history and karma and what he needed to do to learn his lessons in this lifetime."

"Well, that may be," I answered, "but it was horrible for my mother, for my family, and for me. He is truly mean."

"Perhaps, but that was because of his need to survive as a kind of ruler in his domain."

"But he has destroyed so many people," I said.

The old woman was thoughtful for several minutes as she allowed the steam from the tea to caress her face.

"There is one such person whom I want you to meet, and perhaps after you speak with him," Shakkai finally said, "you will understand that, yes, at the beginning it seemed like your father destroyed so many people. His stature was similar to that of a shogun from ancient times. He runs his electronic dynasty with an iron fist. In the end those people whom he hurt learned higher lessons that, perhaps, there was no other way for them to learn."

"Who is this person that you want me to meet?" I asked, wanting to change the subject.

"He is what you might call the new kind of warrior, the new kind of samurai. He worked for your father as a very young man. He was devoted to him as he might have been to the emperor of Japan. In his innocence he was caught in a political struggle and was outcast. It often happened in the old feudal days that a samurai who fell out of favor for one reason or another was sent away from his daimyo or master, his feudal system, and cast out on his own. In the old days of shoguns and warlords, that was a tragic event, because the system was so structured that these men then had no identity. There were quite a number of these samurai without masters, from time to time in history. These men became 'ronin,' as it was called. They were cast out into the world of fate to find their own master within.

"Even though the feudal system has long disappeared, there are still families in Japan where the blood of tradition runs deep. When this young man, this samurai, was sent out into the world, he had to find his own way. He was a victim of circumstance. The unthinkable had happened. He had lost face. It was as if he had to begin all over again. He was an outcast. In the old days such men would use their swords to survive. They would fight to the death, literally fighting for their own lives, for food, and they became expert swordsmen. This young man chose to go back to the old ways, so he found and studied with his own samurai master, someone very different from your father. He dropped his business suits, left Tokyo, and, as you have done, went into the mountains. He even went into China. He journeyed to many mysterious worlds in search of a teacher. Because he had been cut away from his original source of survival, he found that he was more capable of finding his master within. He is, indeed, an extraordinary man, as you are an extraordinary woman."

I looked hesitatingly at Shakkai. Then finally I said, "I don't remember someone in my family being cut away in this way or discharged."

"No, this man was not of your immediate family. He was a very distant relation, and he was sent away from your father in shame, because of this business dealing. It does not matter. It certainly was not his fault, but he felt deep shame, which he had to live with a long time. I think it fitting that you meet, because you will have a great deal to share with each other."

"Is he an apprentice of yours?" I asked.

"He is an apprentice to his own spirit," Shakkai said, "but he comes and enjoys my garden, and we talk together. I think we have learned much from each other. You will see."

I looked to the sky and the billowing thunderheads lined with crimson and gold. For a moment I was overcome with sadness. I thought back to the time my father forced me into marriage with a man I did not love. I was a teenager and had become pregnant with this man's child. I was very ill, and when the child was born—a son, the first grandson for my father—he was born dead. I remembered the agony I lived through, the pain of having this child, giving it life, and having that life taken away. It was almost more than I could bear, even now. When the doctors said I could never have another child, my husband left me. It was my father's suggestion that he marry someone else, because it would represent a good merging for several different large companies. Little did he know that I did not care, because I had never loved this man anyway. I think it was a way for my father to punish me; somehow, in his mind, it was my fault that his first grandchild had been born dead. He never forgave me for this. I don't remember my mother helping me. She loved me as she could, and she taught me how to be a wife and a mother and a proper woman. She was horrified when I stepped outside of the family boundaries and learned about business and how to work in the world.

My thoughts seemed to float with the clouds, and I kept seeing images of my past. I saw my life in the business world, and saw how it was not part of me. I had started to study painting, and I'd learned about haiku and the Tao and my sacred roots in

Shintoism. Zen Buddhism held a certain appeal for me. I had studied meditation with a Zen master in Kyoto, but I had found that my original religion, Shintoism, so beautifully married as it was to Taoism, was of much more interest to me. I loved its respect for animals, and I loved finding the spirit of creation in nature. That is why I painted. I would use ink and a simple bamboo brush on ricepaper or watercolor paper. Later I started to paint with colors, and became well known as a fine artist who painted the subtleties of spirit. My first search for a teacher was really to enhance my painting. It was then that I realized that painting only enhanced my spirit and was just one way for me to express my love for nature and the sacred Tao.

The old woman seemed to have been reading my mind. She sat silently and serenely in front of me, not interrupting my thoughts until I had reached a pause in my memory.

"What is your fear, my child?" she asked, looking at me, still with a hint of humor at the corners of her mouth.

"I have been in great fear because of the world condition," I said. "All around us there is always the threat of war. There is great economic unrest. Throughout the entire world, there is chaos."

"Yes, our great world garden could be taken from us at any moment," Shakkai said. "All the more reason to move into the silence, into the work that is calling you. When your life ends, I want you to have learned what you came here to know. There is a kind of emptiness that has prevailed in your life, that your tradition and your training and your brilliant mind have helped you through. Is that not so?"

I looked at Shakkai, blushing, and turned my eyes down to the tatami mat and the *zabuton* cushion I was sitting on. "No," I said.

She reached across and held my hand. "It is important for you to know who you are. Trust me. I will tell you of your limitations." She laughed quietly. "But it is important that you remember who you are. Women today—wherever they are in the world, through all our centuries of learning, through all of this time of revolution—still do not remember our goddess selves deep within. I am here to mirror that extraordinary image that you are," she said, taking another sip of tea and pouring some more into my cup.

Shakkai had several exquisite wind chimes hanging in the bamboo, in the trees, and from the eaves, the *kaeru-mata* beam supports, of her house. A gentle wind was drifting through one of the chimes. It sent a melody of gentle sound throughout the interior of the room.

"Do as I do," Shakkai said.

She took a very deep breath, and I took one also. Then she settled her hands in her lap, and I did so too.

"Gently," she said, "the wind is calling you. It is calling us to pray, to listen to her. She asks for peace, for peace of spirit. And she asks that you return to your original joy." She closed her eyes, and we meditated together for some time.

Shakkai's voice broke the silence of our prayers. "I am a renegade. I have been a *ronin* all of my life. I speak for no one except spirit, and I will teach you the way of light, the way of great illumination. All you must do is listen with your heart. In a way your pain has brought you to me, and it is good. Without your pain, you could not bear the joy that is soon to be yours."

"Forgive me, Shakkai, but how do you mean, without my pain?"

"Your pain has given you depth, a way to open your spirit. Never think that there is not a reason for everything that happens. Even your tormented father, poor soul. One day you will be able to look into the pond of his being and forgive him."

There was a gentle ringing of the chime at the door. Shakkai waited for her assistant, the old gentleman, Samisan, who is rarely seen, to let her visitor in. A young man of average height, barefoot and wearing simple white clothes, was kneeling in the *genkan*, or entrance room.

"I have been expecting you," Shakkai said, bowing her head as he bowed his.

He entered and handed a basket of fruit to her, which she lay on the table.

"This is Katakiri Nakamura, from a village at the foot of Mount Yoshino on the Kii Peninsula," Shakkai said in introduction. She turned to me. "And this is O Kiku Yoshida of Kyoto. May we enjoy tea together?" The tea ceremony became less a tea ceremony and more a way of relaxing my hands, as I looked discreetly at this man that was so handsome and so charming.

"I understand that you knew my father once," I said, wondering what his reaction would be and wondering, after I had asked the question, if I perhaps should not have.

"Don't worry, O Kiku. There is nothing you cannot say when we are together," Shakkai said, perhaps in response to the worried look that passed across my face.

He raised his eyebrows almost imperceptibly, and leaned back on his cushion. "Yes, I knew your father once. He changed my life. You could say that he was one of the greatest teachers I ever had."

"And why is that?" I asked.

"Because he set me free," he answered. "If it were not for him and the pain he forced me into . . . he threw me out into a world that was foreign to me, without protection. I was the shame of my family. I had no one, only myself. But it is as it should be. I learned much. I became a warrior of the spirit, you might say. I became a samurai, as men did in the old days. Now I am strong. And now I understand my weaknesses," he said, looking into my eyes.

"I think he thinks you're very beautiful, to be your father's daughter," Shakkai said, laughing.

I was horrified with her words and took another sip of tea, my cheeks blushing crimson.

"Yes, it is true. I am afraid it is true," the samurai said, looking away, obviously not wanting to embarrass me.

"Sometimes at dusk, I feel the demons, the hundreds of ghosts running through the streets, as if they were running through my heart. And they fill me with terror," I said. "Sometimes I feel that that presence is my own father." I hoped he would understand that I was trying to say I was sorry for all the pain that had been caused by my family.

He looked at me a long time and nodded. "Yes, I understand." Then he turned to Shakkai and said, "I think I should go now." Turning back to me, he bowed his head and said, "Thank you," then he stood up and was gone.

Shakkai looked across the table at me and began to laugh.

"Why are you laughing, my teacher?" I asked.

My words made her laugh even more. Shakkai seemed so free with her emotions, with her thoughts, with her movements. Even though they were controlled and serene, they were only controlled when she wanted them to be. Now, her head flung back, she laughed deep in her soul, and it made me giggle. I began to realize that I must have looked pretty silly for a grown woman, acting like a child with her first infatuation.

"I knew it," Shakkai said, clapping her hands. "I knew it."

"What did you know?" I asked.

"I knew that you and the samurai had much work to do together."

"Are you pleased?" I asked.

"It is what you need. You need the balance of the male shield."

"The male shield?" I asked.

"Yes, there is a teaching in the samurai tradition. It is the teaching of the swords. There are many teachings throughout history. Basically, they say very similar things. In this teaching it talks about the woman carrying not only a female blade, but a male blade within to balance the power."

"It is the same for a man?" I asked.

"Oh, yes. For this samurai to have power, he must understand his female blade, and he does not. That is what you can teach him."

"And what would he teach me?" I asked, almost afraid to hear the answer.

"That is for me to know and for you to find out," she laughed.

"That's not fair."

"Who said anything about being fair?" the old woman answered, squinting at me.

Picking up her basket of fruit, she carried it to the other end of the house.

I sat in front of the little table, thinking how different Shakkai was from any woman I had ever met before.

"Is your family from Japan?" I asked Shakkai when she returned.

"My family is from Japan. I may even have an Ainu ancestor." She winked at me.

"Are you part of a specific religion?"

"I have studied all the religions in the world," she said. "The Tao is my spirit, Shintoism is in my heart, and the Great Spirit embodies my soul, all of which I find reflected in the world of nature. My temple is the sacred garden, and I have no beliefs. For to believe is to limit my knowing."

"But don't you believe in love?" I asked.

"Why would I believe in something that I am made of?" She smiled at me. "Come, we will go outside and wash the tea service in the stream."

"But why do you do that, Shakkai? We can wash it here."

"No. Come."

I followed the old woman outside. She would not let me carry anything. Although most of her things were very simple and made of earthenware of her own design, this tea service was of Victorian silver, and she obviously loved it very much.

"Why do you not use a traditional Japanese tea service?" I asked, as we knelt by the stream on the grassy bank, my knees enjoying the feeling of earth beneath them.

"I often use a traditional tea service. But I also like the color of silver," she said, looking at me after several moments.

"The color?" I asked.

"Yes, the flash of light in the sun, the color of silver as it reflects colors in the room. It is beautiful when it is polished. It is like the sacred melôn used by the monks of Tibet."

"What is that?" I asked.

"It is a combination of metals melted together into a medallion that produces a mirrorlike surface. It is a way of teaching," she said. "When we drink tea not in the tea ceremony or the *chanoyu,* I like sometimes to teach with the mirrorlike quality that the silver provides. It is exquisite, like the face of the Goddess of the Sun. You will see." She took the running water and splashed it over the silver.

"Why the stream water?" I asked.

"The energy field in running water washes away any tension. It is sacred, this water, and it holds the reflection of the sky and the trees as it passes by. And it imparts the nature of life to our ceremony."

· 6 ·

Garden of Serenity

♦

The Way is patterned on Nature.

— LAO TZU,
TAO TE CHING

♦

We sat at the edge of a reflection pond, my teacher and I. Shakkai wore a red scarf around her head, her hair tied up neatly on top. The old woman's hands were elegant; she had long, soft, artistic fingers, with deep pads on the fingertips, gentle pads that could feel with intelligence and correctness. She had the hands of a musician, of someone who has played the piano for years, as she told me she had done as a younger woman. When she approaches a plant or a stone or something in her home, she treats it with a profound sense of reverence, completely unself-consciously, yet with a sweet sense of humor.

The night before, we had lit lanterns around the main room in the house, and Shakkai had done a welcoming ceremony with me. We wore short white kimonos and long red skirts that glowed in the semidarkness and reflected the central fire that was contained within a square metal grate, perhaps fifteen inches on a side. Square paper lanterns were placed around the fire, with candles burning inside, and they flickered and cast a shimmering glow for the ceremony. The fire blazed away.

Shakkai's face beamed with light as she smiled, her round cheeks glistening. She danced and chanted, honoring the Goddess of Fire. Her movements were very precise, very simple, very controlled, just like the gardens. She would sing in long, unceasing tones, almost like the wind. She raised the power like any other shaman in the world, making the powers stand up and take notice. She awakened the different elements. She awakened her drum, the heartbeat of Mother Earth. She danced with the powers of the earth and welcomed magic and beauty to live within us. Then she held up her wand of sacred bells, which sounded like the east wind dancing through the wind chimes, and we moved in a ceremonial

way into the sacred temple of her garden to give thanks to the
great Tao that had brought us together.

As we sat by the pond, the afternoon sky was filled with billowing white clouds. A craggy granite outcropping and smooth river
stones formed the northern edge of the water. Around those rocks
were carefully planted junipers, sacred *sakaki* trees, and rounded
bushes of flowers, fuchsia-colored, with dots of white. A large acacia tree formed an umbrella of yellow filigree over our heads. We
sat on a large bamboo mat, meditating on the reflection of Mount
Fuji in the water.

"Shakkai, why have you devoted your life to the art of constructing sacred gardens?" I asked, unsure whether I should break
the silence. I could feel the gentle southerly winds against my high
cheekbones as I spoke. My long black hair was pulled severely
into a knot on top of my head, held there by two black and red
lacquered chopsticks. I was wearing a white kimono jacket that
fell just below my knees, and wide-legged black slacks and *getas,*
or sandals, woven of straw.

"You are an accomplished woman now in your thirties," the old
woman answered. "I have watched you for many years, from a
distance, even before I left my city life and came to the mountains.
As you know, I knew your family socially, and I met you as a
child. I know you have wondered many times in the past why I
would isolate myself in this way from the world to prepare sacred
gardens for the gods."

A tiny leaf fell from a maple tree above onto the bun carefully
fashioned on the top of her head. The old woman's eyes crinkled
at the corners with her ever-present humor. She watched me as I
struggled for the correct words to express myself. "You be silent
now," she finally said, reaching her hand out and gently touching
the back of my wrist with her graceful fingers. "You see, the garden that we sit in represents a universe to me. The stones there"—
she pointed to the black and gray stones on the other side of the
pond—"represent a sacred mountain. Every steppingstone represents a moment in my life when something sacred has happened. It
is history, it is future, and it is the eternal Tao represented in a
microcosm of reality. So many of us move outside ourselves to find
truth. We go out into the world in search of something larger than

ourselves. We do not realize that truth lies within, so I have contained myself. *Shakkai* means, literally, 'captured landscape,' and that is, in essence, what I have done with my life, is it not?"

I nodded, intent on her words.

"You see, in a way I have created my own paradise. You understand, do you not, O Kiku? What we create in the world, we must first create within ourselves. A long time ago, I realized that we can either live in hell on this earth or we can live in a land of peace and joy, what one might call a paradise. There are really only two ways to live."

She smiled at me, waiting to see if I agreed with what she was telling me. Finally, I nodded almost imperceptibly, as I had been taught to do, and looked down again into the reflection pond. "You see, O Kiku, I do not believe that we go on to a hell or a heaven, such as many religions speak of. I believe that we create our own hell through obsessions, jealousy, hatreds, judgments, and fear. Long ago I decided to build my own monastery, and the monastery that I built is this garden. It is a garden of serenity. Each plant represents some aspect of my joy and my love, because, in actuality, if one is to find heaven, one has to open one's heart to love. That is the moon gate that one has to walk through to find eternal peace."

"But, Shakkai—or is it better, since you are my teacher, that I address you as *sensei*?"

"Shakkai, *sensei,* or Mama-san—whichever pleases you." She smiled.

"Why do you call this a captured landscape?" I asked.

Shakkai took a small, rounded river stone and turned it over and over in the palm of her hand. "Captured, in a sense, means that you have lost your freedom. I realized early on from my teachers, who were originally from China, that in losing one's freedom, you gain it. In capturing the spirit, you free it. That sounds strange, doesn't it?"

I stared at my teacher for a long time, weighing the words in my mind, and I came to the conclusion that that was true. "It is like falling in love, isn't it, Shakkai? When you open yourself to a love relationship, you find total freedom, but in a sense your freedom is transformed into something even more powerful," I said.

"Yes, this is true, O Kiku. It is as it should be. It is a way of learning. It is a way of teaching. You have chosen in this lifetime to be with me, to learn what I have learned, and I hope that it is a proper path for you."

I smiled at my *sensei*, and a kind of wordless love and understanding passed between us. "But I still don't understand, exactly, Shakkai, how that pertains to a garden."

"What happens when you meditate, my child?"

I thought for some time and then answered, "When you meditate on a beautiful flower, you, in essence, become that flower, if your meditation is deeply felt."

"Yes," Shakkai answered, "go on."

"I would imagine that when you understand what is needed in your life, if you even have the opportunity to make that conscious choice, you would then see that you need to surround yourself with your tools, with your elements of transformation. Is that correct?" I asked.

"Yes, my daughter, that is very good. It is true. It is exactly what I did. I love nature, and I realized that nature represents the goodness of the human spirit, a perfection of the Tao that is within each of us. So what is better than to spend my life meditating on nature, meditating on a beautiful flower until the fragrance of that flower becomes part of my own spirit? You see, all that we love is here. The sacred mountains and the spirits of the mountains are represented here with the stones, and we can see the reflection of our mountain in the water beside us. All I need is to move out of my house and sit here and meditate with the most high. What could be better? But it took me a long time to reach past the reflection and down into the source."

Shakkai got up and, taking my hand, led me down to the pond, where a beautiful lotus blossom, pink and moist and perfect, reflected Mount Fuji in the tiny droplets of water on its petals. She placed her hands lovingly beneath the water and held the lotus blossom up.

"See, my daughter, as you well know, this lotus blossom for a long time germinated in the mud, out of the mud into the light of day, into the magnificent, innocent flower that you see before you."

"I don't understand," I said.

"The chaos of life, the madness, the pain, the agony, the evil that surrounds the human condition on so many levels, is represented by the mud."

"I understand," I said.

"Put your hands in the mud," she ordered. I knelt down by the pond and dipped my arms deeply into the water and dug my fingers into the wet, murky mud on the bottom.

"Run your fingers through the mud. Feel the stones and the grit. Does it seem that there is life there?" she asked.

"No," I said, "it feels foreign to my skin. It feels cold and lifeless and rough, and yet there are smooth places."

"You see, O Kiku, it is a wonder, it is a miracle, isn't it, that something so beautiful as this lotus blossom could grow out of that mud? And yet it is so." The old woman closed her eyes and sat back on her heels, her arms outspread, feeling the currents of air around us. The trees rustled in the breeze. The bamboo swayed behind me, giving me a sense of wilderness and space. "Life is a miracle. The world is as it should be," Shakkai said. "It is so hard for us to find our way through the mud, to celebrate the innocence and the seeds of knowledge that we plant there. We must foster those seeds. We must find those seeds and give them life."

"But how do we do that, Shakkai?"

She opened her eyes and leaned toward me, placing her wet palms on either side of my face. "Don't you see, you have spent a lifetime nurturing those seeds. You have delved deep into the murky depths of your own being. You have searched out the karma that is there, and now that you have performed your social duties in life, now that you have educated yourself and lived with your family and done as you should have done, you are here for spiritual training. This is training that you have chosen. It was not chosen by your society or by your status in life. You have left public life, as I did, to understand your *tamashii,* your own soul, and I think we are very close in that endeavor," she said, sitting down now in front of me. Taking both of my hands, quietly she washed the mud from my fingers and then held my hands in hers. "I will teach you. I am a woman of power. I have been a woman of power throughout history. I will lead you to the knowledge of your own lifetime. I am very proud to be with you. It is our first year together as teacher and apprentice. Now perhaps your life will be changed forever.

"Sit by this pond and meditate on the unity of your body, as you will, and visualize this eight-petaled lotus flower. Meditate carefully. Gather your energy and your spirit. Let your mind be at ease. Meditate until you feel the essence of the flower that is truly a reflection of your own essence. See it blooming within your womb. This is the beginning of a long process, so take your time. When you feel accomplished, come into the house and we will share tea together. Take your time. If it takes a day or a night or an hour, let it happen as it will."

The old woman smiled at me, her face looking not much older than my own with her joy and the excitement that was expressed in every movement she made. I felt secure and at home with her, as if at long last I had come back to my roots. How fitting that I should be meditating now, with this magnificent woman of knowledge, on the lotus blossom.

Timelessness

Only the one who fully comprehends
the difficulties of awakening can understand
that long and arduous work is needed to wake up.

— G. I. GURDJIEFF

I came out of my journey very abruptly, as if shaken out of a day's sleep, back into the Dreamlodge in Manitoba. I was very sick to my stomach. Ruby helped me outside, where I threw up, and then she pushed me into the creek and doused me with ice-cold water, bringing me sharply back into ordinary consciousness and reality. I sat on the riverbank, shaking my head as Ruby put two blankets around my shoulders to keep me warm, and dangled my feet in the water for some time, trying to regain my equilibrium. I said nothing as Ruby sat beside me. Suddenly, Agnes burst through the branches between two poplar trees, carrying some beef jerky with her. She thrust it into my hands.

"Eat, Little Wolf; it is important that you eat."

I chewed on the jerky and realized that she was right. I felt better almost instantly.

"Why do I feel so lousy?" I asked the old women.

"It is just the stress on your body. After all, little one, you are not as young as you used to be."

"Oh, thank you," I said to Ruby. "But I guess you're right," I pulled the blanket even closer around my neck. As I began to feel better, a thrill of excitement ran through my body, and I beamed at the two women, eager to tell them my story.

"Well?" Ruby said expectantly as she walked me back into the Dreamlodge and we sat by the fire.

"Ruby, this old woman reminds me so much of you," I said, looking at her suspiciously. Ruby only smiled and said nothing. "I don't know why you both can't just tell me things," I said. The two old women laughed and poked each other with their elbows. "We spent our time sitting by a pond somewhere in the mountains of Japan. It was a reflecting pond with beautiful stones and trees around it. There was a wooden house in the distance with low-hanging fog around it, but I didn't pay much attention to it. I was sitting with Shakkai, my teacher—*sensei,* as I called her. We talked about the 'captured landscape' and the meaning of gardens and what it means to be a 'captured landscape.' It was fascinating. I felt the same great love for her as I feel for you. The thing that is so disorienting to me, Ruby, is that I am going into a future life and it does not feel that different. My desires are the same, my needs are the same, and even though I'm in another body— Japanese, with long black hair and beautiful bronze skin—I don't feel any different. I just feel like me, as if my spirit can simply put on another body like a suit of clothes. The clothes look one way or another, formal or informal, but I don't feel any different, because they're simply a different color or a different cut. I'm fascinated with this. It gives me a real sense of continuing life through lifetimes. It isn't such a big deal, is it?"

Both of the women smiled at me and giggled at each other and to themselves.

Finally Agnes looked at me and placed her hand very gently on my shoulder. "My daughter, we make such a drama out of life. For some reason the human being has to develop an extraordinary ego just to exist. Because of that ego, we think we are better than the flowers, better than the animals and the birds, and certainly better than other human beings and races that are not our own, but in fact life is simply life, and life is sacred. Beyond anything, life is sacred. In a sense, I wish I had another word for *sacred.* It is given to so many things that are really not special, but I think that, because of these experiences, you will begin to understand that there is a sacred form to everything. There is a reason, as I have said so many times, for all the pain and terror we experience as a result of the societies we live in. These societies don't have much to do with the greater vision of existence, do they?"

"No," I said. "I can't believe it. I'm getting such a sense of timelessness. Oh, I'm so excited. I can't wait to work with Shakkai. She is so lovely and gentle and serene. It is like taking a great long drink of water when you have had none for three or four days. I am so thirsty for her. It is beautiful. Thank you, my teachers, for making this possible, for making it possible for me to experience this and for asking me to write about it. What a beautiful, exquisite gift for me and for my brothers and sisters! I only hope I can portray this feeling through words, because I can't even find the words to tell you about the beautiful quality of what I've just lived through. I feel very limited."

I turned to Ruby and was stunned with surprise as I saw big tears rolling down her cheeks. I leaned over and lifted one of the tears onto my finger and placed it on my own cheek. "My dear teacher," I said to Ruby, "what is your sadness?"

For several minutes Ruby said nothing, her eyes reflecting the light in the lodge, like the reflecting pool that had reflected the sun in my dreaming. "My tears are of joy," she said. "It is the joy of communication, of knowing that finally, through our work with you, you are beginning to see, to truly see, what we are all about. It is a great joy to me because, as you know in your own life, when you work in the world of power as a woman of power, you make a few dear friends and you isolate yourself from the world, because very few can understand your commitment, your pain, your desire for compassion and love. Few can relate to your life and what you seek. When I look at you, I see a woman who understands my heart, and that makes me very full." She placed her fist over her heart. I turned to Agnes, who smiled at me.

"This is a long path that we have walked together," Ruby continued. "It is a ribbon, a shiny ribbon of time, that goes through history. You need only to follow that ribbon to reach your illumination. We do not know how long we all have together, but never will there be a true separation. We are part of each other now, through the wisdom of understanding."

With these words, Agnes and Ruby got up and put out the fire carefully. We did a short ceremony at my altar to the Great Spirit, Mother Earth, and the powers of the four directions. Then we left the Dreamlodge and went to Agnes's cabin, where we ate well and slept dreamlessly through the night.

· 8 ·

A Gourd Womb

◆

*When an ordinary ignoramus
meets an immortal sage
and does not recognize him,
that too is in the order of things.*

— NIEH

◆

The next morning, before dawn, Ruby came crashing through the front door, making an inordinate amount of noise.

"Rise and shine!" she yelled at the top of her voice. "Rise and shine! Come, come, now, Little Wolf!" she yelled, giving me several nudges with the toe of her boot.

Agnes sat up straight on her cot, staring bleary-eyed at Ruby. "What's the matter?" she asked.

"Nothing is the matter! It's just time to work! Time to get moving! Idle hands are the devil's workshop," she said, putting down an enormous basketful of gourds in the center of the table.

"You needn't be so rough, Ruby," Agnes grumbled as she pulled on her clothes, washed her face, and walked outside.

"God, Ruby, take it easy," I said, pulling on my clothes and rolling up my sleeping bag.

Ruby was busy trying to light the fire under the tea water. The cabin was cold, so I threw some wood in the potbellied stove and lit it, rubbing my hands together, trying to wake up. Finally we were all seated around the table and the huge basket of gourds.

"What do you want us to do?" Agnes asked. "Make five hundred rattles for the youth club?" She picked up a gourd and looked at it carefully, turning it over and over in her hands.

"Very funny," Ruby said. "This is a teaching. Isn't that what this is all about? Teaching? We are going to teach Lynn something today."

I raised my eyebrows and said nothing as I picked up one of the gourds and looked at it carefully. It was large and pear-shaped, about eight inches long.

"I want you to become familiar with gourds," Ruby said.

"Okay," I answered. "But it's not as though I were unfamiliar with gourds, Ruby. I have made a few rattles in my life."

"It doesn't matter. I don't want you to make a rattle out of one of these gourds. I want you to feel them with your hands. I want you to *become* a gourd. That shouldn't be too hard for you," Ruby said, knocking the top of my head with her knuckles.

"Ouch!" I said. "Stop it!"

"Do you remember when Red Dog had July's spirit in a gourd, when he had stolen her spirit?" Ruby suddenly asked, getting more serious.

"Yes," I answered.

"I want you to remember that," she ordered, rubbing the gourd ominously with her fingers.

"What do you mean?" I asked. "Are you trying to scare me? Are you saying that you want to take my spirit and put it in a gourd?"

"No, Little Wolf. I just want you to think about all the things you know about gourds and their uses. This will help you understand the next journey you are to take."

"It will?"

"Yes."

"You mean they have gourds in Japan?"

"Yes, they do, but they are used differently. I want you simply to become familiar with these gourds. Take them outside. Put them on a blanket all around you. That is your lesson for today. Tonight we will talk about what you have learned. Class dismissed!"

After eating a couple of biscuits, I took a blanket and the basket of gourds, left the cabin, and headed for Dead Man's Creek. I found a soft, mossy place beside the running water, where I stretched the blanket out and emptied the basket of gourds. Maybe fifteen or twenty gourds lay all around on the blanket. I took out the small handsaw I had stored in the smokehouse, and sawed several of the gourds in half, some lengthwise, some crosswise. Then I examined them. I lay down on the blanket and rolled around with them, pretended that they had names, and talked to them as if they were my children. I found that some gourds were happy, some were male, others female, and some seemed to be rather sexless, actually. After several hours of working with them, I saw that they very definitely had personalities. Like everything else in life, they had spirits. Finally, at the end of the day, I put all the gourds back in the basket. Then I folded up the blanket and walked back up the path to the cabin. A stream of smoke was coming out of the chimney, so I knew that we would most likely be eating soon.

After a very wonderful dinner of smoked salmon, Agnes, Ruby, and I sat around the table. Ruby became very serious after we had spent several hours laughing together like carefree children. She seated herself next to me as she always does when she's going to get intense, on my left this time. She squinted at me and said, "Well, Little Wolf, are you out of your gourd yet?"

I glared at her and she said, "Just kidding, just kidding. All right, tell me."

I took a deep breath, trying to still my stomach, which was nervous in the face of Ruby's now confrontational attitude. I told her about the gourds, how I had felt, and how I had named them. Ruby nodded and said nothing. Agnes simply sat in the shadows, almost as if she were not there, she was so still and quiet.

"And I felt," I continued, "that they were containers for life force, a kind of environment for something very, very special. They contain the seeds of life, and I realize that the gourds are a womb. In a way, they create a womb that allows them to contain history and past and future lives of young gourds, of little life forms that are most special and extraordinary. Even we, as human beings, with all of our scientific knowledge, could not produce what a single gourd can produce. I found it very soothing to have these gourds near me. I thank you, Ruby, because never would it have occurred to me to place these gourds in such a way in my life. I have learned something very wonderful today. I've learned not only more about the power of the rattle, but about the power of Mother Nature and the Great Spirit in every form that is created on this planet."

When I was finished, Ruby sat there quietly for several minutes. I couldn't tell whether I had pleased or displeased her, but finally she nodded and said, "Yes, yes."

Without another word she got up. Then, taking the basketful of gourds, she turned to me and said, "My daughter, you are ready for your next journey. We will work tomorrow in the

Dreamlodge." She smiled at me very subtly, and I relaxed. I knew I had pleased her. Ruby turned and, carrying the basket, left the cabin without another word.

I looked across at Agnes, who was sitting straight upright in her chair, her eyes closed. I assumed she was asleep. Very quietly, I got up from the table and started to get undressed for bed. Agnes began to speak, her face still obscured by the shadows. Only her gray hair was visible, shining like a halo in the firelight.

"Lynn, that was very good. I want you to know that Ruby was pleased with what you said."

"I know that, Agnes, but thank you for telling me."

"You needn't be afraid of Ruby," Agnes said. "She is only here to be your guide with the deepest love and respect."

"Agnes, I understand that, but I can't help it. There is something about her power. It is like a brilliant flame, and every once in a while it burns me."

Agnes laughed, her shoulders jiggling the way they always do, and I laughed with her as we got ready for bed. I went to sleep feeling good and very full in my heart.

The next day I worked in my Dreamlodge. I prayed with my sacred bundles for guidance on my dream journey with Shakkai. I placed a tiny red river stone on my altar to represent her and hung a beautiful dream-catcher that was woven within a willow hoop as if Spider Woman herself had sent us her blessings. A herkimer crystal dropped from the center of it, casting rainbows of light on the old hide walls.

At last I felt centered and empowered enough to begin another process of double dreaming. Ruby joined me and picked up her Star Rattle as we began the ceremony.

The Tea Master

◆

Knowing the male,
keep the female.

— LAO-TZU,
TAO TE CHING

◆

The moment I saw Master Hara Kyoshi of Izu Province, I was filled with an unreasonable anxiety. He was a handsome older man with a cold, piercing light in his eyes, and he moved with extraordinary grace. He was nearly as graceful as Shakkai. They obviously were old friends, but their relationship seemed tenuous. We sat together in the *hanare* pavilion of the garden, beneath a weeping willow tree, its delicate branches trailing in the water as a thin plume of mist drifted like smoke across the pond. It was a lovely and serene afternoon. Master Hara spoke of his childhood and of Shakkai and her extraordinary talents. Why, then, was I put off by this man? In fact I was not only put off, but the back of my neck would crawl as he looked intently into my eyes. His shoulders were slightly hunched, belying his youthful grace. I thought he must be older than he appears. He was extremely perceptive of the world around him.

"In beauty is truth," he said, handing me a pink rhododendron flower from a vase on the low table next to us. I did not blush with Hara-san, because I was not flattered.

For several minutes, Master Hara looked at me from the periphery of his vision, from the left side of his line of sight, and finally he said, "You are beyond flattery, and that is good."

He smiled at Shakkai, who maintained a more austere presence than what was normal in my relationship with her. Then he promptly changed the subject. He said, "I would be entranced to see your sacred *hu*. You promised me a long time ago that I could visit with her."

Shakkai smiled and, bowing her head, said, "I would be most pleased to share her elegant beauty with you, Hara-san." She left the garden, leaving us alone.

"What is a sacred *hu*?" I asked, not knowing what else to say and not wanting to sit in silence with this man.

"A sacred *hu* is a gourd, a gourd garden. It contains a miniature version of this monastery, this captured garden, that Shakkai has built for her being. I am very excited. She shares this sacred *hu* with very few. In beauty is fullness of spirit," he said, looking at me again. "Shakkai can teach you to *see*. To *see* is the mastery of the tea ceremony. It is an ability you can learn once you remove yourself from the objective world." He pursed his lips and sat back a little, looking very serious and intent.

"Yes, I have removed myself from my world," I answered.

"Mastery of the tea is mastery of self. Mastery of self is learning to move your mind into that place of the sacred witness, deep within your own being. When you live in that sacred witness, then you begin to see without beliefs, without doubt. For doubt is what clouds your vision even now. Is that not true?" he asked.

Now I blushed, for he had touched a place of truth within me, and I was embarrassed at his ability to see me.

"You see? I have killed you, because I have the ability to see you, to truly see you. I do not think anything about you. I simply look at you. The veils of illusion have been torn away by the tea. I have mastered the ceremony. It no longer is my master, as it was for many years. And that is what you must seek to do with your teacher."

Feeling a little disarmed, I watched the setting sun glowing orange behind Master Hara's head, moving slowly toward the horizon. He was sitting in silhouette, a dark figure against the gathering clouds.

"I can see that you have learned well, Master Hara, and I thank you for your concern with me."

Shakkai returned, carrying a white pillow, upon which rested an object covered with a white cloth. She placed it before Hara-san and myself; then, ceremoniously and with a perfect, graceful motion, she removed the white cloth, and there sat her sacred *hu* for us to see. It was very beautiful, a large gourd polished with the touch of her hands. Very gently and with extraordinary control of every movement, Master Hara gently placed his fingers on the gourd, touching it with great respect and reverence. He turned it gently on its pillow, and then, looking to Shakkai, who nodded, he picked it up very gently, held it to the light, and said a prayer over it, then looked inside. Several moments went by. A gust of wind blew through our hair and stroked our skin, feeling like fine silk. A bolt of lightning, like a dragon's tail striking the ground, split the sky above us. Rolling thunder in the distance gently shook the ground. Tears fell from Master Hara's eyes and splashed onto his white kimono-styled shirt. He was deeply touched. He needed to say nothing. He looked into Shakkai's eyes as she looked into his, and a moment of great understanding passed between them. I felt invisible. I had never seen the *hu* before, and yet it was oddly familiar to me. I could not imagine where she kept it in her house.

Shakkai took the *hu* from Master Hara, then passed it to me. My fingers touched the gourd. Its surface felt like human flesh over taut muscles. I turned it slowly in my hands and looked inside to the beautiful garden in tiny miniature contained within. I was entranced with the tiny reflecting pool, the mirror reflecting my own eyes. It reminded me of something and jolted me. For a moment I saw a falcon. I saw a great bird in flight and a woman standing on a hill, dressed very strangely in a long gown, and then the vision left me. I looked toward Shakkai, who smiled at me. I didn't know if she had seen the vision with me, or what the explanation was for the experience, but I said nothing, feeling that she knew, and I handed the *hu* back to her, my hands shaking slightly.

Shakkai placed the cloth again over her beautiful gourd. I could see from her movements and the expression on her face that this *hu* meant everything to her. It was the embodiment of the garden that she had worked on—this magnificent temple she had built, that represented her love for the Tao, for her goddess spirit. She left us once again to return the *hu* to its place.

Master Hara looked at me, his cheeks still moist, his eyes cold, like a black reflecting pond in the mountains. "You would do well to learn the tea ceremony," he said to me with an ominous tone in his voice. For a moment the image of Master Hara fringed off into the light of the sun, and he suddenly appeared to have a red beard and tanned skin. But that apparition disappeared like a ghost as I shook my head.

"Does Shakkai teach the tea ceremony?" I asked in a weak voice.

"Yes, but it is my way. It is not really hers."

"Oh," I said, "you mean I should learn the ceremony from you?"

"I am suggesting that it would be of interest on your path," he said very carefully.

The clouds were gathering above us. It was going to rain soon. I could smell moisture in the air. I took a deep breath as I looked at Master Hara, wondering what it was about this man that disturbed me so.

"Where do you live?" I asked finally.

"I live closer to the mountains. I live much as Shakkai has lived. I have separated myself from my people and from the busyness of urban life. For many years I lived in Izu Province, then in Kyoto. But now I live with the trees. You see, it is power that you are after," he said, a glint of red sunset shining in his eyes.

"Power?" I asked.

"Yes. Power," he said, his eyes pinning me.

I did not know how to answer him. Finally I said, "Yes, power over the false self."

"Well, I do not mean simply power over the self," he said. "That is only the first step to true power."

Then Master Hara did a disturbing thing. He reached out and touched my hand, and rubbed his fingers on my knuckles. I was taken aback and moved my hand away, as if I were moving a strand of hair out of my eyes.

"It is not often that you find someone with your dedication," he said, "or with your ability to focus. It is needed to perform the ceremony properly. So, for the tea to become your god, you must remove all doubt from your life. It is doubt that puts you into your mind, that makes the mind work, that makes the mind have power over you. You must learn to use your mind to gain power over your mind. Then you must move out of the mind and into the sacred tea. But first you must learn to see what is real and not what you only think is real."

"But how do you know what is real and what is not?" I asked.

"That is something that you need to learn. Look at the intensity of the garden. Shakkai is a real person. She can teach you about color, about seeing the deep vibrance of green and how it moves into your heart. She can teach you about the depths of blue, like the pond that we are sitting next to. She can teach you to see, but it must become your experience, this process of seeing, because otherwise it will be nothing to you, and you will doubt my words as you do now. Each of us must learn differently. We focus in different ways, but we come to the same end. That end is always power. And I can teach you about power better than anyone else."

I thought it was very presumptuous of him to speak to me in this manner. It was as if Hara-san were trying to steal me away from Shakkai. I did not like this man.

Just then, Shakkai returned. She was laughing. She sat down in front of us and looked at Master Hara and shook her finger at him. "Hara-san, you are trying to steal my apprentice, and I would like you to cease. A *tengu* mountain goblin might come and play tricks on you."

She bowed her head and looked at him with great force. For a moment the humor was gone from her face. Just then, as the lightning struck behind us again and cut a path of jagged gold into the great mountain, I saw for a moment a light pass from Shakkai's eyes to Hara-san's. He opened his eyes wide and fell backwards, as if he had lost his balance. He scrambled to his feet most unceremoniously, his fine silk clothes stained from the grass. Then he sat back up again, looking stunned, and for the moment very frightened, but only for a moment. Had I not been staring at his eyes, I would have missed the expression that moved fleetingly across his face.

As if nothing had happened, Shakkai smiled and reached out to him, touching his hand. "You must be more careful in the way you sit. I wouldn't want you to hurt yourself."

"The lightning spirits have always been yours, Shakkai. And I have mine," he replied.

"You are a Master of the Tea," Shakkai said, "and I honor you." But her eyes were not smiling.

"You are a good friend," he said, bowing low, "and I honor you and your great mastery of power. Shakkai, you are a true mistress of the spirit of the captured landscape. May you sleep well in your sacred *hu* tonight." He bowed and, looking to the sky, addressed me. "I must leave you now, before I am drowned by the rain. It has been my pleasure to speak with you, and I will see you again." He turned, and Shakkai led him out of the garden.

I sat next to the pond, considering everything that had just happened. I watched the light show in the sky. The lightning was coming more frequently. Thunder rolled down the sides of the mountains and shook the earth that I sat on. I wanted to stay outside and enjoy the rain, but I knew I must go into the house with Shakkai so that we could have our dinner together. When Shakkai returned, we walked up the path toward the house.

"Come. Let us place some cheesecloth over the irises to protect them from the storm that is surely coming."

So we did not return to the house, but went around the other way, to the other side of the pond, where purple and white irises grew by the dozens. They were beautiful and gentle against the landscape. Their blossoms unfurled in the evening light. We placed huge sheets of thin cheesecloth across them to protect them.

"It may hail tonight," Shakkai said, looking up at the sky and testing the temperature, which was getting deeply cool. Then we turned toward the house.

"How did you like Hara-san?" she asked, looking at me with her head cocked sideways.

"I enjoyed Master Hara," I lied.

Shakkai stopped me and looked at me, holding both of my shoulders. "Never lie to me," she ordered. "It is not becoming to you."

"I apologize," I said. "I know he is your friend."

"He is a man of power," Shakkai said after a moment of consideration. "He is a great Master of the Tea, and I want you to observe him. Just watching him do the ceremony will teach you many things. But beware. He is, as I say, a man of power, of dark power. He is capable of doing anything to acquire power."

"What do you mean?" I asked.

"It means that I have power, and you have power, or you would not be working with me. To gain more power, he likes to set himself against people. He likes to try his mettle, if you understand my meaning. He is a very dark soul."

"Do you mean he is a *shih,* a sorcerer?" I asked.

"He is a man who defines the light by his own lack of it," she said. "Some call him *yen-shih,* or the master bent backward."

We laughed together as she squeezed my hand.

"What is it, child?" she asked, looking at my face in my obvious confusion.

"I don't understand how you could like a man who could do you harm."

"Because he keeps me on my toes. And I enjoy that, to a point," she said. "But when I found him trying to take you away, to hypnotize you, that made me angry."

"Yes, Shakkai. You frightened me," I said. "Did I actually see what I thought I saw?"

Shakkai laughed and placed the back of her knuckles gently against my cheek. "And what did you think you saw?" she asked.

"I saw lightning, or light like lightning, move from your eyes to his. And that's what dumped him over backwards," I said, very pleased.

"Yes. You saw me move with my intent and give him a shove. I wanted him to know that I see him as well as he sees me. I do not want to be fooled with, like a *saizo* clown in a *sengu manzai* stage performance. It is a trifle and it is not important, but I do protect what is part of my world. You are part of my world, my dear."

I took a deep breath, not wanting to think much more about this strange man. "Your sacred *hu* was most beautiful, and filled me with much joy," I said.

"Yes. It is going to be part of your teaching. You will learn later about the sacred *hu.* I am glad you saw it today. I had not shown it to you before because you were not ready. The sacred *hu* lives at the center of my personal womb mandala, my personal power painting. It will become very important to you in your work, and you will soon make your own sacred *hu.* It is part of what we will do together."

"Is your sacred *hu* an embodiment of your spirit, so to speak?" I asked.

"Yes. How wonderful that you can see that. It is part of what I am. It took me a very, very long time to be able to make that *hu*— the balance of the elements, the balance of the stones, the tiny

ones, and the pond, the great mirror. Yes. I had to know the great
spirits of the mountain very well. I had to know the *tengu* spirits
that live in the trees. I had to be able to speak to them, to know
their heart, so that I could see where they belonged in the design
of nature. It was the breath of nature that taught me. You cannot
just *design* a garden. It must be created from the inside, not the
outside. To truly see, you must see from the inside of your own
being. When you have true vision, the outside matters very little.
But when it is constructed by the interior of your being, the outcome is magnificently beautiful. When Hara said that within
beauty is truth, that is what he meant. For me, the sacred *hu* represents the evaluation and manifestation of my own femininity. It
represents the dreams of all women, the mysterious female. It is of
woman. The sacred *hu* represents the womb, the eternal womb of
Mother Earth. It contains the mystery of life in symbols and in
spirit. It is the essence of who I am."

"Then how could you have shown it to Master Hara?" I asked.

"Because power begets power," Shakkai replied. "He is a great
master. He has worked as hard as I have, but in very different
ways. For light to exist, there must also be darkness. So you must
honor all the sides and all the faces of God. Master Hara is the
dark face of the Tao."

"But I don't want to do that, Shakkai. I don't want to honor the
dark side."

"If you do not honor the dark side," Shakkai said with great
seriousness, "then you will be *ruled* by the dark side. You must
look at it and understand it, and then turn your face away and let
the light be your guide. To understand the darkness does not mean
you become it. You can paint a picture of a horrible *oni* demon.
You can describe him in every gruesome detail, but that does not
mean you *become* that demon. You only describe it, paint it, and
see it. Examine it carefully, knowing what it is made of, understanding its power and its limitations."

"Are you speaking of a conflict?" I asked.

"Only if you have ego is there a conflict between the dark and
the light. If there is no ego, there is no fight. There is only a divine
vulnerability, which is your very best shield and defense."

· 10 ·

Celebration of Life

◆

You won't discover the limits of the soul,
however far you go.

— HERACLITUS

◆

For several days, Shakkai and I had been making a pilgrimage to the shrines around Mount Ontake, or the Honorable Peak. It had been raining. The thunderheads were billowing white and dark gray above us, moving across the sky like *kami* spirits at play. During this journey I had felt the spirits of the mountain more than I ever had before. They were giving me a sense of anticipation that I felt in my stomach, almost fear, because I could feel them playing with my hair as they moved with the wind. But I could tell that the *kami* welcomed us and that they felt they lived in spirit form within our beings, as I was beginning to see and understand that our souls also lived within this sacred mountain.

We rested beneath a juniper tree alongside the path near a Shinto oratory. We took out our lunch. Sensei heated water for tea over the small fire that she diligently made whenever we paused to eat. She carried a tiny earthenware tea service, and heated the water in one of the tiny bowls after we had had some soup with tofu and seaweed. The scent of the pine and juniper was pungent in my nostrils. It was the fragrance of the mountain that was giving me a heady feeling, or so I thought. Sensei was looking at me sideways in a way that I had become accustomed to as if she were an old crow or an owl. Suddenly she burst into laughter, and leaning back on her heels, she slapped her thighs in a boisterous manner that startled me.

"Shakkai, you scared me," I said.

"Many things happen to a person when she falls in love," Shakkai finally said to me, handing me an ivory-colored bowl of tea. I held the bowl in my hands, feeling its granular surface and letting the steam rise and cover my face with a gentle cloud of moisture. I said nothing, knowing that my cheeks were reddening in the gleaming afternoon sunlight.

"When you fall in love," she continued, "an opening begins to happen in your heart and in your body. It is that opening that frightens people. They think they are losing control in some way."

She paused for several minutes, watching the effect of her words. I continued to look into the tea and listen to the wrens hopping about in the tree branches. Only a few bird notes were missing, so many were gathered around.

"Think of the sun, O Kiku. Look at the sun with me." She pointed toward the sun, low in the sky. "The sun never ceases in its movement, as the earth never ceases in hers. The sun comes up and you can worship her; you can love the sun and her goddess Amaterasu Omikami. She can bring life to the earth, and warmth. And then the sun goes down. Every day the sun is the same."

"I don't understand, Sensei," I said, still not looking up from my tea.

"The sun," she went on, "is a being of great power. She is always in her center and never leaves it. Whatever happens on the earth, whatever changes occur—whether there's an ice age, whether we are traveling to Mars, whether there are wars, whether there is love on this great Mother Earth—the sun rises and sets, because the sun never loses her power center."

I nodded in understanding, eager to hear what Shakkai was about to say.

"I am sure you cannot imagine that the sun would ever do anything other than rise and set. But a person is like the sun, if that person stands in her power. Whatever happens around her in the world, she goes on living, never moving out of that center, never moving away from that place of bliss that is her sacred witness in the world. Over and over again, O Kiku, I try to show you, to mirror to you, this experience."

"Are you saying I am off my center?" I asked, finally looking toward Shakkai. Again she burst into laughter, until tears rolled down her cheeks. I felt disconcerted by the way she laughed at me, and said, "Sensei, you are embarrassing me."

Shakkai reached out her hand, touched the backs of my knuckles, and gently stroked them. "You need not be ashamed of being in love," she said.

"But, Sensei, I did not come here to fall in love. I gave away my

worldly possessions to the poor. I gave away all of my life, everything I had created in the material sense, so that I could come and
be with you. I gave it all away to the people in the world who need
so very much, and I renounced my physical life, in a sense, to
come join you. And I am not in love. Besides, I only just met Kat-
san." I hesitated a moment before using the familiar form for Kat
and then decided it was appropriate.

Shakkai laughed even harder. Now I was beginning to feel a little angry, because I was very proud to have given up so much to be
here. Now what was I finding? I was finding trouble of the heart—
the last thing in the world that I ever anticipated. I did not want to
be in love with Kat-san. I did not want to lose my center in some
worldly love affair. I was here to elevate my spirit, and I told
Shakkai that.

"I am here to become enlightened. How is it that this could be
happening to me? I went through my twenties in Kyoto and in the
world looking for someone to be in love with, looking for a family, looking for all of these things, and instead it was all taken from
me. Then I renounced love for professional success. And now that
I am here, look what happens. This is not what I want," I said
very firmly. I had fallen in love with Kat-san the moment I saw
him, but I fiercely denied this to myself.

At this point Shakkai was rolling around on the ground, laughing hysterically. I was very disconcerted by her behavior. It was not
what I expected of my teacher, and I said so. Of course, this made
Shakkai laugh even more. Finally she settled down and took a sip
of tea. Looking for all the world like the ancient queen of the forest, with twigs in her hair and dirt smudges on her elbows and her
knees, she folded her hands in her lap and looked at me with a
smile of compassion.

"My dear O Kiku, what do you think enlightenment is?"

I thought for a long time and then said, "The realization of my
center."

"Who is this person perceiving your center?"

I looked at her, feeling frustrated because I knew what I meant,
but had great difficulty putting my thoughts into words. After a
long time I said, "I know that in my center is an emptiness, a
space, a nothingness that is pure love, pure grace, and I sit here in

the center of my being when I am with you, Sensei, knowing that the person perceiving me is an illusion, that this person is my personal myth, who for some reason is around to make difficulty for me."

Shakkai laughed again, unable to contain herself. Then she said, "Yes, O Kiku, it is around to make trouble for you, but there is a reason for that, and the reason is that the physical body is an extraordinary mirror, a tool to enable magic to come into your life, if only you will let it. We think, when we go on a spiritual path, that we should denounce everything and sit in meditation, and finally we will be God incarnate. That is one way; but it is not my way. My way is the celebration of life, the dance of life."

"But, Sensei, then why would you live here in this garden that you have created? Why would you not be living in Tokyo?"

"Ah, because there are different kinds of life. There are different ways to celebrate. I did live in Tokyo and Kyoto, in the centers of the world, as well you know. But I chose to experience this, finally." She swept her arms around to the wilderness surrounding us. "That does not mean I am sorry for the life I once led. It just means I want to experience something different now. It means I want to commune with the wilderness of peace in my soul. There is an abundance of joy in my heart, and I want to express that in the most meaningful way I can, and this is my way. It is my celebration. It is not a retraction from life. It is an opening of my heart. That is what I want you to learn. You are feeling something so very wonderful. You are feeling love for the first time."

"Yes, it is true, and I am very afraid," I finally admitted in a whisper.

"But, you see, Kat-san is afraid too. Kat-san is afraid of the mirror that you create together. That's why it is all so beautiful," Shakkai said, rolling up her things and putting them in a little pack.

We started to move up the trail. I wanted to sit and talk, but Shakkai obviously felt the need to move on up the mountain. We climbed around one craggy granite outcropping that shielded us from a great waterfall on the other side. We could hear the beautiful fall of water, in a constant rush that reverberated through the canyons. We rounded the cliffs to see birds floating in updrafts in the mist created by the torrent falling hundreds of feet to the river below. We stepped carefully on a fairly wide trail cut into the side of the mountain. As we walked, Shakkai would point out certain things to me to illustrate our conversation.

"Look at the birds," she said. "Look at that hawk circling above. It is pure in its essence. It is in the center of its being, as if it were focused on the opening between its eyes, called the Hall of Brightness. If it swoops down for its prey, it never moves off its center. But you see, what is happening with Kat-san and you—you are tending to move off of your center the moment you open to love. That is your mistake, and this is what you will learn—to stay in that center, even though you are open."

"That idea is wonderful," I said, watching the hawk circle high above us, making infinity designs in the air.

I was listening to Shakkai so intently that I didn't see a place in front of me where the trail fell away gently, and as I put my foot down, I slipped, and suddenly I was sliding very fast toward the edge of the trail and the precipice and certain death on the rocks hundreds of feet below. Shakkai, instead of helping me, stood ready to reach out her hand, but she did nothing. As I started to slip and fall, I became totally panicked, reaching out in all directions. Shakkai moved just far enough back so that I could not reach her. Finally I grabbed a tiny, gnarled pine tree, secured in a crevice to my right. It held and kept me from falling. I looked up at her questioningly from the ground, horrified that she would not help me.

"Why didn't you lend me a hand?" I yelled as I scrambled to my feet.

"Because you must learn to stay aware. That happened just now because you were again off your center. You must find your way back to your own strength, or you may as well be dead. You cannot always reach out for someone. There are times when that is appropriate and times when it is not." I was very shaken by the incident. Tears ran down my cheeks as I brushed the mud off my clothes and picked the stones out of my *getas*. My feelings were very hurt. As a woman, I had always been given assistance. As we walked down the trail, neither of us saying anything, her words boiling in my mind, I began to realize that indeed it was true. I had moved off my center, and I had expected help instead of turning to myself. When I saw that she didn't help me, I did turn to myself, and I found my own safety. It was a bitter lesson, but one I grudgingly admitted I needed.

"Follow me," Shakkai ordered, leaving our conversation in mid-thought. She struck off the trail at one point. "Walk carefully," she said. I picked my way behind her, feeling the trail continually moving out from underneath my feet, gravel and stones slipping underneath my *getas*. The shock of having almost fallen made me hold my attention and center myself as we walked.

Finally I said, "Sensei, we should not have worn *getas* on this journey. It is very hard for me to keep my footing."

"It will make you pay attention," she said, walking quite quickly down the very narrow winding path that led down along the edge of the waterfall. Suddenly I looked up and saw that she had disappeared. I realized that the trail led into a cavern filled with sacred herbs beneath the tumultuous waterfall. The dampness in the air was heavy, and the smell of moist earth and herbs was pungent as I walked into the darkness.

The cave was actually high enough for me to stand comfortably. I stopped a moment to adjust my eyes to the shadows, and found Shakkai already seated on a spiral-woven mat on a ledge just under the falls. The falls were cascading in front of her, down hundreds of feet into the turquoise blue river below. The water was far enough away so that she remained dry, and she indicated for me to sit next to her. I did so, the vision of aquamarine water before me. We were looking out at the sky through a translucent window of moving water. It was as if this cave were here for a very special reason. Shakkai, as if reading my thoughts, put her hand on my knee for a moment, assuaging my ruffled feelings with a look of deep compassion.

"This is a sacred cave. It is here that many old masters reached enlightenment. It is here that I have worked with my teacher. This is our destination," she said.

"Sensei, I feel as if we were in the womb of the mountain, as if the river, the falls, the water, were her blood and life force."

"The fall of the water can be like your love for Kat-san. It is a flow of life that should not be stopped. Were I to reach out and try to stop this pounding river, it would be very difficult, but it could be done," she said.

"Yes," I replied.

"We have talked a lot, O Kiku. It is much for you to digest in one day. Sit beneath this waterfall and allow the power and flow of this water to enter you. Allow your thoughts to fall away and your heart to expand, and experience your own truth. Let your mind and body be set free. Let your being be supple and empty. Let your mind flow downriver with the water. Allow yourself to be in touch in the most loving way with the real 'living midnight' that lives inside you. It is the arousal of your positive energies. You do not need me. You do not need anyone. Because of that, you are ready for love."

· 11 ·

Old Holy Crooked One

♦

The mountains, I become part of it. . . .
The herbs, the fir tree, I become part of it.
The morning mists, the clouds, the gathering waters,
I become part of it. . . .

— NAVAJO CHANT

♦

I was sitting one afternoon with Shakkai in her garden in a small detached area called a *hanare*. We were resting by the pond, watching our reflections rippling on the surface of the cobalt blue water. For a long time we had been meditating together, uniting our spirits and receiving energy through a mystical opening in the body called "the mysterious female." The immortality of the valley spirit is based on this foundation of receptivity. As she said so often, we were coming to understand and have knowledge of each other's hearts and energy fields. We sat listening to the birds in the trees, feeling the gentle wind against our cheeks and blowing in our hair.

I finally asked, "And how is it, Shakkai, that a person can go from one lifetime to another, and yet never seem to learn the more important things?"

"What do you mean by 'important things'?"

"Why is it that we don't become enlightened more quickly? Why is it so slow?"

My impatience must have showed in my voice. Shakkai laughed at my consternation. There was the now-familiar twinkle in her eye.

"You remind me of someone," I said.

"And who is that?" she asked with a smile at the corners of her mouth.

"I don't know," I said, "but it is true—you are so familiar to me. Is it possible that we have spent lifetimes together?"

Shakkai looked away. I could have sworn there was a glint of tears in her eyes. She said nothing for the longest time, as if her thoughts were going back to some pleasurable moment long ago.

"You know, when I look at you, Shakkai, I feel such love for your presence. I open my heart. I see your Ainu ancestry shining through your eyes. I see you looking almost like the pictures of the Native Americans who roamed the plains of North America so long ago."

The old woman cocked her head sideways, like a crow listening in the treetops. She looked at me sharply for a moment and said, "Is that so?"

"Yes," I said. "It is as if you were from another world. Perhaps I'm from another world as well. I'm so confused, Shakkai. I get flashes of another reality in my dreams and when I am in your presence. I see you sometimes as someone other than who I know you to be."

Shakkai took a stick and drew a design in the sand beside her. It looked as if she were considering whether to tell me something or not. She looked up at me for a moment and then looked back down at the sand. Finally she nodded, as if making an agreement with herself, and said nothing. I wished so much that she would share her innermost thoughts with me, but I felt that would be presumptuous and that it would not be appropriate for me to ask such a thing.

"It's all a problem of weightlessness, isn't it?" Shakkai finally said as she watched a leaf from a golden maple tree behind us float through the air and onto the surface of the water. It floated there like a tiny boat, waiting to carry the light of the sun to the other shore.

"What do you mean, 'weightlessness'?" I asked.

"There is light," she said, "and there is light. One kind of light illuminates the shadows, and another kind of light illuminates the spirit." Shakkai picked up the stick, held it high in the air, and let it fall to the ground. "You see, it's also a matter of gravity. If the stick is long and large, it becomes heavy, because more of it is exposed to the pull of the earth. In instructing you on how to meditate, I ask you to sit directly on the ground, to sit with a straight spine, in a lotus position. Is that not correct?"

"Yes," I said, placing my legs into a more correct position and straightening my back and locking my fingers.

Shakkai smiled with approval and then asked, "Have you not wondered why I tell you to sit in such a way?"

"No, not actually," I said. "I just thought you were supposed to."

"There was a time when you would have asked me," Shakkai said. "There was a time when you never would have accepted anything I said without an argument."

Surprised, I asked, "What do you mean, 'there was a time'?"

Shakkai shook her head and laughed and slapped her thigh in a raucous manner that again surprised me. She explained nothing more, but continued, "You see, my child, I cannot talk about time in a relative world. I cannot teach you the way a professor teaches a student, because then your knowledge would be merely borrowed; it would not be of your experience. Just to tell you about the truths of spirit and the wisdoms of the world would not help you. They would only feed your intellect and make your ego even bigger."

I wondered if it was so obvious that my ego was big. I looked down at the sand and remained quiet.

"To tell you of time," she went on, "would be to waste your time. So I am going to help you experience time and, perhaps, timelessness. To experience what is timeless, what is beyond the relative world, is joyous. It is an illusion that you and I sit here separated. It will help you to understand the idea of weightlessness."

"I would like to do that," I said. "I am fascinated with your words."

"Whether you are fascinated or not," Shakkai said, "it is true." She smiled and reached over and pinched my arm very gently. "You think that the world is not as it seems, and that you want to know more about that. Am I correct?" I nodded, and she went on, "In the practice of meditating, if I ask you to sit straight on the ground, sometimes without clothes on so that you can be closest to the vibration and energy of Mother Earth, do you question me?"

"No," I said.

"You believe that what I say is real, and I thank you for that, but when you do not understand something in its totality, I want you to ask me, so that you will understand things in a circle. You will know things from the center of that circle and all of the

aspects of the directions around that circle. Otherwise your knowing will not be complete."

Shakkai stood up with amazing agility for a woman of her age.
She lifted her arms to the sky, closed her eyes, and, holding her
arms out to her sides, her white kimono-style sleeves floating out
like a bird's wings, turned slowly in a circle. Then, furling her
arms down, she looked at me.

"You see, when I stand like this, there is less gravity pulling at
my body. It only comes up through my feet. I want you to stand
and practice something with me."

I stood up next to her, my body and limbs much more stiff than
hers had been. She giggled at me as I straightened my knees, which
cried in pain from having been folded for so long.

"Now stand straight," she ordered. I did so. "Close your eyes,
and let's meditate for a few minutes. Follow your breath in and
out. Just let yourself totally relax, but stay very straight, with your
shoulders directly over your hips and your hips directly over your
feet."

I did so for some time. As the breeze blew through the small valley, I felt like a proud tree standing against the wind. Then, slowly,
I began to lose a sense of my attachment to the earth. It was a
wonderful feeling that I had never had before. I wondered if,
because I was meditating with Shakkai, she helped me to move
into this trancelike state more easily. Then Shakkai asked me to
tilt my body to the left. "Lean to the left," she said, and when I
did, I felt the pull of the earth. I could feel it. I could almost sense
an unseen connection between my extended body and the earth
below. "Now," she said, "lean to the right." I did so again, feeling
a heaviness. "Now, my child, do you feel the difference? Do you
feel how much heavier you are when more of your body is
extended over the earth's surface?"

"May I open my eyes?" I asked.

"Yes," she said.

"When I lean to either side, I feel the heaviness very definitely. It
is as if I have gained several pounds."

"Yes," Shakkai said, clapping her hands, "that is exactly right.
That is what happens, so you are more full of weight. Is that not
right?"

"Yes," I said.

"When you meditate, I want you to sit with your spine straight, or you can meditate in a standing position. Some people even meditate standing on their hands."

"They do?" I asked.

"Yes, they do."

"Well, it will be a long time before I can manage that," I said.

"Yes, I am sure that is true," Shakkai laughed with me. "You see, our nature as human beings is to lean. When we relax, we spread out all over the place. We lie down, and we feel the full pull of the earth against our bodies. It's gravity, nothing complicated, very simple, but it is not the state of weightlessness that we are looking for."

"But again, Shakkai, why weightlessness? What does that have to do with anything?"

"It has to do with your mind. Your body is your mind. It is matter. It has weight and substance. When you move into higher consciousness, when your soul becomes illuminated for all time, you will be in a state of weightlessness. When you move into emptiness, you move into that process. You begin to let go of the body. You let go of the mind and its control over your thoughts, your emotions, and your physical self. When that leaf left its mother tree, when it floated off the branch and into the air, it was as if its spirit took flight. Watch," she said. "There, that leaf, high in the tree, is beginning to float towards us. It's floating with the currents of air. In a sense it has let go of its connections with its body, with its larger physical self, and has moved into the source of power. The source of power floats on the wind. The source of power is like the wind itself. It can move mountains and change the surface of the oceans, but it is unseen. You cannot prove it, but you can feel it. It is like magic. Believe in the Great Spirit. Believe in the Tao in the same way. Believe in the integrity of your own soul. Believe in the movement of the winds from the north and the south. Those winds can change the surface of the earth, just as spirit can change the surface of your mind.

"Kat-san is sometimes called 'Spirit Wind,' because he has learned to harness the ally of the wind. When he uses his sword, he uses it like a giant wind. It is invisible, yet it cuts through anything and you cannot see it move. You only know that it has happened, because you see the effect. You may feel it on your body, but again, it is transparent, without form. Weightlessness is learning to be without form."

"But how can that be, Shakkai? We cannot exist and be without form."

"Ah, yes, therein lies the question, not only the answer. Do you know why we have form?" she asked, picking up the leaf that had floated from the tree. She held it up to the light, examining the veins, testing the texture of it with her fingers, and finally she held it to her forehead, feeling the coolness against her skin.

She stood up and indicated for me to follow her. We began to walk on the smooth stones placed for each footstep around the lake. We walked beneath the trees, through the shafts of sunlight, moving through the leaves, smelling the flowers, the fragrance on the air.

"What a magnificent garden!" I said. Shakkai nodded, pleased that I enjoyed her temple, her gift to the world.

"You see, weightlessness is not a part of form. It's what happens after you have had form. To have weightlessness, you must first have form. A teacher will take on an addiction, a problem, so that she can have form in this lifetime, so that she can be seen by an apprentice, so that he can teach. I have taken on certain aspects of karma so that I can be here for you, my apprentice."

"I don't understand," I said after several minutes, thinking about what she had said. "What do you mean, you take on an addiction?"

"Haven't you ever noticed," she asked, "that a great teacher—a truly enlightened being—may have an alcoholism problem, a disease, or perhaps a problem with sex or food? These great teachers have an addiction, usually a pretty big one in one area, so that they become heavy, so that they give away their weightlessness and take on a more opaque quality, the quality of form. To stay in form, you must have difficulties. If you are clear in your spirit, if you are truly weightless in your being, then you will leave your form and you will move on to another dimension, but if you have achieved weightlessness in this lifetime, you can also learn to take your body with you. When the great teachers of the past have gone on to the other side, they have often taken their bodies with them. Sometimes they have even taken their horse, as Mohammed did. He took what he needed, what he loved, to the other side, because he had learned to be weightless. Buddha, though, left no remains behind him. He simply disappeared as many teachers have done. Traditional Taoists do not believe in reincarnation, but in great longevity, such as is found on the Isles of the Immortals. It has been my experience that we do have other lifetimes, so I had to depart from one of my beloved masters at that point. I think you can move between the dimensions. You can move into the other world with your body and come back to this one at will."

"Really?" I asked. "Is that really true, Shakkai? Why would I want to take my body with me, anyway?" I said after several minutes of thinking about it.

Shakkai laughed and then said, "Well, I can understand that consideration. If you are a perfected being, your body is perfected, and it gives you a chance to manifest back into the physical when it is needed."

"But I thought you could choose parents and reincarnate," I said.

"It is not exactly that simple," Shakkai said. "It is a great privilege to be on this earth. It is truly a schoolhouse that we have here for every person alive. Even if they are unaware of that gift, it is the truth and they are learning in spite of themselves. Eventually, all sentient beings may learn what they have come here to learn, but that is a lot to ask," she said smiling at me. "There are only a few who are truly aware of our plight as physical beings and our gift as physical beings, because in truth, it is both."

We took a turn in the path and walked across a beautiful bridge that was built over one end of the pond. It was made of river-smoothed stones, fit together like an intricate puzzle. I traced my hands over their flat surface and smiled at Shakkai with enormous respect in my eyes.

Shakkai looked at me and said, "There will be a time, not long from now, when you will build your own garden. I will help you. It is good that you appreciate what this is all made of."

"It is made of spirit, and it is made of love. How could any human create a garden so beautiful?" I said, and I felt it in my heart. The old woman beamed at me, very pleased that I appreciated her talent. "Why is it important to transcend the mind?" I asked.

"Because in transcending the mind, you transcend your confusion. It is the mind that is the troublemaker. It is also the mind that moves you toward power," she said with a soft tremor in her voice. "It is a fine line, you see. Like all things, it is a choice. You can choose your bad habits. You can choose to waste your energy by being muddled and retracing old mistakes, or you can move on into the world of power and take your stand as a woman in this universe."

She turned to me. Her face had gone very serious. There was no emotion around her eyes or her mouth. She looked at me intently, and then led me to a small hill that looked out over the lake toward the mountain, snow-capped and serene in the distance.

"It is here," she said, "that I want you to sit and meditate, thinking about the concept of weightlessness and the source of open emptiness. Protective *oni* spirits will surround you. Think about our words together and what your own form means to you. Be aware of the edges of your spirit and where they meet your body. Sit now."

I sat in the lotus position atop the small hill, directly on the ground, which had been smoothed to perfection. I disliked disrupting the pristine quality of the earth, so I sat down carefully and arranged my feet and my hands until my back was perpendicular to the earth, and I faced the great mountain.

"Close your eyes," she said, as she sat down behind me, her spine against mine. And very quietly she began to talk to me. She told me to take deep breaths and to follow my breath in and out—to visualize the color blue as I breathed in and, as I breathed out, to visualize the color green. Then she asked me to clear my mind completely, to let any thoughts float away like debris in the wind, to set my emotions and my judgments aside until we were finished.

"If you could clear your mind of all thought for ten minutes," she said, "you would be enlightened. It is that profound to sit in a state of emptiness."

Then she called in the Goddess Who Makes the Flower Buds

Open, who is sometimes called the Goddess of Mount Fuji, and she asked the Goddess to sit across from me, to help me and to bring me clarity. She asked me to open my heart, to open my mind, to the thought of this resplendent Goddess and to let her come to me and become part of my conjuring. Then Shakkai left me alone in my meditation, telling me that she would come to me when the time was right.

"Remember to ask the Goddess of the Mountain for a message. I expect that she wants to ask you or tell you something very special. Be sure to listen for the message that she wants to show you," Shakkai said as I heard her turn with gentle grace and depart down the path toward the pond.

After a long time of contemplating the beautiful garden, I continued to meditate. But every time I closed my eyes, instead of seeing the Goddess, I thought I heard a voice whispering on the gentle breeze, calling me to come. Finally I opened my eyes and looked all around. I followed an irresistible urge to walk down a series of *tobiishi*, or steppingstones. Thick *shiba* grass and green moss grew luxuriantly between the stones. I could feel the soft coolness on my sandaled feet, and I knew I was to continue walking. When I came to a fork in the path, small *toneishi*, or marker stones, had been piled carefully as barriers to my taking the right-hand trail. Still I heard the gentle calling on the wind, and I followed the path around to a more wilderness-like area of the garden. The garden was acres wide. From this vantage point, Shakkai's house was hidden from view. I stopped for a moment, letting my spirit glory in the creative power that had defined such a work of art as this garden. I felt like I was standing overlooking the ocean and a wilderness shore on a northern island. I listened to the fresh spring water trickling onto flat stones. Then I followed the curving path through clumps of sweet clover displaying pink blossoms, and then the path sloped up to a rugged incline. I followed it.

I came to a stand of gnarled juniper trees that looked stunted in their growth, perhaps because they were growing in shale and very rocky ground. The path led me through a bonsai forest. I threaded my way through the twisted trunks of larger dwarf pine trees and was stopped by a cloud that seemed to be hovering in the tree branches. I looked at it curiously, wondering what a cloud was doing in the middle of the forest garden, with no other clouds around. I walked slowly around the tree, looking at it suspiciously, and wondered at the lavender color in the center. As I focused on that color, I realized that there was a light beginning to emanate from the center of the color, and then it began to glow, a pinpoint of light that became larger and larger. I blinked, and suddenly saw the figure of a very old crooked woman sitting on a branch, leaning against one of the upper trunks of the tree. She wore a long white kimono, and her hair was frizzled and wild, forming a halo of gray around her face. Pieces of twigs and grass and even a little dirt were caught in her hair. It looked like a mane around a lion's face. Her eyes twinkled like a young girl's with a wonderful sense of humor. I looked at her in amazement and stopped dead in my tracks, I am sure, with my mouth hanging open. She began to laugh louder at me. Her whole body jiggled on the branch, and I thought for a moment that she was going to fall from the tree.

"Old One," I said, "what are you doing in that tree? You're going to fall."

She looked at me, laughing even harder, slapping her feet, which were curled in front of her. "I am not a dream, you know," she said, toothlessly at me.

I was horrified by her appearance, but fascinated at the same time. "Are you an *oni* spirit?" I finally asked, a bit tongue-tied.

"Oh, perhaps that's part of me," she said, "and perhaps not." She just stared at me. And then I noticed that she had a staff with her, an old bamboo staff, tapered from top to bottom. The four sides had been notched, and a sacred *hu* gourd was tied to one end. It appeared to have nodes on it, seven nodes. I asked her about it.

"Your staff is very beautiful, Old One."

"Well, thank you." She nodded to me. "Not many people understand fine art these days," she said with surprising gentility in her voice. Then she leaped from the tree, landing on her toes. I reached out to grab her, but she didn't need my help. Then, taking her staff and twirling it around through her fingers as if it were only two feet long, she said, "This staff is very sacred. Perhaps it will teach you something. Would you like to hold it?"

"Oh, yes." I would not have presumed to ask her. I reached out and she lay the beautiful staff in my hands. "I love bamboo," I said.

"Yes, it is most sacred."

"Why is that, Old One?"

"It is because the bamboo is hollow. Its beauty and usefulness are not unlike all of life and not unlike ourselves as human beings. Our substance, our knowledge and wisdom, and all that we are comes from nothing. The bamboo is a living symbol of what we are."

Very lovingly she ran her gnarled old fingers across one of the angles of the staff. The old woman sat down on a smooth stone and patted the rock next to her for me to sit. I sat down, still holding the staff and looking at the carving on it, noting how it had been rubbed to a beautiful burnished, tawny color. And I began to feel oddly sleepy.

"Old One, I do not know your name," I said.

"Let it suffice that I am an Old One. That is plain to see," she said, throwing her head back and laughing uproariously.

Then I looked back down at the staff and turned it over again and again in my hands, liking the feel of it. It was very light. But as I did so, I became more and more sleepy, finally looking at the old woman, who was staring at me intently. I said, "Old One, I am becoming very tired. Why is that? What is happening to me?"

"The staff wishes to teach you. Whenever that happens to you, my child, you must always look at the object or the person, the sacred one, that has presented itself to you, and simply say, 'Teach me.'"

"Oh," I said, looking back down at the staff, thinking it odd for a moment to ask a staff to teach me, but I did so nevertheless. I centered myself and looked at the staff with respect and said, "Teach me, O Sacred One." The moment I stopped speaking, my eyelids became very heavy, and I lay down on the ground, unable to help myself. I lay down next to the staff.

Very far in the distance I heard the voice of the Old One. "The staff wishes to teach you in your sleeping. The staff wishes to teach you about the other world. Travel to the Isles of the Immortals. Move inside yourself. Become very small. Walk with the stick and become the sacred staff."

I felt myself go into a very deep sleep, but I did not lose my consciousness. I was totally aware of what was happening, even though I could not open my eyes. I felt myself going inside the hollow center of the staff, and suddenly I became the staff. It was as if the staff and I became one, and the hollowness of it became my interior, as if I were born from and lived in nothingness, with the substance of the world around me, but not me.

Then I simply heard a very soft whisper, and it said, "Play dead. Simply pretend that your body is dead. Say 'I am dead.'"

I heard my voice far in the distance saying, *I am dead, I am dead.* And my body became very heavy and simply melted away into what felt like the cloud and moved off into the sky and into infinite space. I was the hollow bamboo, the wind moving through me like a flute. I was the sacred staff, and I walked the teaching trails that wend their way through the world. I was the sacred staff, emptiness within me and strength around me, giving me structure in the world, and hiding my serenity and the source of open emptiness within my womb.

Then suddenly I began to wake up. I felt my body as the staff began to slowly fade away, and a separation was reborn. I found myself again in my body. I was no longer a bamboo staff, and when I awoke, I was curled on the ground in a fetal position next to the stone. Quickly I looked around for the Old One, but she was gone. A beautiful lotus blossom sat on the granite rock where she had been. I reached over and picked up the white, eight-petaled blossom. I held it, pristinely beautiful and perfect, in my hand, close to my heart, and I knew that it too was speaking to me. There was a message in the lotus for me, and somewhere inside me I knew that it was through sensitivity and the sweetness of our spirits that we can truly know another person or an object. It is with our ability to remain vulnerable and receptive and open that we can truly merge with any object or another being. It is the true basis of love.

I also felt an odd sensation of fear surrounding the presence of the lotus blossom. I had a sense of foreboding, as if the flower had something to tell me. It seemed a matter of life and death. I could not understand the message. I looked around to see if the Old One could be perched in a tree or down the trail. I wondered if she were an *oni* spirit or some aspect of the Goddess Who Makes the Flower Buds Open. I couldn't wait to ask Shakkai about her, and yet there was a part of me that thought better of that, that perhaps I should not speak of her to anyone, that if I spoke of her, maybe she would never appear to me again.

I moved on down the trail.

The Female Blade

◆

The great sea has set me in motion,
Set me adrift,
And I move as a weed in the river.

The arch of sky
And might of storms
Encompass me,
And I am left
Trembling with joy.

— ESKIMO SONG

◆

Shakkai and I were walking up a path that wound around and eventually found its way to the top of our sacred mountain near our home. A halo of clouds had settled around the top of Mount Fuji. There was a dampness in the air and a pungent smell of earth in my nostrils. More birds than usual were chirping in the trees above us. We were walking in a stand of very old and tall bamboo, its branches forming a canopy of leaves and filtered light over our heads.

"There are many ways to learn a discipline," Shakkai said. "In the old days, ritual meant that every ceremony that was done had to be performed exactly like the one before it without a shift or a change; even the blink of an eye at the wrong moment was an outrage."

"Did Katakiri Nakamura learn to be a samurai in that fashion?" I asked, remembering his visit the night before, when we had talked a long time about our respective feelings about the universe.

"He did and he didn't," Shakkai said, smiling to herself. "In the beginning he learned the traditional way. When he was disgraced by your father and cut off from his master, he was thrown out into the world, as I have told you, and he began to do *ronin*—he began to find the master within himself. Of course, what he learned was based on his tradition. He found much more, however, as he walked into the world of self-mastery. He learned that a sword has two faces, two cutting edges, both equally powerful and severe and both very different. He learned that there was a female blade and a male blade. He has mastered the male blade. He is strong and powerful in his extension of his own male spirit and ego. He moves well into the world. He acts well. He has been able to contain his ego in a very colorful way."

After walking for several minutes, Shakkai looked up at the sky through the branches of bamboo, the light playing in strange, unworldly patterns across her face, and I finally asked, "It sounds as if there was something missing in Kat-san's training. Am I correct?"

"Yes," Shakkai said, folding her hands in front of her as she walked carefully, each step completely silent as we moved through the leaves strewn on the path. They felt damp beneath our feet. "It is his receptive side, that side which is feminine within all of us, the side that is forgotten within most of our warriors. They might laugh at the thought, and definitely these ideas do not come from the samurai tradition, but nevertheless they are missing something essential. You see, Kat-san can give action into the world, which is a comfortable male movement for his mind and his ego. It is difficult for him to move into his humility, to sit back and receive love, receive peace, or receive his own power in a way that empowers the female blade of his sword."

"But what does that mean, Shakkai? I don't understand. I thought that when you wielded a sword, you did it with great force from your center of power, from your *ch'i*."

"Yes, but often it is better to allow someone else, your opponent in this instance, to attack you and to use his force to defeat him. Here, let me show you," she said, suddenly twirling around to face me, her body and arms in a stance that I had seen often in aikido or karate. I did not know what to do, so I just stood there. "See now, if I move toward you," she said, "you move back. Say, you move away and out of my way." I did so. "When you do that, when you move away from me, my force has nothing to move against and rushes through, and I am off balance." She twirled around again, with the agility of a much younger woman. "Now, you come toward me—fast," she said.

I moved toward her, my arms outstretched, and she took my own momentum and power and I was on my back on the ground, and I didn't even know how I had gotten there, it had been so fast. I had not even felt Shakkai touch me. She had picked me up and thrown me. I looked up from the ground, partially dazed.

"Shakkai, I didn't even feel you move or see you move."

"Yes, you see," the old woman said, "I used the force of your movement, but I could not have done that if I had not been receptive. It was not an action directed toward you. I allowed your energy to give me power."

"Well, it certainly worked," I said, scrambling to my feet, brushing the dirt from my pants.

"Come, we will walk on." She took my hand and we walked down the path, now more densely populated with bamboo. The light came in sparse dapples on the ground. The glow from the sun reached the outer leaves of the bamboo that we could see through the tops of the temple like ceiling of curved branches. It was a breathtaking yellow-green glow that gave me a feeling of being outside normal time and space. Wind had come up from the west, and the branches were rattling together above us in a primal rhythm of forest sounds.

"Our people speak of making peace," Shakkai said with a serious tone to her voice, searching carefully for the words to impart this knowledge to me. "It is comfortable and easy for us to talk about making peace, making love, giving love, giving action out into the world. That is where the mind is comfortable, and the ego is very comfortable with that idea, because in fact ego is mind. It is a much more difficult thing to put oneself into a humble stance and receive that love, receive peace into one's own heart and being. That is why I am here, my daughter, that is why I have chosen to live in my own garden, surrounded by the temple of my own creation. It is here, in my tranquillity and serenity, that I can receive the love from the Great Spirit, that I can receive the peacefulness of a Tao-like existence. That is what I needed to learn, and that is why I see its absence so clearly in our young samurai. He needs to learn to receive, and that is hard for a man, because a man has been taught in the societies of this world that ego is so important, that he must go out and make a mark for himself."

"But, Shakkai, that's important, isn't it? The ancient teachings talk about the act of power and how important that is to provide mirrors for growth."

"Yes," Shakkai said. "An act of power is very important, but remember, you can only give up something that you have, and if you do not have an act of power, you cannot give it up." I nodded in agreement and took a stick that she handed me. "Here, feel this stick with your fingers; feel her warmth. Feel the receptivity that this branch has to the life-giving force of rain and air, and to the earth. Think about it a moment—how the trees, the sacred bamboo, receive the wind." Shakkai made a sweeping motion with her arms. "Look above us at the wind moving through the leaves and the branches that sway so gently in a dance of love. They receive the wind and move at will. That is what our spirits can do, but you should not blow like a reed in the wind."

"But that's a contradiction, is it not, Shakkai?"

"It depends on your point of view. If your point of view is one of knowledge, of understanding, if your point of view comes from an open heart and a place of love, then you begin to see with the eyes of love. If you simply manipulate and consume the goods of the earth, then you will miss the teachings that are all around you, that are in the trees, in the light, in the wind, in the earth that we walk upon. The first lesson of power is that we are all alone. You have heard this spoken before, I believe." She looked at me and winked. "The feeling of duality, of being alone in the world, comes from movement into the world with mind and ego. It is through this movement and action that we find ourselves separated forever and ever. It is the tragedy of human beings that we separate and confine ourselves to belief structures that limit our growth. That encompasses the male blade, and that male blade is powerful and has great lethal ability in the world."

We walked with our faces to the westerly wind for some time.

"There have been many sciences of death," Shakkai went on. "There was a time when we believed that death would take us to the heavens, where the almighty God would give us eternal bliss. I personally feel that death is the end of our story of this lifetime, and it is important to have a feeling about death—for death, like the end of a book, is a conclusion. When you write a story, you have a beginning, a middle, and an end, and you progress toward a certain tension at different points in the writing of that book, all of which is put into perspective by the end of the book. That is just as it is in life. Our feelings about death give us a point of view, a stance in life as a warrior of the spirit, as a samurai. We have different feelings about death. We look at things in ways that will help us to grow. So, when you talk about the samurai and about the male blade of his sword, you talk about action and all that we have just spoken of. But when we speak of the female blade, we talk about the receptive power of the warrior that wields the sword in the first place.

"Being a great swordsman is not just a matter of technique; it is not just being impeccable in your movement. It is understanding that the sword is the extension of your own arm and body. The female blade is created and given power by a swordsman's ability to build his integrity, his wisdom, and his strength. That is done with receptivity to the earth's power. Receptivity allows you to set aside your thinking and go swiftly to the heart of your prey. Power is always the same, as truth is always the same, and the source is always female. If a swordsman does not understand the power of woman, the power of the female, the receptivity of life, the womb of life that exists between man and woman, that swordsman or swordswoman will not be very powerful. A swordsman knows this with his intent, but would never verbalize it or admit to the primal power of woman. It would almost be a heresy."

For a long time we walked down the trail, not saying anything more. I digested everything I had received from Shakkai, and realized some very important things from her words.

"So part of being a samurai, a warrior, is to become receptive to your prey," I said.

"Yes," Shakkai said, "that is true. When you have a prey, an important prey, whether it be an enemy, food in a hunt, or a state of being, you must make a place for that prey to live within your own body. You must know where it lives in your body. Does it live in your solar plexus? Does it live in your heart? Does it live somewhere in your groin or your stomach? These things are important, because if there is no place for the prey to live within you, you will be unsuccessful in your hunt. It will not matter how powerful and perfect you are when you pick up that sword and wield it. Without the female strength behind it, that receptive quality of womb that has been given the seeds of knowledge and power, your sword will be impotent."

As we rounded a turn in the path, we gazed down the distance of trail, like a narrow, amber-colored ribbon lying at the feet of the high bamboo trees. Coming toward us was Kat-san, carrying his sword, walking with firm, strong strides. My heart filled with love at the sight of him. Suddenly I realized that the nervousness I had been feeling, the lack of sleep, the fullness of energy and light that I had felt in my chest was because of him and my feelings for him. Suddenly he seemed to be a beacon of pure light, walking in the semidarkness of the forest. I knew beyond a shadow of a doubt that one of the reasons I had come to Shakkai was to meet him, and that he was to be a great part of my learning with her. He looked at me and I knew without words that we were of one thought, and it was as if, suddenly, out of time and space we committed ourselves to each other forever. There was a bond between us, as if Shakkai were no longer standing there, as if we had spent years in courtship, as if we had known each other from the day we were born. We were together as if a divine marriage occurred in a sacred circle surrounding the forest. A ceremony was created between us through our eyes and our eyes alone, and we performed a ritual together, as if it had been planned for a very long time, as if we had been promised to one another, and as if we had always known this. I cannot explain the feelings that rushed through my body and mind, but there was no doubt, no question, not a moment of wanting to turn back. It was there, and the two of us created something that was much greater than our simple circle would have indicated only moments before. And somehow we were married there, by the bamboo, by the light that streamed down like zebra stripes onto the ground with the reflection of our sacred mountain looming in the distance. My life was changed, as it had been changed the moment I met Shakkai. Suddenly, out of nowhere, without warning, like a bolt of lightning striking the ground out of a clear sky, my life path was altered forever.

As Kat-san approached me, he swept the *Katana* sword from its integral sheath, and laying it across both of his hands with childlike tenderness, he held it out to me. Not a word was exchanged. I looked into his eyes, no longer shy, but full of love and understanding. I felt as if I were moving out toward him in a male way, aggressively, in a way that I had never known possible for me. I had always been so shy. I took the sword in both of my hands and, not knowing why I was doing it, took the tip of the sword and turned it sunwise, honoring the power of the four directions, still looking in the eyes of Katakiri Nakamura. Then I kissed both sides of the blade. I don't know why I did this, either, but I wanted to. I wanted to honor the essence of this man who had suddenly moved so dearly into my life.

I handed the sword back to him, and he secured it back into the sash around his waist. Then, slowly, he pulled the sword out again and, stepping back, cut the air with swift and sure movements of his blade, then somehow he communicated to me that I was to stand perfectly still. I nodded to him as if in answer to the thought that I was reading in his eyes. Suddenly the sword swished by the top of my head. For a moment I caught my breath. Then he reached his hand out quickly and cradled the ends of my hair that he had just cut with his sword. I had not felt a thing. He took the hair and placed it in an embroidered red silk pouch that was hanging from his neck. Then I reached into my bag, secured around my waist by a *netsuke,* and took out a *netsuke* that was dear to me, that had been given to me by my closest friend years before. It was of carved bone, very tiny, representing a deer seated on the ground in an attitude of prayer. It was exquisitely beautiful and very old. I had held it close to me as the most treasured object that had ever been given to me. A *netsuke* has two little holes in the bottom, and since Kat-san dressed in very traditional clothes, he could run a string from the cord of his sash through the *netsuke* and carry his change bag on one end.

I gave it to him with tears in my eyes. He held the tiny creature in the palm of his hand, then held it up to the light, the sun glinting off the antlers of the tiny deer. It was almost as if it came alive in the moving light from the bamboo branches still swaying in the breeze above us. Kat-san held the deer to his heart. Then, taking the cord from his waist, he ran it through the *netsuke* and tied a knot at the bottom of the cord. Suddenly the skies turned black above us, and a whining sound like the wind in the mountains, only deeper, as if it were coming from far out in the universe, surrounded us with a crackling sound and then darkness. As if a spell had been broken, I turned, looking for Shakkai. I lost my balance and flailed in the darkness, reaching for Katakiri. I felt his strong

arms around me, and then the sound was overwhelming. A whirl-
wind encompassed the area around us. The branches of the trees
rattled together and created a musical din. I must have lost consciousness, because I remember nothing else.

I awoke in Shakkai's house, lying on a futon with Shakkai kneeling beside me, a smile on her lips and a cup of tea in an earthenware mug in her hands. She held it out to me and helped me to
drink.

"What has happened, Shakkai? I feel so strange. The last I
remember—" I caught my breath as I recalled the extraordinary
events in the bamboo forest, and I looked into the face of my
teacher and asked, "Where is Kat-san?"

·13·

Death and Rebirth

◆

Beseeching the breath of the divine one,
His life-giving breath,
His breath of old age,
His breath of waters,
His breath of seeds,
His breath of riches,
His breath of fecundity,
His breath of power,
His breath of all good fortune,
Asking for his breath
And into my warm body drawing his breath,
I add to your breath
That happily you may always live.

— ZUNI CHANT

◆

I came back into the Dreamlodge in Canada to find that it was late night. A full moon cast an eerie glow on the interior of my lodge. Agnes was waiting. She wrapped me in a blanket and took me to the cabin. We shared some cookies, and I told her excitedly about Shakkai and Kat-san. I slept peacefully for the first time in days.

The next morning the sky was turquoise blue. I awoke to sparrows dive-bombing Crow as he ate his breakfast on the kitchen windowsill. Agnes and Ruby had gone off somewhere. I spent hours with myself, thinking and writing about my journey and trying to adjust my consciousness and my emotions into a balance within my physical body. My physical being was exhausted and stressed, and somehow I couldn't get mind and body to fit together. I walked upstream in the early afternoon and found Ruby sitting on the flat, round teaching rock that she so often used. Ruby was basking in the sun and eating an apple, smacking her lips and feeling good with the taste of it. Smoothing the tiny grains of sand off another flat rock near her, I sat down. She handed the apple to me and said nothing, waiting for me to speak.

"Ruby, I am having trouble," I said, taking a bite of the delicious yellow-green fruit. We always called them banana apples because of their color. It was crisp, and its tangy sweet taste reminded me of my childhood, when I would climb up in the apple trees in Washington State and write poetry to make myself feel good.

Ruby waited several minutes to speak as she took the apple back and took another bite, obviously enjoying it immensely. Then her face lost its happy expression, and she turned to me and said, "There is a sadness in you, my daughter. It sends arrows into my heart and I feel for you. I know of your sadness. I know it well."

"Ruby, in everything that I do and say and experience, beneath that experience is always the knowing of my mother's death. I cannot seem to help it. It is there."

"I understand," she said sympathetically.

Knowing that Ruby understood my feelings—and I knew that she had felt such things deeply within her own heart—made me feel that at least I was not alone in the world.

"Ruby, these journeys into double dreaming, this rebirth into a future lifetime, for some reason brings up my feelings about my mother."

"It is the acquaintance with life and death in that process," Ruby said. "That is why you are thinking these things at this time."

"Yes, I suppose it is," I said, spitting out an apple seed, which I then planted in the earth, covering it with my finger.

"Just as you are planting that seed," Ruby said, "you have just planted the seed of a new life."

"Can you talk to me some more about that, Ruby? Just talk to me. Let me hear what your feelings are about what has just transpired, so that I can more completely understand what is happening to me."

The old woman took a deep breath, as if to clear her thoughts. She faced the sky with her beautiful eyes, which reflected its turquoise blue. Then she sniffed the air and held her hands up as if to caress the currents in the breeze that was gently blowing in our hair. Settling her hands quietly to her sides, she began to talk.

"The Great Spirit has been trying to enlighten the beings of this earth for all time. It is a very difficult task, as you well know, my daughter. When you tear away a veil of ignorance from someone's vision, another one replaces it. It seems that we never get anywhere. As we move through this existence, problems beset us at every turn. For many years I felt the tragedy of this in my heart, and I was filled with anger, and I fought side by side with my people for our lost borders, for the land that is our Great Mother. I could not understand why the surveyors came into my cabin when I was so young and raped me and put out my eyes with the points of their compass so that I could not identify them in a court of law. I didn't want to live. You have heard this story before, Little

Wolf. But remember that I understand your feelings of terror and sadness and your feelings of frustration, for we have all felt them. But there comes a time when you begin to understand the greater patterns in life, the energy flows."

Again Ruby lifted her hands and caressed the currents of air around her.

"We are involved in a sacred dance. We have chosen this dance. We have given over our lives to the preservation of life force and the goodness that exists within each human being. Within each of us is a life force, just as there is life force within that seed you have just planted. All possibility exists within that tiny planting, as it exists within you. In a sense, you have been through a rebirth. Just moments ago the Great Spirit chose that moment out of all others to give you new vision and new life. The shamans say that you are born once and you have a possibility to be human. You have life, and then you have a choice. You have a choice to become a special human being. You have a choice to grow, to become more than just the result of a mating of two people. You have the opportunity for Godness, for the Great Spirit to be expressed through your spirit. That is why we work together, my daughter. That is why we live, and that is why we die to the ignorance that surrounds us. Our lives are filled with violence and anger and rage. It lives everywhere, in every corner of the earth. It is like a child being born, angry at the first blast of light and sound, angry at the loss of its mother and the state of perfection it enjoyed in the womb. You have experienced that again, but this time with consciousness. You experienced the womb and the rebirth, and you are troubled because now you want to return there. Is that not right?"

"Yes, Ruby. I think that is the basis of my discontent."

"It is very difficult to walk with a foot in each of two worlds. You have walked in two worlds in the sense that you had a foot in the material world and a foot in the spiritual. Now you are going to have a bigger stretch, even bigger than you had with the Woman of Wyrrd. You have to step now, one foot still within this present lifetime and one foot in the future. Whatever that means, it truly isn't important. What is important are the lessons that are learned in this process. And that is what we are about—to understand this birth and death process."

"But what is the meaning, Ruby? I understand that I am moving through this, but isn't there an underlying meaning that I am missing somehow?"

Ruby waited for several minutes to answer me, trailing her finger in the rushing stream that was cool and sparkling by her side.

"Yes, I think what you need to see is that life is never-ending, like this stream flowing by. We are in a never-ending current of life flow. We take different forms. Sometimes we have a body and sometimes we do not. But that energy is never-ending."

"Is it different for the saints, for the great shamans, Ruby, from the way it is for regular people?"

"Yes," she said. "When you are a great shaman, when you are a Jesus, a Buddha, a Crazy Horse, a great teacher, when you are the Woman of Wyrrd, then it is different. Because when you die, your spirit lingers on in this earthly plane. It stays, and the lodges that are built to hold the remains do not die. They are alive. When you go to those lodges, they are alive with the spirit of that being, because the spirit does not have to move on to other lifetimes to learn more. It has already learned. It is only here to bring us light and power and to end our suffering."

"In other words, my life force will then move into one body and then another, so that I can learn different lessons?"

"Yes, this earth is a schoolhouse, as I have said so many times, as Agnes has taught you so well. The earth is a schoolhouse and you have a great privilege to be here on the beauty of this Great Mother. She teaches you whatever you need to learn. For each of us, those teachings are different. In this lifetime you have hard lessons—lessons about family, about commitment, about God. You have lessons that we grapple with every day in our work with you. Sometimes those lessons are very painful, because they demand that you change, no matter how hard it may be. You have to shift and change to grow. So this seed that you just planted is not unlike a human seed. It is born, just as you were born into a new world, a Japanese child. And you will experience the possibility of becoming a saint, a great shaman, in that lifetime. You will experience trials, difficulties, and a whole new world that is now unknown to you, and you will learn that we each have that possibility, but only a possibility. If you do not have the intent, the wherewithal, the training, the guidance that you need, that life will be lost and you will simply move to another one."

"Sometimes, Ruby, I don't know who is alive. I don't know who is sitting here speaking to you. I know that my name is Lynn. I know where I come from, I think, and I know what I have accomplished, and yet I don't feel that I have truly accomplished anything."

"But how can you say that, my daughter? You have done so much."

"No, I don't feel that. I feel that I need to do so much more."

"One day, Little Wolf, you will understand that to be loved, it is not necessary to accomplish. It is only necessary to *be,* simply to exist in your state of awareness. If you want to accomplish something out of that state, that is fine, and if you do not, that is fine too. There is unconditional love in the universe, not only from your friends and teachers; certainly we love you, but somehow there are times when you don't feel that."

"Yes, that is true, Ruby. Sometimes I feel very alone, very isolated and separated from everyone and everything. And there are other times when I feel at the center of the universe. I know that I am one with the Great Spirit."

"But you see," Ruby said, "those changes are very important. Those shifts, those movements, are important. Remember, enlightenment is within the process and contained in the process of movement. Without that movement, there is no life."

Later than night, Agnes, Ruby, and I sat around the potbellied stove. It had turned colder outside and very dark. There was no moon. We laughed and talked, sharing stories about our lives, laughing about Ben and Drum and the silly tricks they had played so many times in the past. When I am with my teachers like this, I forget myself and my self-consciousness that plagues so much of my time in Los Angeles and in the world. Time floats away from me, and I forget even what century I am living in. We laugh and talk about simple things—about preserves and working on the cabin, fixing the roof, things that are needed to survive through the winter, what wood needs to be chopped, and so forth. And we laugh.

Kotodama — *The Sacred Sounds*

◆

Trailing down the wind
the smoke of Fuji
vanishes into space
till nothing lingers
of my love's deep fires

—SAIGYO

◆

It was early morning, just past dawn, when I awoke on my futon on the floor of Shakkai's house. Several weeks had passed since my intimate encounter with Kat-san. A golden glow of early-morning light filtered through the screened windows. The burnished wood floors were dappled with pools of light. A movement to my left caught my eye, and I looked toward the shoji screen that separated me from Shakkai's area of the house. I saw a fleeting shadow, a strange form that was there momentarily and then disappeared. I blinked, wondering if I was seeing things. I stared at the screen. Suddenly, in a blush of purple and green, the form came again, dancing in a chaotic manner behind the screen. My mind formed a montage of thought patterns, remembering the work that we had done the night before. We had been doing a practice Shakkai called *kinchen,* a process of pulling the energies of the universe into your body and merging with the divine soul of the Tao. We had worked and meditated in the garden for hours, and I had seen many shadows on the periphery of my vision as we got deeper and deeper into the work. I wondered momentarily if this was a similar shadow of some sort, perhaps a *kami* spirit that had lingered from the work the night before. My eyes widened and terror gripped my stomach, as suddenly the purplish green shadow uttered a vulgar scream and burst through the screen, tearing it into hundreds of torn shreds of paper that transformed into shards of mirror, crashing in tiny pieces, scattering light in chaotic fragments. A powerful wind entered the room, turning everything into a shambles. The table flew to the ceiling. The few paintings that were on the wall crashed to the floor. The bedcovers were ripped off me, and I was flung to the other end of the room, screaming.

I tried to stand up, and as quickly as the apparition had turned violent, it was gone, and I was back on my futon, lying there as if it had only been a dream. In fact, it must have been only a distortion of my imagination, because the pictures were again on the wall. There was no hole in the shoji screen, and the shadow was gone. I tried to catch my breath, tears running down my cheeks. I called out to Shakkai, as I quickly rolled up my mat and dressed for the day.

I found her sitting in the *chaseki* area of her room, before her altar. She was doing her *kinchen* practice, which she did every morning at dawn. This was breath practice and meditation to calm the spirit. She always told me to do this only if I wanted to. I dared not disturb her, so I sat behind her and began to meditate with her.

Presently she turned very slowly to me, and reaching out both of her hands so as not to startle me, she spoke gently. "O Kiku, it is necessary for you to do work today on your dream body. You look very tense, and I am concerned about you."

"Sensei, I had the most awful experience this morning. It was as if a spirit took a shadow form and turned my room into a typhoon for just a moment, but it didn't really happen. But it did." I didn't know how to explain the apparition to Shakkai.

She looked at me quizzically and smiled. "Oh," she said, "the spirits are playing with you. You must understand that when your dream body is not securely connected to your physical form, to your conscious mind, there is a space that is left." She stood in front of me, asking me to stand also, and told me, "Now bend your knees ever so slightly, and place your feet about a foot apart. Now you've centered your ki energy, which is located right around the hara, or navel area. Place your left hand over your center. Just rub it gently." She rubbed her belly in a circular motion around that area, as did I. "Now close your eyes and gather your power. Just gather it slowly. We have all day. Do not rush. Try to let the terror that is in your heart leave through your feet and move into the earth. The earth can handle it much better than you can."

I did so for several minutes and then breathed a sigh of relief as I felt centered again and more in control of my emotions.

"Now," Shakkai said, "you are experiencing your passive spirit. There are also passive spirits in the *kami* world. They are spirits that give you strength and intuition, that help you to be inspired in your life, and there are also very aggressive *kami* spirits that move things around sometimes to get your attention. They don't usually mean to hurt you. We will deal with that *kami* spirit a little later. But I want you to feel the cross of power that is in your body. You see, there is a receptive quality to the female side of you. Stretch your arms out from your sides."

I did so.

"There is a great cross of power formed here from your head down to your feet," she said. "That is the aggressive abode that is vertical within your own being. There are also passive spirit strengths within you that are horizontal, across your arms. Within most apprentices there are tiny spaces of energy loss between the horizontal and vertical energy flows. There are spaces, also, between the sacred sounds, the *kotodama,* that we will learn more about, and spaces between other minute energy forms within your own body. It is within these spaces, these little areas of entropy where sometimes we die a little, little areas that, in a sense, lack energy, and when there is no energy, no swirl or dance of light— positive and negative, male and female, *yin* and *yang*—you experience a dark moment, a quality of emptiness that is quite different from the emptiness of the Tao, because the emptiness of the Tao is actually a fullness. Do you understand?"

"I think so."

"Within these little places of entropy," Shakkai went on, "you can sometimes get lost, and if you get stuck there sometime, such as when you wake up in the morning, you feel a depression. Sometimes you feel a kind of frantic void, and you try to collect yourself and remember who you are. Am I right?"

"Yes, Sensei, that is exactly right. I feel that often when I wake up in the morning."

"Well, that is what's happening to you. That is why you have a need to get up and move and make things happen, because you're trying to move back into the energy flow. But a better way is to just let yourself settle in and experience the entropy, and then the power of creation will follow you, swirl around you, and bring you back into the living world."

Shakkai closed her eyes and, holding her left palm over her cen-

ter of power, around her navel, started to breathe in. It was a practice I had often witnessed her doing, in which she gathered energy
and power. Then she emitted a terrifying sound, a kind of primal
scream. I listened as it echoed through the house and out into the
garden. I was spellbound by the light that seemed to surround her
in a golden radiance. I looked into her eyes, and they were rolled
upward, as if her eyes had turned solid white. Her hair appeared
to be luminous with electricity, and whatever hair was not caught
up in the bun at the top of her head stood out from her face in little tendrils. Her skin took on a golden hue, and with the sunlight
glowing through the paper screens behind her head, she looked for
all the world like a saint about to ascend to heaven.

Then, opening her eyes and looking at me, she said, "Now it is
time."

"Time for what?" I asked.

"Time for you to find *your* sound. I want you to set your mind
aside. Forget that you have a mind, and breathe deeply, like this."

She was exhaling in quick breaths, forcing the air out with the
power of her diaphragm, and I did the same, as I had done so
often.

"All the work you have done with me has prepared you for this
moment. I want you to listen to the celestial music that is within
your own head," she said. "Listen to the sounds. Can you do
that?"

"Yes," I answered. I could hear music in my head. I had always
been able to hear sounds from the ether.

"Good," she said. "Now I want you to hold in your breath. I
want you to emit a sound, a scream. It doesn't matter what tone it
is. It doesn't matter what words are formed with it. Just allow
yourself to scream."

"But why, Sensei?"

"Because we need to find your essential, one-pointed sound. I
call it your *su*. *Su* is a word, a one-pointed word, that is the collec-
tion of all sounds, and in its fullness of sound, in a sense, it is the
absence of all sound, because it is the sound of creation. It is your
sound, the sound of life itself. So now, using the letters *s-u*, I want
you to emit a sound. I will close my eyes and lend my power
to you."

I began to breathe, trying not to be self-conscious. Finally I felt power welling up inside me, boiling like blood in a cauldron. I felt my whole being begin to brim over. I felt Shakkai's energy merge with mine, making my spirit feel pregnant, and a sound was born from I know not where, some place deep inside my personal universe, and I screamed. It was a long, penetrating sound. I felt the tension, the fear, everything negative in my system pour out through that sound until there was nothing left but emptiness. Then I understood. A flash of power started from my feet, spiraling up my spine, out through my crown chakra at the top of my head—a power that I had never known. It felt like a freight train coming through my body, and once it started, I realized that I could not stop it. I kept on breathing.

"Breathe," Shakkai said. "Keep breathing."

As I did so, the power moved through me, and the sound, and finally it was over. I slowly opened my eyes and looked at my teacher wide-eyed and astonished by what had just happened.

"Very good." She nodded and smiled at me. "Now you understand. That is what the *kotodama* is all about, my child. It is the science of the sacred sound. It is said by many teachers that within the word is the power of creation. In Christianity they say, 'In the beginning was the Word, and the Word was with God.' We say something very similar, that the sacred sounds contain the universe, just as within my body is the universe, and in the universe is my body. As above, so below. Do you understand?" she asked.

I nodded, unable to speak.

Taking my elbow, she held my arm and led me out into the garden next to the pond, to the special area she called the *hanare*, where we did a lot of meditation and work together. Our sacred mountain was looming before us, out of the mist of early morning. The waters of the pond were placid and mirrorlike, reflecting the rainbow colors of late spring on its surface. I felt profoundly at ease and at peace with my own spirit for perhaps the first time in my life. I sat with Shakkai on the ground, feeling the damp grass beneath me. It felt cool against my body, which was on fire with an inner heat.

"Listen," she said.

Seven cranes had come out of the trees to walk around in the pond looking for breakfast, their long legs like sticks in the water, their long beaks probing beneath the surface. Once in a while they would raise their heads and speak to one another, a cooing sound that was primitive and lovely.

"Listen to their sounds. They are sacred sounds. You see, the winged ones and the four-leggeds know," she said, glancing at me to be sure I was watching. "They speak to each other through the power of sounds. If you understand the meaning of a sound and can visualize that meaning, all power can be yours. Listen to the birds. See how they communicate. It is as if they merged with one another through innuendos, subtleties, through sound, like the dolphins and the whales. Theirs is a language of love. When a whale communicates with another whale, it sends out a sound and its mate sends it back, reversed. That is an extraordinary ability, very difficult to do. I doubt you and I could do that. I am teaching you to come back to the voice of the world of nature around you."

Just then there was a call from the gate and a tinkling of bells, announcing that we had a visitor. Shakkai's Sami-san let Kat-san in and walked him to the garden to join us. He was wearing beautiful, old-style silk pants and a kimono shirt with patterns of squares in dark maroon and black, a black obi sash tied around his waist, with his sword held by it on his left side. He looked as if he had been doing sword practice in the forest, alive and vibrant with energy. He smiled brightly when he saw me. I knew that I blushed. He came and sat next to us, bowing his head low, touching the ground and revealing the back of his neck in great respect to Shakkai.

"Welcome," she said. "What perfect timing! I have been speaking to O Kiku about the *kotodama,* the sacred sounds."

"Yes, I could not help but hear your call. It echoed mightily into the forest. It was beautiful and sent chills up my spine." He laughed as he winked at her playfully.

"You have been cutting bamboo?" Shakkai asked, eyeing his sword and smiling.

"Bamboo is too great an opponent for me," he said. Then, looking at me, he smiled and said unabashedly, "I have missed you. Will you come and walk with me? The light is so beautiful in the bamboo forest."

"Yes, I would like that very much," I answered, "if you will give me a moment. It has been a morning full of surprises."

I went back into the house and prepared a few things to eat, then, putting on a cotton jacket, I went back to join him and Shakkai. I was almost dizzy with the energy that was coursing through my body. I didn't know if it was the sound that I had been working with or the fact that I was feeling so happy in seeing Kat-san once again, but whatever it was, it was pleasant.

As Kat-san and I walked through the bamboo forest, we looked up at the cathedrallike branches meeting high overhead, the stalks of the bamboo rattling gently together in a haunting dissonance of hollow wood sounds.

"The bamboo sings to us," Kat-san said, watching me and carefully taking my hand in his.

"They bless us with their presence," I answered. "I love the bamboo. Whenever I experience this forest, it changes me."

"I have been very afraid," he finally said, looking at me.

"And why are you afraid?"

"Because of my feelings for you. I never expected this to happen."

"And neither did I," I said.

"Then you feel the same?"

"Yes, I do."

"I feel that we were destined to be here together," he said.

After a long time I looked at him and realized that he spoke the truth, that no matter how I fought this, it was bound to happen and I might as well relax, and I said so. Kat-san smiled and then turned to me, stopping me in my tracks. Placing his arms around me, he held me close. His body felt strong, and I could feel his heart pounding against my chest. Then, ever so gently, he turned my face up to his with his powerful fingers, and gently kissed me on the lips. That moment, of his face touching mine, was so exquisite that I felt it would not matter if I died then and there, because I would have truly lived. I would have experienced what ecstasy was all about. I lost myself in my feelings, and yet I did not move off my center in fear. I simply enjoyed the power that lives in each and every one of us, the power that we so seldom experience.

"Come," he said. "I know of a beautiful place where I want to take you."

We walked off the trail and he led me carefully through the bamboo. It was very dense. We had to walk with great care, until we found a clearing. In this clearing there was a shallow cave and a spring-fed pond and flowers. It was a tiny natural garden within the dense forest. He had brought a blanket and placed it on the ground while I took out a few things to eat. He had brought some rice wine. We sat together and talked—about our lives, about our fears. We talked about everything that mattered, and we laughed together and we played. We became very close in those moments. All the barriers seemed to dissolve in our happiness.

Finally I looked at him and said, "There seems no reason to shield myself from your love. What a foolish thought. There is no reason to protect myself, because I know that you protect me."

Holding my hands to his heart, he said, "I have been with you always, and I will always be with you, whether I am a samurai or a gentleman in England or a spaceman. I am part of your heart and soul, as you are part of mine. And now we can teach each other so much."

"Yes," I said. I had learned so much just today.

Then he held me very close and caressed my body. My skin came alive under his fingers, and I felt a gentle passion such as I had only dreamed of. I embraced him willingly. My body opened like a flower, and he penetrated my spirit with great tenderness and left me feeling complete and adored.

As we lay naked in the sun, I looked over at Kat-san. He lay next to me with his eyes closed, his skin shining like living bronze. I looked at his mouth, serene and full—a mouth I longed to kiss again.

"Do you think I am mad?" I asked, tracing his lips with a blade of grass. Kat-san smiled, never opening his eyes.

"Yes, of course. You are the mad empress of the trees who flies through the night stars with the *kami* spirits."

"You frighten me," I whispered.

"And you haunt me." Kat-san opened his eyes and laughed as he grabbed me and we rolled in the grass.

"You scare me, because I have never believed that love of the flesh and communion of the spirit could live together in one romance."

Kat-san placed his fingers over my mouth and shook his head.

"Your life was not real then. Your life was a social myth, as was mine."

"How mysterious that it was my own father who set you free."

"It has all been written by the gods—only mysterious if you don't believe in magic, my love."

I looked at my arm touching his, the blend of skin, the play of golden light forming a hazy cocoon around us.

"I feel as though we have been born into a new world where all possibilities exist. Oh, Kat-san, I am so grateful. I have never really felt gratitude until now."

"For you to feel gratitude, you must first have love."

Reaching into his pocket, he produced a tiny golden abacus, which he gave to me. "If ever you wonder how much I love you— here is an ancient adding machine to count the ways."

I kissed him. Kat-san was the first man I had known whose affections did not propel me toward a foreboding of death and pain.

When we returned that afternoon, Shakkai appeared to take no notice of the fact that we had been gone all day. She simply gave us both a hug and a smile. Kat-san hugged me and kissed me good-bye and said he would return soon.

Shakkai and I ate dinner together that evening and went to bed early. She said I was too tired to do much work.

· 15 ·

Web of Seduction

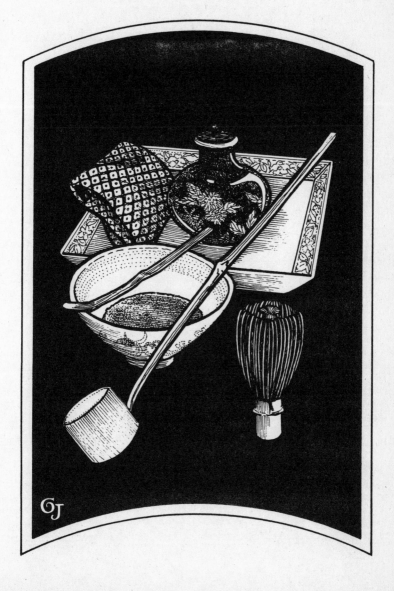

From the unreal lead me to the real.
From darkness lead me to light.
From death lead me to immortality.

— THE UPANISHADS

The next day I awoke in the Dreamlodge in Manitoba. It was a shock to wake out of the dream, so deep, so profound, and look into the faces of Agnes and Ruby. I felt split in half, as though I had a foot in Japan and one in Manitoba, and was being pulled farther and farther from my center as Lynn.

They grabbed me, and taking me down to Dead Man's Creek, they dunked me in the ice-cold water until I was screaming for mercy. They kept looking in my eyes, and not seeing what they wanted to see, they'd dunk me again, every once in a while holding me beneath the surface of the water. I was furious, flailing in all directions, trying to make them stop. Finally they let me sit on the stream bank, and wrapped me in blankets, rubbing me all over until my skin was bright red.

"Well, this is a wonderful experience," I said, coughing and sputtering.

"You didn't want to come back." Ruby glared at me, pounding me on my back and rubbing me furiously with the blanket.

"Don't tell me you've fallen in love again," Agnes said in a fury, her eyes flashing.

I looked at them both with a sheepish grin.

"Great Spirit, have mercy," Ruby said, wrapping me in blankets and pulling me toward the cabin.

It was dusk. I felt a sensation similar to jet lag. My body felt as if it had weights tied to it. I had great trouble moving. They kept prodding me, as if I were a cow or a goat.

"Cut it out," I yelled at them. "I'm doing the best I can."

"That ain't good enough," Ruby said, giving me another prod with her long brown finger.

When they got to the cabin, they stoked the fire and made me sit up at the table. They wouldn't allow me to lie down and go back to sleep, as I wanted to do. They started to feed me.

"You have been gone much too long," Ruby said. "It is dangerous, and we don't know if we are even going to let you go again."

"What do you mean, you won't let me go again? I haven't finished my journey. It's essential that I return."

A thrill of fear went up my spine, as I contemplated the thought of never seeing Shakkai or Kat-san again.

"Sometimes I think you are really never going to learn," Agnes said, shaking her head.

"Agnes, sometimes I weary of all these lessons. Can't I enjoy my journey? I'm learning things, you know."

"Yes, my daughter, you are learning things, but I don't want you to die in the process."

"*Die?*" I said, my eyes suddenly wide with fear.

"As we told you when you were working with the Woman of Wyrrd," Ruby said, "you can only go for so long. The body can't stand the absence of your astral spirit in your dream body for that long."

"Oh, that's funny. That reminds me. Shakkai mentioned that I need to work on my dream body."

"Yes," Ruby said, "that would be a very good idea. It's practically severed from you."

"I feel okay," I lied.

They both laughed at me.

"No, you don't feel okay," they said in unison.

"You're right, I don't."

I felt nauseated, as though someone had kicked me in the solar plexus. I was dizzy. My vision was blurred, and I was miserable. I suddenly realized I was starving. I started eating everything in sight and then got violently sick, ran outside, and threw up. When I came back in, they were waiting for me.

"Great. That's a wonderful compliment for the dinner I made for you," Ruby said.

"I'm sorry. I'll be more careful."

This time I sat down and ate more slowly. I took a long sip of tea and several deep breaths, and became more present in the room. I realized I was very glad to be back in the cabin. Everything was familiar. I liked being Lynn. Even though Shakkai was so alluring, with her refined taste and brilliance, and I enjoyed my life as O Kiku, it seemed very foreign to me. I had never spent much time in the Orient, and it was an unusual experience to look so very different from the way I expected my physical self to be.

I ran my fingers over the wooden table, and got up and touched the rattles hanging from the rafters, which I had used so often in so many ceremonies. I smelled the sweetgrass. I went to the window and looked outside and saw Crow hopping about in the branches of a pine tree. Smelling the crisp northern air, I finally relaxed. It was good to be home.

After several days of strenuous physical work, chopping wood and helping Agnes fix the tin roof, I was ready for more Dreamtime work. This time, when I went into the Dreamlodge, it was a beautiful, balmy early morning in Manitoba. I lay down on the sheepskin and looked around at the interior of my Dreamlodge, grateful for the truths that had been made available to me. I thanked the Great Spirit for my teachers, for their unceasing faith in me and my ability to learn. The morning had been very placid. Agnes had prepared pancakes with honey for breakfast, and Ruby, unusually quiet and serene, had been sitting for the longest time down by Dead Man's Creek in a state of contemplation. When I had walked by her on the path earlier, she had barely nodded her head in recognition that I was about to enter the Dreamlodge. She did not join me.

I lay on my back, looking up at the smoke hole and the soot that had gathered around the edges of the hide and the bent willows. I mused about my life and the extraordinary events that had led me to this adventure in the Dreamlodge, and I felt proud. I reached over and took the gourd rattle I always used in my dreaming with Shakkai. I felt the celestial patterns in turquoise on the outside of the gourd, and then I rattled it ever so slightly in my ear, hearing the dream crystals sing their dreaming song to me. I closed my eyes and lay the rattle over my solar plexus. Breathing deeply, feeling serene and quiet, slowly I moved into the sacred Dreamtime. I had learned well this process of double dreaming. Now I could actually move myself into trance without Ruby.

* * *

Suddenly, before I saw anything in my double dreaming, in my visions of that other world, I found a great darkness around me. I opened my dreaming eyes and could see nothing except an occasional flicker of light here and there, but I heard deep breathing, panting, as if someone were running. Then I heard the crack of something like lightning or branches being torn from a tree, and then, again, I heard footsteps running. Without warning, a feeling of terror engulfed me. I was running. It was my own breathing I was hearing. I was running through a bamboo forest. It was as dark as pitch. No moon or stars were visible, and I was lost. I was running for my life. I couldn't imagine from what, but I had no time to think. I felt certain that I would not live beyond the next few moments. The fright was so exquisite in my heart and stomach that even though I was running, I could barely breathe. My arms and face were scratched from the branches that were slapping me and tearing at my clothes. I had always loved the bamboo forest so much, and now it was as if it had turned against me, as if it were trying to impede my progress and hold me for the person who was in pursuit to catch me and kill me. I struggled against the forest, and with every motion my way became more difficult. It was as if the branches and trees were reaching out to grab me, to imprison me. Part of me wanted to stop this madness of running, but another part of me knew that if I stopped, it would be the last time.

Then I heard a crack of thunder that jolted the ground, and through the bamboo branches I saw a flash of lightning. Then the rain came, drenching me in moments. Now not only the forest was holding me back, but the ground suddenly became slippery. Rivulets of water were running under my feet. I had lost my shoes as the mud sucked them from my feet. My feet were bleeding and I fell facedown in the mire. The air was knocked out of me. I felt the rain pelting on my back. I reached out with my fingers and held weeds in my hands, gripping them with my fists to try to center myself. It occurred to me that this was actually a gift of fate. Then I felt a presence, and I saw a flickering pinpoint of light next to my left side. I knew it to be the *kami* mountain spirit that had been with me since the pilgrimage to Mount Ontake. I couldn't hear words, but the *kami* was telling me this was a good position to be in. Perhaps I would lie here unnoticed, no longer thrashing and creating evidence of my passage through the bamboo.

Moments later, my ears straining, my eyes seeing only darkness, I heard the thud of footsteps. Whoever was following me was running with a steady cadence, moving like a warrior through the bamboo, not like me, in a terror of confusion and chaos. I could hear a blade cutting away branches here and there—the sure, stealthy movements of a warrior. Then I took my power back as I lay there on the earth, replenished by the vibrations of the Great Mother. I let her energy permeate my being. I took a deep breath and found my *ki,* my place of shaman power. I was no longer terrorized into insanity. I lay there, very slowly and gently taking the leaves that surrounded me on the lower parts of the bamboo stalks and covering myself completely. The branches and leaves of the underbrush sheltered me from some of the rain, and actually I felt quite warm.

I knew with my intent that it was Master Hara who was hunting for me. Somehow we had gotten into a situation where he had attacked me. I racked my brain. I couldn't understand the visions I was seeing, but then, with an explosion of imagery and terror and color, I remembered the tea ceremony. Master Hara had been inviting me for a long time to join him for a tea ceremony. He had always said that he wanted to teach me, and with Shakkai's urging, I had gone to his impeccable teahouse, a small, shingled hut that sat on a point overlooking a small lake. There were jumbled outcrops of slate and granite above the hut, high into the mountain behind. A waterfall cascaded down behind the hut, and with the doors and screens thrown open, one could hear the magnificence of the waterfall in its tumultuous search for serenity. I looked out over the lake and the mists rising from its surface. This inspiring scene touched me deeply. I had wanted to open my heart to learn what there was for me to see about the tea ceremony. Hara-san was a great master of his art. I tried so desperately to forget my feelings of foreboding and dread in his company, but as I surrendered to my feelings of awe at his presence, and to the beauty of the scene, Master Hara had taken advantage of me. He had seen the opening, and like a samurai with a great pointed sword, he had stabbed me with his intent. He had moved in for the kill. He knew that his female receptivity was negligible, that in the world of true power he had very little, because he did not understand the feminine. His technical ability was perfection itself, but the power that drives that ability was sadly missing. He saw in me an apprentice who might help him in some way. He saw that through me he could steal power from Shakkai, so he began to weave a web of seduction around me, pulling me in subtle ways that I cannot name, but he danced with my mind and tried to dance with my spirit. As he did this, I closed my heart to him. I moved away into my own stance of power. I sensed the danger I was in. Mentally he had cut off every road to escape. He had even taken down the rope and wood bridge that crossed the abyss of water between his hut and the mountainside where Shakkai and I lived. The only way back to the compound was through a bamboo forest in territory that was unknown to me. When Master Hara saw that through his dance he could not contain my soul or my interest, it became clear that he wanted to imprison me.

I remembered his hands and how fascinating the movements of his fingers were, how he caressed the high-fired vessels and turned them so gently in his palm. He placed powdered green tea in a cuplike bowl, poured boiling water over it, and then whipped the tea into a froth with a brushlike instrument. Then ceremoniously wiping the cup he reached out to me with it. It was as if he were extending to me a part of himself. He turned with the grace of a tiger centered over the energy part of his body. Never for a moment did he lose his center until he began to be agitated with me. Then he lost bits of his power, piece by piece, like sparks flying away from the mother fire. I chose a moment when he had turned away from me to refill the bowl, and I ran, very quietly taking my shoes from the entryway. I ran into the night, and very close behind, he came. Only this time it was not, "Do not be afraid. I will not hurt you." He threatened my life, and I knew somewhere deep inside me that he would rather kill me than lose the opportunity to have me and the lifeline to Shakkai. He was possessed by a demon, a demon called *power*. His whole life had been bent on destruction, and yet there he had constructed a very beautiful shell around that life, a wonderfully honed impeccability in his art, a quality of expression that was only betrayed by his eyes, by his use of negativity. Were you to trust him, his negativity was very subtle. It was only when you attacked him or resisted him in some way that he became ugly. Now his ugliness became a passion for revenge. His revenge was not really aimed at me; it was against all womankind, for his own inability to truly take his power. Instead of building his power in a true way, he wanted to steal it, and if it was taken from him, it only made him more angry. I symbolized all of that as I ran through the bamboo forest in the darkness, terrified.

I remembered that Shakkai was supposed to have come for me earlier that evening. She must have come to the bridge and not been able to cross. I couldn't imagine what she might have done in that instance, but she must have sensed what was happening. Suddenly, gaining control, I stopped running wildly and crawled under a fallen tree covered with low-hung bushes and leaves. I caught my breath and lay still like a stone. Digging even deeper into the ground, I watched for Master Hara. There was no way he was going to find me unless he actually stepped on me. But I knew I could send my intent to Shakkai, and that perhaps I could draw her to me for help.

As I lay there, a sense of power came over me. I heard Master Hara thrashing around. First he was very close, and then he was farther away, and then he would come back. He knew I was in the area, but he couldn't find me. I'm sure he thought I was still running, so he was stopping every once in a while to listen for me thrashing headlong through the forest, but he could hear nothing, and it was making him angrier and angrier. I could hear him cursing under his breath, breathing heavily. I lay there as if I were at the center of the storm, very quiet, very still, completely in my own serenity of spirit, still terrified, but not out of control. I felt a kind of terror that builds strength and power, and I remembered how Shakkai had taught me to build that power out of my own fear. I breathed as she had taught me to. I centered myself, and allowed my receptivity to open to the power of Mother Earth and the *kami* spirit that was helping me. Finally there was no more sound. I couldn't tell whether Master Hara had left or had simply done what I had done. I dared not move, and I thought suddenly,

What if he waits until dawn, then surely he will find me. Terror flowed through my body. I didn't know what to do.

It seemed as if an hour had passed when out of the darkness came Shakkai's whisper. "O Kiku, it is your teacher." Then I felt her hand reaching under the leaves. "Come. Say nothing. He is down the hill. The *kami* spirits found you for me. Come. I will take you home now. You are safe with me."

The next thing I knew, it was morning in Shakkai's house. I had been having a nightmare. Or had I? Shakkai came quietly into the room and knelt beside me with a curious expression on her face.

"What is it?" she asked.

"We haven't been anywhere? I wasn't at the tea master's hut?" I asked.

"No, my child."

"Then I have had a very strange experience," I said, as I took Shakkai's hand and related my dream of terror in the bamboo forest.

When I was finished, Shakkai looked through me with the intensity of her eyes, but said nothing for a long time. Then, nodding her head as if making an agreement with herself, she said, "It is a premonition, O Kiku. We are going to have some trouble, but it will not be like your dream. We know of the coming of this evil, so prepare your spirit and stay strong. This evil lies sleeping. It will take some time for it to awaken."

16

Master Hara-san

◆

Water flows over these hands.
May I use them skillfully
to preserve our precious planet.

—THICH NHAT HANH

◆

One afternoon late in the day, Hara-san came to visit us and sit by the reflection pond.

"It is important for you to watch Hara-san," Shakkai whispered in my ear. "Watch every move he makes. I want you to stalk him like a hunter stalking her prey."

"But why, Shakkai?" I hissed. "I don't like him. I don't want to watch him."

"All the more reason for you to witness everything he does," she said. "Often the person you dislike most in life is your best teacher," she added, as I shrugged my shoulders and resolved to witness him as carefully as I could.

One thing I noticed about Hara-san was that he smiled with his whole face, except for his eyes. His eyes remained cold and piercing. There was definitely power within this man, but it was an unresolved power. There was a quality of imbalance about his demeanor. I didn't know exactly why. I tried to watch him more carefully to try to get a hint. I noticed that his right hand was more gracefully formed than his left hand. I wondered if that had anything to do with the male and female sides of ourselves. I thought that was a possibility. Perhaps that was one of the reasons I perceived him as being out of balance in some way. I also noticed that when I asked him a question, he would never look up to one side or another the way most people do. He was always calculating, always tricky, as if there was a motive for everything he did. There was no spontaneity within this man. As a result, I could not relax around him, because I felt that he was always scrutinizing me, wanting to control me in some way. It was a very unpleasant feeling.

We decided to take a walk through the garden. Shakkai led the way, and I picked up the trail behind them both. Hara-san placed his feet very carefully from one steppingstone to another, so as not to disturb even a grain of sand. It was quite remarkable to watch the control he had over his movements. At one point, as we walked through a small meadow of purple and white irises, there was a tiny ladybug on one of the steppingstones, and I noticed how Shakkai stepped carefully so as not to impede its progress. I gasped as Hara-san, quite to the contrary, reached out with his right foot and killed it, stepping heavily, as if the ladybug weighed several pounds. He turned his face to me. Fleetingly, around his mouth there was a grimace of satisfaction that made me despise him. How unlike a Master of the Tea to do such a thing!

As the afternoon wore on and we sat together sharing some tea cakes that Sami-san had prepared for us, I questioned myself at the sinking feeling that was enveloping me.

"My teahouse is finished now," Hara-san said to Shakkai, "and, my dear friend, you must come and do ceremony with me. It is beautiful, and I have so many new apprentices. They give everything to me," he said. "They have given me their worldly goods. It is wonderful to feel wealthy, not only in the world of spirit, but in the physical world as well. You must come and see. Just yesterday someone brought me a beautiful cloisonné vase from the Ming Dynasty."

As he spoke, Hara-san would look out of the corner of his eye to see if I was being affected favorably by all of this talk. Instead, I wanted to yawn. I could hardly keep my attention on him.

"O Kiku, you would do well to come and do the tea ceremony with me. Don't you think so, Shakkai?" Hara-san looked at me, his eyes flashing black light from within their soulless depths.

As I looked at Hara-san, I blinked and shook my head slightly. He seemed to be changing before my eyes. His face was contorting. It was turning into a gargoyle, sitting there laughing, making small talk. I felt a wrenching tug on my solar plexus. Hara-san reached forward underneath the table. He did not touch me with his hand, but obviously he was doing something with his energy field, and it was centered on my stomach. He was tugging at me to the point where I felt that I would fall forward. I leaned back, perspiration breaking out on my face. Shakkai frowned, sat back in her seat, and glared at Hara-san, knowing full well what he was doing, but saying nothing. I imagine she did nothing because she wanted me to experience something; I knew not what, but I disliked it intensely.

Hara-san went on to say, "And I can snake you into confusion, my little one. I can teach you to be a true sorcerer. I can walk into a room and change the energy field to my liking. I can make you do what I will."

With those words, Shakkai stood up abruptly, and stamping her foot, she glared at Hara-san, who was flung back again on his chair, perspiration breaking out on his upper lip. He looked down for an instant—perhaps, I thought, in a moment of shame. But I was wrong, for he turned to Shakkai with an evil grin on his face and said, "We are good enemies, are we not, O-Sensei?" And he bowed low, but without the respect that I would have expected.

Shakkai's eyes flashed with anger, and then she sat down again on her cushion and waited for me to pull myself together. I was very angry, and I was frightened, because it was true. Hara-san had a great deal of power.

"You are a very destructive man. You have gone too far," Shakkai said finally.

Hara-san threw his head back and laughed. "Oh yes, Shakkai, that is one thing that perhaps I am, but so are you."

"And how is that?" Shakkai said.

"Creativity," Hara-san said. "You cannot create something new in the world without destroying the old."

"Perhaps that is true," Shakkai said, "but my intent is to bring light and order into the universe and inspiration through my creativity."

"Inspiration is looked at in many ways," Hara-san said. "In my destructiveness, as you say, I tear down not only beauty in the world, but also old habit forms, like fear, like lack of power. I tear those assumptions away from the minds of my apprentices, so that they can wield power in the world."

"But when you move into a relationship," Shakkai said, "you eventually destroy that relationship."

Hara-san looked at her coldly, and finally, after twisting a stick in his fingers until it broke, he said, "I build through the process of destruction. It is true, but I do not see that your creativity is differ-

ent from my so-called destructiveness, because out of that destructiveness, something new is born, just as in creativity. You tear
down the old and bring something new into being. I tear down the
old and something new is born."

"Yes," I said, "but the emphasis is different. Your emphasis is
not on harmony, but only on power."

"Perhaps that is true, but power is the only game in town,"
Hara-san said, "and I have dedicated my life to the study of
power. I can snake you into confusion until you won't know who
you are, and that is a fact."

"Perhaps that is true," Shakkai interrupted, "but what is to be
gained by snaking someone into confusion, except to build your
ego? And if your ego needs such a demonstration of power, I pity
you, because your own ego will implode upon you and be the very
obstacle that keeps you from ultimate power and oneness with
the Tao."

Hara-san shrugged and laughed, throwing his head back. His
laughter sounded almost like someone vomiting. I was repelled.

"I am at one with the Tao," Hara-san said. "How could I have
such power, if the Tao were not part of my spirit?"

Shakkai leaned forward, looking Hara-san straight in the eye.
"We are all a piece, a sacred part, of the Great Spirit that has created us, and if I were to say that your darkness was not part of my
own soul, I would be fooling myself," Shakkai said. "But I strive
in this lifetime to bring light into those dark corners of karma that
we have all been born with. You instead take that darkness and
spread it over the light. For you to be happy, there would be no
light, and then all would be lost, including you yourself, because it
is your destructiveness that gives you life. If you are not destroying something, then you feel small, because it is only in someone
else's destruction that you grow, and that is a tragedy, Hara-san.
At some point, ultimately, there is only one person left to
destroy."

"And who is that?" Hara-san asked.

"It is yourself," Shakkai said very gently, "and I ache for you,
Hara-san, because you will bring about your own demise one day,
if you do not change your ways."

Hara-san laughed again. "We shall see, O Empress of the Spirit Garden, we shall see." Hara-san stood up.

As Sami-san escorted Master Hara to the moon gate at the far end of the garden, I turned to Shakkai. The setting sun was behind her, forming a halo of brilliant light around her head. Her face was lost in shadow, except for a momentary glint of brightness from her eyes. I reached out and touched her hand.

"Shakkai, I do not understand. Please explain to me why we must allow Hara-san into this sacred temple that is representative of your spirit. I just do not understand. Please enlighten me," I said.

Taking a small red and pink porcelain bud vase that was resting on the table in front of us, and moving the plum branches rich with pink flowers, Shakkai gently rearranged the flowers and set them off to the side. I was waiting for an answer.

"I do not blame you for your confusion," she answered, "but you will understand in time. You see, Hara-san needs to be taught like anyone else. He is an extraordinary man in his way, and a great antagonist. He adds a certain flavor to the pot, if you will. He needs to grow, and there will come a day when he will either die or understand that he has taken the wrong fork in the trail, but I do not judge him, O Kiku. Who am I to judge anyone? Somewhere in history, perhaps I represented the darkness in some way; perhaps you did. Perhaps that was a lesson you needed to learn in one lifetime or another. So all that we can do is witness him and love him, because after all, power, true power, is the man-ifestation of true love and can be nothing else. If I did not love him in some way, if I could not open my heart to him, there would be parts of myself that I would have to disown."

"But, Shakkai," I interrupted, "you are not filled with darkness. How can you say this?"

"My child, don't you understand that darkness defines the light? For all of his madness, it creates a surreal atmosphere that punctu-ates with great clarity the light in the world. His darkness is so great that one cannot avoid the light that is created just by his existence in the world. None of us is perfect. We are striving for perfection. By denying the darkness of our own souls, we create a negative energy in the world. All of us have felt jealousy and greed. All of us have lost our way at one time or another. It is a very good thing to witness someone else walking down the wrong path. If there is love in your heart, you will do what you can to bring him back to harmony and balance in life."

"But, O-Sensei, I feel that his darkness could harm us, that perhaps in trying to help him, he will bring us down with him."

With this, Shakkai laughed from the center of her being and slapped her thighs, which surprised me. It was as if she were another person when she did this. It seemed so familiar. I could not put my finger on it, and I would stare at her. She would watch me with my mouth agape and laugh even harder and leave me almost senseless with surprise. Finally she stopped laughing and came over and gave me a hug.

"Oh, my daughter," she said, "do not worry. At least you are not bored. We have much left to learn together." Again she laughed and led me into the house for dinner.

When I took my clothes off to go to bed for the night, I noticed with shock that the area around my power center, my navel, was bruised, as if Master Hara had actually physically grabbed me with his hands. I ran to Shakkai to show her.

Shakkai shook her head and said, "I am sorry, little one." She took out an herbal salve she had resting on her altar in an amber pot, and rubbed my stomach gently. I was amazed at the heat that I felt, and happy to find in only a few hours that the bruises were gone.

The next morning, when I walked down toward the pond, to the place where I often did my *kinchen,* my breathing exercises, and my meditating to quiet my spirit, I abruptly stopped in my tracks. There was a tiny lizard lying dead on its back on the trail. I knelt down and saw with horror that his mouth had been sewn shut. I picked up the little fellow in my hands and ran into the house to show Shakkai. She took the lizard and meditated with it a moment. An angry light flashed in her eyes.

"What is it?" I asked her. "I have never seen such a thing. Who would do this?"

"It is from Hara-san," Shakkai said. "A message for you. He's telling you that he is watching you."

"I cannot permit this," I said. I was very angry. I felt so sorry for the little lizard. Shakkai and I took it out by the stone wall where it had enjoyed sunning itself, and buried it.

"Sit down with me for a moment," Shakkai said, looking at me intently. "Tell me how you're feeling."

"I'm frightened," I told her. I hadn't realized it before, but there was a quaking in my gut.

"I want you to close your eyes," she said. "Take a deep breath. I want you to move your consciousness down into the area of your body where you feel that fear."

"I hurt inside my stomach, Sensei."

"Take your consciousness into that area, and tell me what you see inside yourself," she said.

I looked around for several minutes and found a dragon breathing fire. It was not a good dragon, but a creature of power and destruction, and its tongue was lashing out, burning everything in its path. I told Shakkai what I was seeing.

"I want you to become that dragon," she said, "and talk to me."

So I did. I became the dragon and said, "I am a dragon, and I am fire-breathing and destructive. I am sent by Hara-san, and I am sent to destroy O Kiku and to drive her away from Shakkai, her teacher. I am going to cause her great pain until she leaves her teacher."

A fleeting moment of angry shadow crossed Shakkai's face as I watched her, and then she said, "Now, O Kiku, I am going to join you in your stomach."

I closed my eyes and visualized my teacher inside my stomach. I watched as Shakkai drew a long sword and stabbed the dragon in its heart. I watched it die.

"And now," she asked me, "what would you like to do with this dragon?"

"Oh, get it out of me," I said.

"Yes, that is a good idea," she agreed.

Together we took the dragon out and buried it in the ground outside the compound. We came back and sat again in the same place. This time, when I went into my stomach area, I found only golden light. The stomach area was healed and the tissue of my stomach was normal. I took a deep breath of relief and hugged my teacher.

"How do you feel?" Shakkai asked me, eyeing me closely.

"I feel relieved," I said, "and the fear is gone. I really do understand that his destructiveness has actually turned on himself, even though he hurts other people. I can see that really and truly he is on a self-destructive path. Eventually he will destroy himself, won't he, Sensei?"

"Yes, I'm afraid that is true. In the meantime," Shakkai said, "it is important to stay aware. He is testing himself by pitting himself against you and me. He is sharpening his claws, and one day, perhaps, we will have to face him in true battle. But never mind. That is not something that we cannot handle. In the meantime, stay aware of what you're feeling and thinking, and if he moves into your mind and your heart, you tell me. In the meantime, your goodness and vulnerability are your greatest defenses."

"How is that?" I asked.

"Come," she said, "stand in front of me. Make your body rigid in a position of defense."

I held up my arms. My body tightened. Shakkai pushed against me hard, and I fended off her advance. It was as if she were running into a stone wall. She pushed again and again, and I pushed her back again and again.

"Now," she said, "stand limp and at ease and in your center. Bend your knees ever so slightly, and just be like a reed in the wind, soft and compliant and open."

At this point Shakkai lunged toward me, pushed, and with her own energy, she flew right by me, as I flexed easily to the side.

"You see, you are vulnerable in this stance, and when I push for you, trying to hit you, I cannot, because there is nothing to fight back against me. You are open and fluid, and you do not respond in a rigid way to me. Therefore I cannot hurt you. It's like striking at air, and that is your vulnerability. If you stay open and not shielded and tense, there is nothing to hit against. Your vulnerability is your greatest shield. It is your actual stance in the world. Therefore his energy will defeat *him,* because as he attacks you, he has to move off his center. Look. Let me show you."

She stood straight, with her knees slightly bent. "You see I am standing, now, in my center over my *ch'i,* the area of power around my navel. This is what the martial artists talk about, but it is the same in terms of spirit, because as we are in our bodies, we are in our spiritual being. When I move toward you to attack you, watch what happens."

She moved toward me, setting her right foot in front of her, and she was off center instantly.

"There was a great teacher who was the founder of aikido. His name was Morihei Veshiba. He talked about allowing the other person to move off of his center to attack you. You never attack. You never attack, because you are never off of your center. You are never out of your own state of power. It is the same way in the world of sorcery. When a sorcerer moves to attack, moves off of his center to harm you, you can defeat him easily with his own power. His own momentum will carry him into great difficulty. That's what I want you to learn about Hara-san. You will begin to feel this energy coming toward you, and when you do, just let it go on by, and he will tumble off into the bushes as surely if he were standing there with his sword drawn. You see, O Kiku, you are the one who is in complete control. You are the one who will be defeating him."

"But I don't want to defeat anyone," I said. "I want there to be harmony and love."

Shakkai laughed at my obvious naïveté. "There are times when you must learn to fight," Shakkai said, "because we are human, and out of the ignorance of being human there are times when people will be angered by your goodness and your light, and they will try to defeat you, but you have to stand in your own truth. You know about your integrity. You know that what you are doing is true and right in the world. And that's, in a sense, all you have, and no one can take away what you are. No one. No one has the right to do that, so if someone comes toward you with ugliness and pain and tries to encircle you in his own aura of discontent, simply understand in your spirit that that is his problem. That is his energy, and it has nothing to do with you. Just let him pass right through. Even a judgment lends power to such a person. Even a discussion lends power. Do not allow yourself to move off your center. Live within your center all your life, and you will be learning the lesson of this lifetime."

* * *

The next morning, instead of waking in Shakkai's house, I found myself back in Manitoba again. Again, I was very disoriented, and after several dowsings in the ice-cold creek, I sat in the grass wrapped in blankets, staring at Agnes and Ruby, shaking my head.

"There is a man in my dreaming, Ruby, who reminds me very much of Red Dog. He's a very dark soul, and though he is different in many ways, there's an energy field about him that reminds me of that terrible person."

"Funny you should mention that," Ruby said.

"Guess what?" Agnes asked.

"What?" I looked at them rather alarmed with the expression on their face.

"We have something funny to tell you," Agnes said with a mischievous grin on her face. She elbowed Ruby, who slapped her leg and laughed in return. "While you were dreaming," Agnes said, "I came back to the cabin to get some jerky, and who did I find but Ben, climbing in the kitchen window. I snuck up behind him, shut the window on top of him so he couldn't move, and tied his legs together. Then I unlocked the cabin door—it's strange, because I never lock the cabin door, but I did this morning—and I walked in, and there was Drum, standing in terror against the sink, with your writing clutched to his chest."

"You mean they broke in the cabin to steal my writing?" I said in astonishment.

"It looks like it," Agnes said, giggling to herself. "It was pretty funny, I must say. I told Drum to tie Ben's arms behind his back. Then I grabbed my .30/06 rifle that I had sitting behind my jacket by the door. Boy, they were scared. Even Crow joined in. He landed on Ben's ass and started pecking on his back pocket, looking for food. It was pretty funny, indeed." She laughed hilariously.

"What happened to my writing?" I asked, dreadfully concerned.

"I took it away from Ben and went through it carefully. Nothing was missing."

"But did he read it? I don't want them to read my writing. Not now—not ever!"

"It's hard to tell," Agnes said. "I don't think they had the time. I think they thought they could take the writing, and then they would read it when they got back to their cabin."

"But why would they want it in the first place?"

"They just wanted to aggravate us," Ruby said.

"No," Agnes interrupted, "I think there was more to it than that. Red Dog never knew how to double dream. That was something he wanted me to teach him just before he stole the marriage basket. And I couldn't teach him. He didn't have the ability. He didn't have his female side, as we all know. That's one of the reasons he stole the marriage basket. He thought he could invent the femaleness he needed within himself by stealing the marriage basket, and then he could learn how to double dream. It was his great desire to move into the next hoop of power with his physical body and be able to move back and forth at will. Whether he ever learned that, I do not know. I could not teach him that, because he was incapable of doing his homework. He couldn't open himself to what he needed to learn."

I sat there staring at Agnes. My mind was racing back to Shakkai and what she had said about Master Hara-san.

"That's incredible," I said out loud.

Agnes's head swiveled around to look at me. She observed me carefully. "What are you talking about, Little Wolf?"

"It's Shakkai and Master Hara-san."

"Master who?"

"Master Hara-san."

"That's a funny name," Ruby retorted.

"He's the tea master, Ruby."

"Oh."

"Why do you have that strange look on your face?" Agnes asked.

"Because it's as if history were repeating itself. Here I am in this future life in Japan. It's so different. It's so strange to me. I look so different. I've got black hair and I'm Japanese. Yet Master Hara-san is like Red Dog. He doesn't look like Red Dog, but his personality is very similar."

"Ah," Ruby said. "Don't you understand, my child, that when you pass on to other dimensions, you retain your personality? Your personality lives in your 'shadow being.'"

"By 'shadow being,' do you mean in the etheric body?" I asked.

"Well, you could call it that. You could call it whatever crazy thing you want," Ruby said. "I call it shadow being."

Agnes nodded and added, "Yes, Lynn, to Ruby, the shadow being is the same as the etheric body is to Shakkai, at least as you've explained it to us."

"Then is it possible that the tea master is in fact Red Dog?" A chill ran down my spine with the very thought of this.

Agnes, with her dark piercing eyes, and Ruby, her expression remote for a moment, stared at me as if they were waiting for me to say something. Then I realized that was exactly what they were waiting for—they were waiting for me to *get it*. I suddenly realized that Master Hara-san could, indeed, be Red Dog. A chill of fear numbed my hands and the back of my neck.

"Do you mean to say I am in this future life without the two of you, and I have to face Red Dog again? I thought that was all over with. I thought we were finished with him."

After a long pause, Ruby tapped me on the top of my head with her finger and moved to a position where she was sitting squarely in front of me. "What do you think this is all about?" Ruby asked, gesturing expansively to the world around us.

"Well, I don't know . . . it's about life and death and what it all means."

"Well that's an interesting explanation for all these years of struggle and work," Ruby said. "And if you want to be painfully simplistic, it's true. That's what it's about—life and death."

"And it's about a lot more than that," Agnes interjected.

"What do you mean?" I asked.

"It's about the *meaning* of life and death. And that's different," Agnes said. "There is a reason for all of the struggle."

I looked at her, and something inside me deepened and opened. I suddenly realized that if you don't solve a problem of hate or love or a struggle in one lifetime, it moves on to the next dimension. It moves on to the next life, depending on your abilities.

"So, in other words," I said, "we continue to unravel our obstacles in life until we learn to deal with them properly. Is that what you are saying to me?"

The two old women nodded in unison, a little smile curling the corners of their mouths.

"I remember something else," I said, pulling my Pendleton blanket around my shoulders as a cold breeze came down from the north. "I remember what Shakkai was telling me. She was saying that when you die, it is simply a passage into the next dimension where you will not have only three dimensions, but four—four different aspects of perception. Is that true?"

Ruby nodded and Agnes agreed. "Yes, it is true, but not in the way you think."

"What do you mean?" I asked.

"There are lifetimes of being reborn into this physical world, and once you've learned what you need to learn in physical relativity, then you move to the next dimension. Sometimes it takes a long, long time to get to that so-called fourth dimension or second hoop of power in the sense of your rebirth patterns. There's also a second hoop of power just in the physical world."

"I see," I said, not completely understanding. "Are you saying I still have some kind of karma with Red Dog?"

"There is no karma, unless you hold on to the way you feel about that person. In other words, if you still hate him or are angry with him, then he is going to reappear, just as he would if you loved him. Any strong emotion creates a connection, and that connection is going to pull him to reappear until it is resolved one way or another."

"But I don't hate him. I simply don't like him, and I think that that's healthy, because he has tried to hurt me and he has tried to kill me."

"Ah, but you see, *he* may hate *you*," Ruby said.

"Oh, terrific, but I can't be responsible for how he feels."

"No, you cannot. You can only deal with the reality of the moment, and if it comes up, it is power just testing you again," Agnes said.

"But I don't want to be tested again. I don't want to go through another war with Red Dog."

"Well, if Master Hara-san truly is Red Dog, you really have nothing to fear," Ruby said.

"How do you mean?" I asked, still terrified.

"Because he still has the same problems he had in this lifetime," Ruby said.

"But how do you know?"

"Because . . . because I know," Ruby answered, and got up and helped me to my feet.

Agnes and Ruby led me up to the cabin, not saying much of anything.

"Agnes, tell me what happened to Ben and Drum. Finish your story. We got sidetracked."

"You could call it that." Ruby winked at me.

"Well, I held them at gunpoint for a long time, and I took out my seven sacred feathers. These are feathers that Ben and Drum have wanted since they first found out about them, about twenty years ago. They were given to me by a Mayan trader, and they have great magic power for ceremony. Supposedly, if you use these feathers in a ceremony for good, they will make it the most powerful ceremony possible. But if you use them to do harm, they will destroy you. I've never used them. I'm saving them for a very sacred moment. Sometime, and I don't know when, it will be proper to use them.

"I took them out and did a smudging ceremony with Ben and Drum. Of course, they were terrified. They thought they were going to disappear at any moment and rot in the fires of darkness forever. I took the pages back. I was careful that each page was there, and I smudged them. Finally I untied Drum and sent both of them on their way."

"Is that all?" Ruby stamped her foot. "You just let them walk away?"

"Well, I took a few shots," Agnes admitted with a sheepish grin, "just shooting into the ground. I made them dance a few steps. They were scared. Let me tell you, they were terrified and doing a jig all the way down the trail."

She laughed uproariously and slapped her legs. We laughed with her, imagining Crow pecking at Drum's rump, thinking how silly those two men were. They knew a lot in their way, and they could certainly scare me too, as they had from time to time, but they missed the point that there is a much higher design to life. Power is only important in respect to your resolution with the Great Spirit, with your own illumination. Power in itself is only another game, unless you have a higher understanding of the balance and harmony of existence.

Later that night, Agnes and Ruby took our medicine healing drums down from the rafters near the stove. We did a short ceremony, sitting outside on the porch, watching the orange streaks of the aurora borealis through the towering pines that surrounded the cabin. Each of us passed the drums around to the other. I took Ruby's drum, which had red pyramids painted around the circumference, representing the balance of male and female energies. The drums have two faces—male and female. On the female face of Ruby's drum is a stag deer. Agnes's drum has a whistling elk on the female side, and hummingbirds on the male side in reds and yellows. My drum has wolf tracks on the male side, and a wolf and a morning star on the female side.

We touched the drums respectfully, and then, taking our own, we began to sound a heartbeat. For a long time we played together until that sacred moment came in which the space between the worlds opens up and the void is created. It is a place of no sound within the sound. It is a place of power where intent is born. When this moment happens, I have been taught to sharpen my shaman intent and will. This time I asked for strength in my dreaming, and renewed power to understand this new teaching. Then I took the heartbeat down into my solar plexus to work with my White Star Woman shield. Hours went by before the ceremony ended and we went to sleep.

The next morning, Ruby and I were in my Dreamlodge before dawn.

17

A Theft of Spirit

◆

He who lives on the earth,
but is not of the earth;
who is not known by the earth,
but has the body of earth,
who rules the earth from within,
he is the Self, the inner guide,
the immortal Self.

— THE UPANISHADS

◆

Upon entering the sacred dream, I found myself on my futon in Shakkai's house. The mists lay soft, like lavender gray cotton, over the garden and the pond. I looked over to where Shakkai slept and was very surprised to see that she was still asleep. She was usually up long before dawn, working in meditation out in the garden or in front of her God-shelf, or altar, inside the house. After I had dressed and folded up my futon and put it away, I moved around the house rather noisily to awaken Shakkai, which usually would have happened in a moment. I went over to her and knelt beside her bed. For a moment a bolt of terror struck through me. I thought that she might be dead. Her eyes were partially open, and her breathing was so shallow that it was almost unde- tectable, but I could feel a pulse in her neck. She was in a very peaceful sleep, so peaceful that a very slight smile was on her lips. I was alarmed, but then I thought perhaps she was in a deep trance for some reason. I decided to make some tea, and then I thought I would go look at her sacred *hu* in the other room and perhaps meditate a while in front of it.

I walked into the room where the *hu* lives. Bars of sunlight streamed through the windows, and birds welcomed the sunrise outside. A slight wind had come up, blowing the fog into waves and swirls of filtered light. Shakkai had built a small altar for her *hu,* with candles and various icons set around it. I gasped as I looked at the altar. The white cloth was opened and the space where the *hu* normally sat was empty and still. A note in black ink on rice paper was set on a tiny tripod in the center of the white cloth. I walked closer, almost afraid to read it. I felt something in the air, a negativity, a darkness, as if the room had been desecrated by an alien presence. As I came closer to the paper, I read the note, written, as I had feared, by Master Hara Kyoshi.

"You are the Mistress of the Shakkai, and I honor your *oni* spirits. And now take heed, for my *kami* spirits have become angry."

I knelt in front of the altar, stunned by what had happened. How could the Master of the Tea have actually done such a thing? He was obviously a Master bent backward, a black sorcerer. I felt a wave of terror that turned to sadness. I closed my eyes, wanting to move myself into my center. I breathed deeply, as tears streamed down my cheeks. It was as if an ancient memory were knocking at the back of my mind. Somehow I had seen this event before it happened. I had sensed his evil and his darkness, and I knew that he meant to hurt us. It was as if he had stolen the sacred *hu* to represent his woman power. But he had no idea how to be receptive to the powers of Mother Earth. I realized that he needed the power of woman, and he could not have Shakkai or me, or any other woman of power, because she would shun him. So he had taken the sacred *hu* for his woman power to balance his male shield.

I was shocked with this realization, and yet I knew that I had to retrieve the *hu* in some way. Why was Shakkai asleep? Had he put a spell on her? I did not know what to do or whom to turn to, and then my thoughts moved to Kat-san. Tears of frustration washed my face. I wanted to be able to fight for Shakkai. I didn't want to have to turn to anyone. I wanted to be able to pick up the sword of fate and deal with Hara-san in an appropriate manner, but I was afraid, because I didn't know enough. I prayed for a long time, asking for guidance, asking my allies and the Tao to give me the wisdom to return the *hu* to its rightful owner.

As I stood up from the altar and turned to go back to Shakkai, I heard the tinkling of bells at the door. Kat-san stood there, and I welcomed him. An intense frown was on his face, as if he knew that something had happened. Taking him by the hand, I led him to Shakkai without a word. We knelt on either side of her. He held his flattened palms above her body, feeling her energy and sensing her deep trance as I watched. Then, very tenderly and lovingly, he stroked her hair back from her forehead, as if he were touching his mother.

"I don't understand," he said, shaking his head. "What is happening here?"

"I think I know," I said, and taking his hand, I led him into the altar room and showed him the note. He picked up the rice paper and held it up to the light.

I had not seen the dragon watermark imprinted into the paper. After a long time he set the note back down on its tripod, and taking my hand, he led me out into the garden, where we sat next to the pond for some time in silence.

"All things are blessings in their way," he said finally. "There is a teaching here."

"It is disguised very well," I answered, looking into his face with great admiration for his strength.

"Has anything unusual happened with Master Hara-san in the last few days?" he asked me.

"Yes, we met a day or so ago in the garden, and he had a test of wills with Shakkai."

"Over what?" he asked.

I blushed and gazed at the reflection of our beloved snow-capped mountain in the pond, and wished I felt as cool as it looked. "Several months ago, Hara-san seemed to want me as an apprentice, and when Shakkai went to prepare to show him the *hu,* he prevailed upon me to work with him. When Shakkai returned, she was quite angry, although she didn't say much, but I saw lightning flash from her eyes and knock him over onto the ground."

Kat-san threw his head back and laughed in spite of the seriousness of the moment. "Aha!" he said. "No wonder! The Master of the Tea is an egoistic man. He could not bear to be embarrassed in front of you, let alone Shakkai. You see, O Kiku, he has declared war. He has stolen Shakkai's most sacred symbol. This is something that should not have happened. It shows him to be the black sorcerer he is. Their friendship will never be the same. He is trying to steal her power and claim it for his own. She has extended herself in friendship and trust for all these years. We have all warned her about Hara, but she believes in the goodness of humankind, and she always sees that side of a person. Her innocence is her greatest shield and protection, but Hara has taken advantage, and he has declared war without warning her. This is unforgivable, and it dishonors him. He has dishonored power, and power will turn in on him. You wait and see. In his posturing and egoism and

constant negativity, he will be destroyed by his own sword. It will
be so." Kat-san stared into the sky, his face lean and brown, like
burnished pecan wood. His demeanor was that of a coiled snake,
ready to strike. I could see that he was gathering his power.

I smoothed the sand around me where we were sitting and then
picked up a flat river stone and held it in my hand, smoothing it
with my fingers, feeling the warmth of the morning sun coming
from its center.

"But why would he steal the sacred *hu?* Why not just attack
her? Why not just try to kill her?" I asked.

"Because it is the way of power. He wants more than her life.
He wants her essence, her spirit. In that magnificent gourd shrine
is her essence."

His words struck me to the quick. I felt something moving
inside me, an old memory, so dark that I could not see its face, but
something resonated within me that made me afraid. My eyes
must have betrayed my feelings, because he reached out to me and
touched my shoulder.

"Do not be afraid, because Shakkai can handle this. We can
handle this. We are, all of us, warriors of the spirit. For some, the
way of building power is to test one against another, over and
over. You and I and Shakkai teach ourselves about power by pitting ourselves against ourselves. You, O Kiku, move toward illumination by testing yourself. You do not need to hurt someone to
grow. You do not need an opponent. You have learned the way of
light. Shakkai will teach you how to grow through the proper use
of power. You do not use power to hurt or manipulate people, but
to enlighten your own being so that you can begin to heal the
world and all those around you. Hara is too stupid to do that. He
needs what he calls a 'good enemy.' He needs a reflection, someone else's reflection, because he doesn't have the courage to look
into his own mirror and heal his own spirit. That is the true warrior. It takes true wisdom to battle with your own reflection and
become whole. That is the path of heart, the path of the peaceful
warrior."

"It takes a very strong female shield, doesn't it," I asked, "to be
a warrior on the path of heart?"

"Yes, O Kiku, it takes the receptivity of woman, of the sacred void, to open yourself to the primal power of all things. This is something that you are teaching me, and I am forever grateful. The primal power of the source of wisdom is held and carried by woman, and that is why Kyoshi took the *hu,* because the *hu* symbolizes the power of woman. As Shakkai has often told me, it is the womb of Mother Earth and gives birth to all women. What could be better for a warrior who has no female shield?"

"But why is Shakkai asleep? Is there danger for her? Should we find a doctor?" I asked.

"Shakkai only chooses to be asleep, and if that is her choice, then I can only surmise that she is giving us the sword of defense. She is asking us to take our power and return the *hu* to her altar. I would imagine that until then she will lie deep in slumber in another world, perhaps even in another lifetime, until the *hu* is safely returned to her."

"But couldn't she die?" I asked, frightened. "How could she be asleep for so very long? Are you saying that she will be asleep for days and days?"

"Only the gods know such things," he said. "But come, we must devise a plan."

·18·

The Sacred Hu

We are close to waking up,
when we dream that we are dreaming.

— NOVALIS
(FRIEDRICH VON HARDENBERG)

Kat-san took me up into the mountains near where he lived, about an hour's walk through the forest from Shakkai's garden. It made me uncomfortable to leave her alone in her house without one of us being there, but at least Sami-san was nearby. We reached a clearing in the forest high up on the mountain, where an ancient Shinto shrine with a thickly thatched roof and oddly curved eaves had been built. It was expertly tended, very small, and the temple was built of beautiful burnished wood and polished blue tiles.

Kat-san asked me to enter the temple with him. I followed him up the steps, and we sat inside the temple, facing the altar. He lit several lanterns, and after meditating for some time, he turned to me and whispered, "I need you to meditate and stay in your place of power. I must go out into the forest, where my *kami* spirits live, and speak with them."

I asked nothing. His intensity belied his calmness and his careful movements. I went into deep meditation.

As Kat-san stood, he whispered to me, "I need to borrow your female power. You will feel a tugging in your chest and solar plexus. I will be using your strength. Do not be afraid. I will not hurt you. I will return the energy to you when I'm finished." Then Kat-san left.

Not more than fifteen minutes later, I began to feel a tugging such as he had described. It was not uncomfortable, but I felt a bit drained, as if my life force were slowly being taken from me. Had he not described this to me, I would have been very frightened indeed, but instead I mustered all the strength and power I could, and sent it to him. I imagined a silver cord leading from my solar plexus to his, and I let the strength from my body flow into his.

Not long afterwards, Kat-san returned to my side, and we left the temple together and sat outside in the grass. It was late afternoon, and I knew we had to return soon. We spread a white cloth, and he placed some sweetmeats there for us to eat, and some water.

"Do you wonder about the *kami* spirits?" he asked.

"Yes," I said. "Would you explain to me what is happening? I am most concerned."

He smiled at me briefly as we ate, and said, "My very special *kami* spirit is a rascal who plays with people and enjoys it, and one of his great talents is to sit on something and make it disappear. Even though it is still placed in front of you, you cannot see it, so I feel very grateful for the energy you have given me. It helped me, and the *kami* spirit has been sent. Now we must work very quickly. This is the plan . . ."

"What plan?" I asked excitedly. This was all very mysterious. "How can we help Shakkai?" I asked.

"The *kami* spirit has been sent to sit on the sacred *hu* in Hara's house. Hara will go soon now to pray, and he will see that the sacred *hu* is gone, and he will be in a rage. He will think Shakkai has come to take it, and he will not understand why she is not still sleeping. He will rush madly to her house for a confrontation. He will find me there, and while he is at Shakkai's compound, you will reclaim the *hu*."

"But how will I see it, if the *kami* spirit is still sitting on it?"

"You will see it because the *kami* spirit has been instructed to allow you to see it, because it belongs to you and to the sacred dreams of all women. Hara lives alone. He is the Master of the Tea. He is not a stupid man, but because this was an act arising from extreme rage, from reaction instead of action, I am not worried. I think he will act on impulse, which is usually very unlike him. I would ordinarily never tell you to go there, but I think we are safe. The *kami* spirits do not always protect, but this time they will protect you. The spirits do not like Hara. He is not a good man, and though he is a sorcerer and he has beings that do his bidding, they will follow him and come to me, and I can handle them."

"But I've never been to his teahouse. I don't know where it is."

"I will take you there now. Come. It is getting late."

He wrapped everything up in the white cloth and hurried into the temple, left it there, and came out with a coat for me and another for himself. I looked up at the sun, lowering behind the horizon.

"How far is it, Kat-san?"

"Only a short run from here, I assure you. Follow me."

I ran after Kat-san down the trail. Terror was beginning to rise up in my stomach, but I knew I must follow him. Perhaps this was our only chance to help Shakkai and to restore the sacred *hu* to its rightful owner.

When we stopped to catch our breath at the top of the trail, looking down at the azure lake below, I tugged on Kat-san's sleeve and asked, "Is there no other way to regain something stolen?"

"This is the way of power," he said, looking at me with very kind dark eyes. "This is a struggle of the forces of power. Though it is not the way I would have it, and not the way I would choose my mirrors, this has been chosen by Hara, and because he and Shakkai are both masters, they must honor each other in a fight of wills. It has always been that way. It is the game of life, and we all play these games in one way or another."

"But, Kat-san, this man is not just playing," I said.

"This is true. He wants to take whoever has power. He wants to claim their gifts as his own. But he will not be allowed to do this. We must play by the rules of power, nevertheless. So come. It is getting dark."

I followed Kat-san down the trail, struggling to keep up with him. Once in a while he would take my hand to help me down a steep area where my feet tended to slip on the pebbles. I had the sense that we could have been running down a trail six centuries before or six centuries hence, that these trails had been here for eons, that truth, somehow, was always the same, and the games of power were always the same. I was furious and yet intrigued by this event, fascinated to see if I could actually find the sacred *hu* and return it to Shakkai. My heart was beating almost out of my chest with anticipation and fright.

Finally we came to a fork in the trail, where we took the right-hand path, which moved down into a lovely clearing. I gasped. A little house was built there on the edge of a cliff, looking out over the beautiful lake with the mountain in the distance. It was the house I had seen in my dream. It was a very fitting place for a tea master to live. We came closer, and then Kat-san took my hand and walked me around to the far side of the house, behind a mulberry tree and some low, very carefully clipped bushes with red blossoms on them.

"He will be doing his prayers in just a few minutes," Kat-san said. "Hold yourself very low to the ground. He must not see us. He is going to be very, very upset."

We crouched underneath the bushes to wait.

"How are you going to get back to Shakkai's without him seeing you?" I asked. "And how do I get back there?"

"The trail that we just took," Kat-san said, "where we went right, you go back to that fork and take the left-hand trail. It will lead you directly back to Shakkai's compound. We walked part of that trail today. Always take the left-hand trails. There will be two more forks. Always bear to the left, and you will find her house about twenty minutes from here, if you run. I know a secret trail. I can enter from the back and be in her compound before Hara arrives."

"I can't believe we're doing this," I whispered to him. "I feel like I'm in a Kabuki drama."

He laughed and pinched my cheek. "Yes, it seems so, doesn't it? Let's hope this play has a happy ending."

Suddenly we heard a bellow from inside the house, and two lanterns were lit in different rooms. There was a lot of thumping. I was surprised to hear such a ruckus.

"Ah, you see, he has discovered the *hu* is gone." Kat-san settled into his place of power and asked me to do the same. We meditated for several minutes. Then he took hold of my hand and kissed it. "Now, in a moment Hara will burst through the door and run down the trail. I am going to leave you now. The *kami* spirit knows of your presence and will be with you. Trust me. Do not be frightened. As soon as you see him run up the trail, go directly into the house. As far as I can tell, there is no one there. I cannot feel the energy of anyone. When you go in the door, go straight back, and you will find his altar room. Right there you will find the sacred *hu*. Take it and run."

"What if for some reason I should run into Master Hara on the trail?"

"The *kami* spirit will let you know. The spirit will run with you. Do not be frightened. If you see anything around you, just maintain your intent and go. This is a lot to ask of you, I know, but I also know that you are ready for this, or it would not have happened. I wish you well."

Just then there was another bellow, and just as Kat-san had prophesied, Master Hara, carrying his sword, moved out of the hut at incredible speed and disappeared up the trail. I turned to say something to Kat-san, but he was already gone. My heart was thumping, and I kept getting glimpses in my mind of an ancient memory, something knocking, almost as if I had done this before. It was very strange, and I was petrified. When both of them were gone from my view, I crept up from the bushes and ran toward the house. Hara-san had even left the screen open at the threshold to his house. I ran up the stairs and entered the house. The lanterns were lit, and light was still flickering in the impeccably furnished, shoji-screened rooms. I looked for evidence of someone, but there was no one. I ran through the house. It was beautiful and simple and had the feeling of darkness inside it, but I paid no attention. Given a chance, I would never have entered this house, it made me so nervous, and it repelled me to my very soul.

I ran back to the farthest room, and sure enough, there was the altar, and on a white cloth made of what looked like linen lay the sacred *hu*. I saw to the left of it some sparks floating in the air, little white sparks, but I remembered what Kat-san had said to me—that I might see something strange and to pay no attention, that it was only the *kami* spirits, so I proceeded. In a moment, I wrapped the *hu* in the white material, placed it under my arm, and ran.

I ran through the night, up to the fork in the trail, my heart beating, gasping for breath. I took the left fork as I had been told. I felt something around me, and I looked up into the trees and saw little white sparks following me. I was happy that they were there, because I was very frightened. I couldn't imagine how I had gotten myself into this, and yet I knew that it was a very sacred event, that there was karma here. Some sort of justice was being done, and I was a part of that, and it filled me with joy to be able to do this for

Shakkai. So I ran almost silently down the trail. I came to one and then two more forks, and took the left-hand turn at each one. The *kami* spirits were just ahead of me every step of the way. I felt great relief at their presence. Finally the gardens of Shakkai appeared in the distance. In the moonlight the leaves on the trees shone silvery, and the pond was welcoming in its peaceful reflection.

I ran down the path, being careful now, not knowing what was happening ahead of me and feeling a sense of dread, as though something very violent were occurring. Carefully I came around the edge of the house, and I heard screams and yells and odd sounds and the clinking of metal on metal, and I remembered that Hara-san had very stupidly taken his sword, and sure enough I saw the flash of sparks from the clashing blades. I realized that Hara-san had actually taken on the samurai. I couldn't believe it. How stupid, I thought in my mind. This man must be very, very stupid. Then, much to my absolute shock, as I rounded the edge of the house, I saw that it was not Kat-san who was wielding the sword, but Shakkai herself. Somehow she had awakened, and I saw her run the sword through Hara-san's right shoulder and out through his back, and pin him to the ground. Then I shuddered, because Shakkai was covered with blood.

In horror I ran from the bush, totally forgetting that I was supposed to be secretive. I handed Kat-san the sacred *hu* and ran to Shakkai, who turned to me, her eyes as wild as those of an animal, with a red glint in them, the likes of which I had never seen. Her field of power was awesome and threw me backwards for a moment.

I looked back at Kat-san, who held out the sacred *hu* to me. "Take this and give it to Shakkai," he ordered.

I took it back and, with my hands shaking, presented the sacred *hu* to Shakkai, who bowed low and took the *hu*, then kissed me on the forehead and looked at me with a love in her eyes that I would never forget. She was covered with blood. I knew not where the blood was coming from, and I could not stay in that sacred moment as, perhaps, I should have.

"Shakkai, you are hurt. Let me help you," I said.

"Oh, it is nothing. I am simply scratched." She smiled a bit, but she was very weak, I could tell.

In the meantime, Master Hara was on the ground, moaning in agony.

"Do not worry. I will take care of the Master of the Tea," Kat-san said. "I will make sure his wounds are tended to. I will call my men now and take him from this sacred place. They will take him where he needs to go. If he is lucky, he will not die." He turned to me. "But he has been taught a lesson that he will not forget."

I helped Shakkai into the house. Fortunately she had only scratches on her arm and head, but they were bleeding profusely. We wrapped and dressed them carefully, and then, with what little energy Shakkai had left, we returned the sacred *hu* to the altar, and I put her to bed and collapsed on my own futon, only to awaken twelve hours later, still completely exhausted from the night's events.

I spent several days tending to Shakkai. Thunderstorms filled the skies with deep rolling thunder, and zigzags of yellow lightning split the lapis blue heavens. It was as if the gods had been angry and were reminding all of us of their invincible power. It was during these days that Shakkai taught me about the sacred *hu* and the Dancing Bowl. She had Sami-san bring a basketful of gourds so that I could choose one for my own. I spent several days with the gourds, meditating with them. This was a difficult teaching for me, and I worked a lot by myself in the garden.

Dance of the Deer

♦

Spring flowers and autumn chrysanthemums smile upon me,
The moon at dawn and the breezes of morn cleanse my heart.

— KOBO DAISHI

♦

Returning to the cabin in Manitoba after being in such an intense and upsetting emotional situation with Shakkai was painful. It was early morning; just as in Japan, there was fog outside, surrounding the valley in which the cabin sat. Inside the cabin it was warm enough, but it felt cold to my heart, because the fog was so thick outside. Everything looked gray—the old board and log walls, the bundles of herbs and rattles hanging from the ceiling rafters, even the sky. It felt like the coast of California in the wintertime. Agnes, wearing a bright red ribbon shirt and a denim skirt, was sitting at the foot of my bed with a quizzical expression on her face. Ruby sat at the small wooden table, tapping her fingers impatiently. I looked at her blurry-eyed, with the covers up under my chin, not wanting to get up, not wanting to face the day, not wanting to think. I was too tired. Finally I started to hum quietly to myself, as I often do when I'm depressed.

With a heave of her shoulders, Ruby guffawed, shaking her head, still looking at me with her milky white, blind eyes. She said, "You sound like an old bee trying to get off the ground."

"And I love you, too," I retorted, still humming.

Suddenly, Agnes reached forward and pulled the covers off me. Ruby leaped toward me, and the two of them dragged me out of bed, one holding a leg and the other an arm. I settled to the floor with a thump. I looked up at both of them in disbelief and started to cry.

"Oh, poor *placita,*" Agnes said in Spanish.

"Poor little lamby," Ruby laughed.

I just cried harder.

"Let's dress the little girl," Agnes said, putting a yellow shirt on me and buttoning it roughly.

Finally I stood up angrily. "Thanks, ladies, that's just what I need. Thanks so much."

"Come, little one. Sit down, and we will feed you a good breakfast."

"I don't appreciate being treated like a child," I replied. "This is very hard for me."

"Well, it's hard for us, too," Agnes said, elbowing Ruby, and they laughed as they prepared some eggs and biscuits with honey and tea.

Forty-five minutes later we were still sitting at the table. They were staring at me as if I were some strange specimen that had entered their cabin. I was still sniveling.

"Well, now what?" I finally asked.

Ruby got serious, suddenly. Her demeanor changed from that of a trickster to a wise old shaman woman. The reflections of the sunlight on her face were fascinating. Her expressions and movements changed from those of a young, petulant girl to those of of a very ancient woman. Wrinkles suddenly defined themselves across her brow and around her eyes and mouth, as she settled into her place of power. The skin on her face seemed to descend with her. She looked old and almost stonelike in the morning light.

"A long time ago, Little Wolf, we told you that you could not live in the wilderness with us, that you had to go back to the great cities of the world, where the true healing is needed."

I nodded in agreement.

"And you have done interesting things with your life," Ruby said. "When power has tested you, you have been able to move around the obstacles and continue on your path. Do you remember what you told us about traveling on the freeways of Los Angeles?"

"No," I said, as I thought fleetingly of hundreds of cars and trucks speeding down the Ventura Freeway.

"Well, you told us that even the freeways had become pleasurable to you, that you have been able to use those hours spent on the freeway to your advantage."

"Yes," I said, "that's true. I have been able to do that."

"Describe that experience to me," Ruby said.

"Well . . ." I sat back in my chair and took another sip of tea, feeling a little better. "I have learned how physical movement can stimulate spiritual progression. I have realized that concealed in movement is the mystery of enlightenment. There has to be movement, particularly from the north on the sacred wheel to the south. The north is spirit, where inspiration comes from, and in the process of movement from the manifestation of those ideas into the physicality of the south, I create books; I create a life for myself and move toward illumination. On the freeway there is movement, a continuous vein of life force, with all those cars and people going in the same direction. The flow lulls me, if I allow it to. I find myself in a place of power where I can tap into parts of myself that are hard to find when I am in a static position—at home, for instance."

"Come," Ruby said abruptly.

Agnes and Ruby, walking on either side of me, took me out of the cabin and down to the creek. We sat on our customary teaching stones, watching the water, which was moving quite rapidly this season. We looked upstream as the water flowed out of the fog. We watched the cool mist as it lifted slowly from the carpet of green moss edging Dead Man's Creek. The trees swayed in the morning breeze like ghostly phantoms moving in and out of the shadows.

"Listen to the sound," Agnes said. "Listen to the sound of the wind in the trees. That is your sound."

"Yes."

"But it makes you happy?" she asked.

"Yes, it does. It lifts me from my sadness."

"Ah, movement, the movement of the wind. The trees are talking to you as they move, and they are telling you of their truth."

Ruby was trailing her finger in the icy water of the stream, making tiny, pewter-colored ripples.

"You see, this river, this creek, speaks to you of movement," Ruby said. "It is life force reflected through the water, and as it flows by you, it, too, tells you of truth. You are surrounded by truth. You are surrounded by your teachers, and the teachers are in nature, in the trees, in the grass that moves in the gentle wind." She held the palms of her hands flat over the tips of the grass and gestured for me to do so as well. "You see," she said, "movement is very different from activity." She looked at me for a reaction. "I don't understand," I said.

"If you are moving around in a fit of anger . . ." Agnes said. The mist had collected in dense pillows around her teaching rock. She looked as if she were sitting on a cloud. "If you are angry and moving around in a fit, scrambling things, throwing things, stomping around, that is activity," Agnes said. "Movement is quite a different thing. It is like an action that comes from the heart and soul of your body. It moves out into the world as an expression of power. Do you see that?" she asked.

I thought for several minutes and finally chuckled to myself. "Yes, I understand what you're telling me."

"So, movement, then . . ." Ruby started.

I turned my head toward her. Just then a doe appeared in the clearing. It was hard to tell whether the mist had been surrounding the deer and she had been there all along, or whether she had just entered the clearing and stood there surprised at our presence. She was upwind from us. The doe stood as still as a mountain, her tiny fawn next to her, its ears moving back and forth, looking with great curiosity and surprise at these strange two-leggeds sitting by the creek.

"There," Agnes said, whispering, trying not to frighten the deer. "Watch their movements now. You will not see what I call activity. You will not see mad terror, I believe. This deer is very centered. She does not want to create harm for her young. She will move from a place of power when she does move. Now, you watch her carefully."

All three of us watched quietly, trying not to frighten the deer, just watching and waiting to see what would happen. A leaf from the top of one of the poplar trees floated down gently through the mist on the gentle air currents, to land on the back of the doe. I thought she would be startled, but she didn't move a muscle. She looked first at Agnes, then at me, and then at Ruby, moving her eyes and not her head, but her ears moved gently, catching the sound of the wind. Then, slowly, Ruby stood. The doe did not move, and by now the fawn was fascinated by our presence and stood still also. Slowly, Ruby closed the distance between the creek and the deer. She walked with careful, deliberate movements, very

slowly and very gently. She moved up next to the doe and placed
her fingers on her neck. Very quietly she spoke to the deer in her
mother tongue.

I remembered my first meeting with Ruby Plenty Chiefs. She
had tested me through a frightening initiation in which she had
had me skin a deer, and then, taking the heart out of the deer, she
had asked me to take a bite of the meat, offering it to the spirits of
the deer, to the lightning spirits, and to the sun and to all life that
gives away so that we may live. I had been told much later about
her healing and how she had been blinded by white surveyors, by
the point of their compass, when she was a young girl, and how it
had ruined her life for so many years. But as all things come full
circle, it was through this tragedy that she had become the woman
of power who now stood before me.

The intensity in the air was so amazing that I don't think I could
have torn my attention away if I had tried. As I watched, the two
deer circled around Ruby, as if they were in a ceremonial dance,
and then Ruby very carefully moved around the deer, creating a
symbol of infinity, like a figure eight. I felt a wind coming up from
the south that swirled the fog into eddies of golden glow, mixing
with the morning sunlight. The fog undulated in a swirl around
the deer and around Ruby and began to thicken. First their legs
disappeared from view, and all I could see was the doe curling her
neck around Ruby. I remembered the words of Agnes years ago
when she had told me, "It is the spirit of the deer that has taught
Ruby to see better than I can see you, or you can see me. The deer
spirit gave away to her, and for many years she was told to eat
only deer meat. It is the spirit of the deer that has healed her soul."

There was a dance of sacred movement going on, in a magnificent choreography unknown to my experience. It was a dance of
Ruby's medicine, or perhaps Ruby was the power symbol for the
deer. It didn't matter; the balance and harmony were evident.
Suddenly the fawn leaped into the air, its front feet held tight to its
belly, its hind legs projected out behind it, its tiny hooves flashing
in a glint of sunlight. Ruby raised her hands to the sky and sang
her lightning song. For a moment I could see the three of them as
the mist shredded away like tissue paper. Then suddenly the winds
came up again and swirled the fog around them like an ostrich

plume. Agnes and I watched as the fog became gray and impenetrable. I realized that they were completely obscured from my vision. I looked toward Agnes for a moment, and then Agnes, nodding, said, "Look, look." I looked back toward the clearing where the fog and the deer and Ruby had been. The mist had cleared away, and they were gone. Not a track was left.

Agnes reached out and held my hand briefly, and looking into my eyes, she said, "That is a true act of power. That is movement. It is not wasted; not a moment was spent in activity in which energy was lost forever."

She and I sat for a long time in silence, listening to the water, waiting for Ruby to return. After some time I asked, "She will return?" A moment of fear seized me as I looked around frantically for some sign of my teacher or the deer.

Agnes chuckled, her shoulders moving up and down. "She won't let you off that easy," she said.

"How could she disappear just like that? And the deer? They must have walked away in the fog."

Agnes cocked her head sideways and raised her eyebrows, saying nothing.

"That was stupid of me," I said as Agnes and I exchanged a smile of understanding.

After a long time it was clear that Ruby was not coming back for now. I turned to Agnes and asked, "I often feel an overwhelming sadness inside. I feel it when I move out of the dream, when I come back from Shakkai. I don't understand it, and it scares me."

"What are you angry about?" the old woman asked me.

"I'm not aware of being angry."

Agnes just looked at me and didn't say a word, so I thought for a while, and I realized she was right. I *was* angry.

"Okay, let's have it," Agnes finally said.

"I'm angry about life and death. I'm angry that I don't understand better. I'm angry because I don't want people to die. I am angry even though I am moving through these lifetimes and I realize beyond a shadow of a doubt that there is a much greater process than I was ever aware of before, that I will experience people again and probably again and again. I still cannot seem to get over the fact that experience as we know it, say, in this lifetime, my experience of you, will end one day. Perhaps I will not remember in my next lifetime about you; it will be over with. My heart hurts. I am sad for this. I can't seem to help it, Agnes. I don't know what's the matter with me."

"I understand your feelings, Little Wolf. I felt that way for years, when my child was taken from me, and my beloved husband. The pain drove me toward wisdom. I know now that it was all an illusion, a dream, and part of the mirrors of learning in this lifetime."

I stood up from the rock and stamped my foot. "I don't want to hear, Agnes, that it is all an illusion, because it doesn't feel like an illusion to me. When I pinch myself, it hurts. Is that an illusion?" I started pacing back and forth.

"Nice activity," Agnes said.

"I don't care, Agnes. It makes me feel better to move."

"Ah, I see," she said with a crisp smile on her face.

"Maybe it's all wasted on me," I said, sitting down on the rock, feeling desperate. "Maybe I'm never going to get it. I see it intellectually. I understand. Truly, I understand, and I can teach it, but sometimes I fail to feel it, even now. It's so extraordinary, what Ruby just did. My God, I can't imagine being able to have that kind of power. She is so extraordinary, and she teaches me so much, and she scares me to death, and sometimes I wish she wouldn't do these things."

"Don't you know that we are all the same? Don't you realize that we are all perfect mirrors for each other? Your sadness is my sadness, your impatience is mine, and yet there is a passage of time in this relative world of ours, and I have quickened much beyond your years. There will come a time when you will understand with your heart and not just your mind. You won't buy into the dream of everyday life."

I stared at her for several minutes. "And not only that," I said. "Now I feel sad that I won't see Shakkai for much longer. I have become attached to her, as I do to everything else. Is that all this world is about, this beautiful earth that I love so much? Is it just about attachment?"

"Well, you finally got the message," said a voice behind me. I twirled around to see Ruby standing there with her hands on her hips. There was an unearthly glow about her. I thought it must be because she was standing in silhouette against the sun.

"That was quite a disappearing act," Agnes said.

"Oh, it's nothing," Ruby said, polishing her nails on her jacket and holding them up to the light.

The two old Native American women laughed together. Ruby came over and hugged Agnes, leaving me out very deliberately.

"Now what have I done?" I asked.

"Well, it's certainly not anything *you've* done," Ruby said.

"I'm sorry, Ruby. I am obsessed with myself. That was magnificent, and I will never forget the lessons that you teach me. Never."

"You've already forgotten them," Ruby said, seating herself back on her stone.

"What do you mean by that?" I asked. "I won't even ask you how you did what you did."

"There is no explaining what you just saw. There is no explaining the world of mystery that surrounds us. All you can know is that life is magical. How that happens is beyond words, beyond explanation, but one day it will also be part of your experience. It is your emotions that keep you from so much of the mysteries in life."

"I thought emotions were part of life."

"They are. They're part of the great beauty in life, but you must be in control of your emotions, not the other way around. You live in the lodge of emotions a great deal of your life, and that is the lesson here today. It has to do with movement. You know the teaching of movement. You have experienced that, but you do forget."

I heaved a big sigh. I knew she was right, and I could see what I do. I could see how I torture myself. I could see it clearly.

"Is losing everyone the only way to learn how to get over attachment?"

"No, you will give it up long before that, because you will see that you never had them," Ruby assured me. "Mostly, you are attached to things out of habit, and those habits are broken as reality changes, and reality changes through your own perceptions. Whether you know it or not, you have changed greatly. Now sit down and tell me the story. Tell me everything that is happening with Shakkai. Tell me everything, and do not leave out a single detail."

Agnes got up from her stone. "I will go make some sandwiches while you talk with Ruby. I will be back in an hour or so, when the sun is overhead."

Agnes came over to me and touched my cheek with her knuckles very gently and looked into my eyes for a moment with her own sadness. I was stunned by her expression. I had rarely seen that look in her eyes, and I couldn't fathom its depth. It was so stunning that I knew I was to say nothing, but was to think about what I saw in her face. She was a mystery to me.

20

The Dancing Bowl

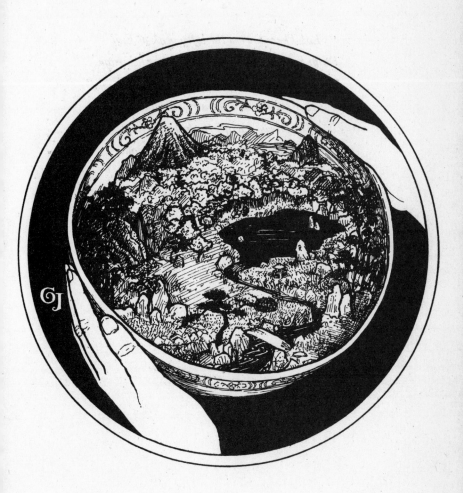

◆

Lo! There towers the lofty peak of Fuji
From between Kai and wave-washed Suruga.
The clouds of heaven dare not cross it,
Nor the birds of the air soar above it.
The snows quench the burning fires,
The fires consume the falling snow.
It baffles the tongue, it cannot be named.
It is god mysterious.

—THE MANYOSHU

◆

On my return to the Dreamlodge, I was refreshed and ready for the teachings that were to come.

The weather had turned cold and blustery, making it an even more perfect time for the teachings of that most miniature of gardens, the sacred *hu*. The first day that Shakkai began to speak to me of this ancient and sacred art, she brought out an old blue and white cloisonné bowl. Turning it gently round and round in her hands, feeling its surface with her fingers, she slowly filled it with pebbles, sand, and pieces of agate and crystal.

Handing it to me finally, she said, "O Kiku, this is a process called 'dancing in the bowl.' I want you to turn it carefully in your hands, look at the stones, and begin to move your consciousness into the world of the miniature. It is an ancient, sacred process for bringing your eyes and your vision off the exterior world, the macrocosm of our universe that we call reality, into the center of our being, into that place of silence and stillness and creativity that lives within us. This is something I want you to practice several times today. I am going to ask you to do this for an hour or so, and then I am going to ask you to go out and work in your garden, leaving the bowl behind. Then come back and hour or so later and begin to do the dance of the bowl again, moving your consciousness out of reality and bringing it back into this miniature world again and again, forming a bridge between those two states of consciousness, those two ways of seeing.

"Find a stone that can represent Mount Fuji. Then arrange other stones, twigs to look like trees, and sand to recall the movement and memory of a trail or winding stream. Create your miniature garden world in the compound inside the bowl. Draw it again as your will takes you."

"Why is it so important, Sensei, to make everything smaller and smaller?"

The old woman did not answer me immediately. Her eyes glossed over and became momentarily opaque, like the pond covered in low-hanging fog at dawn. Then, looking at me with a piercing stare, she said, "Because in smallness is power. To contain the universe, this temple of worship and pain we call life, is to create a mirror of flowers."

"A mirror of flowers? What a beautiful image, but what does it mean?"

"I want you to meditate on the idea of a mirror of flowers, O Kiku. There is a message for you within the seeing of the mirror. Tell me when you find it. Study the bowl. It will give you the answer."

I spent half the day contemplating the bowl, with no results. At last Shakkai came and sat next to me on a cushion with a spiral design.

"Let us meditate on the garden in the bowl," she said, "and then we'll try again."

I began to meditate on the dancing bowl sitting in my lap. I was breathing carefully as I had been taught, but I felt strangely uncomfortable. I had a sense that Shakkai was watching me, so briefly I opened my eyes, and sure enough, she was looking at me with a quizzical expression, almost laughing. She leaned over and pressed the flat of her hand against my solar plexus.

"Breathe," she said. I did so. "Aha." Shakkai closed her eyes and nodded.

"What is the matter, Sensei?"

"You are not breathing correctly," she said, sitting back on her heels.

"Not breathing correctly! What am I doing wrong?" By now I was getting impatient with the whole process.

Sensei threw back her head and laughed loudly. I did not think this was at all funny.

"Sensei, what is so funny? Now I can't even breathe correctly."

"Don't worry, my child."

She reached over and took the bowl from me and set it down on a white silken cloth that was laid out in front of us.

"Sometimes when we breathe in the Taoist manner, we breathe the way men breathe. Occasionally, if a woman is carrying her female shield very strongly, this breathing can be injurious, and I am afraid that is what is happening here. I think what we need to do is to teach you how to breathe another way, and if you find yourself having troubles in the future with learning something, shift your breathing from your solar plexus up to the area around your sternum, between your breasts. I will show you what to do."

She took her fingers and pressed firmly on my sternum or breastbone. "It is there that your female receptivity and power dwells. Because you are learning to be a healer and a shaman, I have had you breathing down into your power center, in your shaman center, where your ki concentrates around your navel. But there are times like this, when the dreaming is very feminine, that it is useful and perhaps, very important for you to bring up your breath and hold it between your breasts. Take a deep breath now, as you usually do, and close your eyes, O Kiku. Center yourself and calm yourself. Everything is going to be fine."

Again, Shakkai giggled a little. This time I could hardly help giggling with her, she sounded so silly. "All the breathing exercises we have done are aimed at transmuting the breath into spirit so that you may become one with the universal breath of the sacred Tao or the *ch'i*. I call this the 'breath of the womb.' It is circular breathing which, if done correctly, will give you the flexibility and the innocence of a newborn. It is as if you are drawing your breaths from the earth, breathing with your feet, with the soles of your feet, bringing the air up into your body and out, up the right side of your body and down the left side of your body, always in a circular motion. The ancients said that in womb breathing, the air should be inhaled and exhaled completely without thought of the nose or the mouth or the body, so that you become like a child, like the life of the fetus in the womb that breathes completely independently of its mother."

As I began breathing, Shakkai picked up the bowl and laid it back on my lap. I took hold of it gently and held it quietly as I breathed.

"Now," Shakkai went on, "I want you to bring your consciousness down into your breasts. Think first of the area between your breasts and your sternum and see a beautiful green light circulating there. Breathe in the green light and focus on your sternum and the energy in both of your breasts, and as you breathe out, I would like you to see white golden light breathing out, and at the same time visualize the energy moving down into your nipples. When you breathe in, bring that energy back into the sternum, into your heart, into that whole area of your chest. Hold that breath and count your heartbeats. It would be good if you could get up to holding your breath a hundred heartbeats. Then breathe out, but never breathe out as much air as you breathe in. Now, O Kiku, breathe in and hold that breath in your sternum, and count."

I was having a very difficult time following her instructions, but I did the best that I could. I held the breath, and then I breathed out, visualizing the energy going into my breasts and into my nipples. I felt my nipples becoming erect as I did this. Tremendous power and strength seemed to gather in the area of my chest. I realized that it was true, that I needed to work with this area of my body much more than I had been; but I had become a bit unbalanced, centering all of my energy down around my navel.

"Women and men do not necessarily breathe or need to breathe the same," Shakkai said very quietly, still seated beside me. "Women and men are of the same spirit, but very often they need to be taught differently. Even the breath needs to be different. It is very evident with you. At times we need to do this breathing, so concentrate, my child, and I will leave you now, because the bowl is beginning to dance for you. I will go out into my garden, and I will not return until the sun is low in the sky."

I meditated for a long time, doing the best I could with my breath, finding it increasingly difficult to maintain my concentration. I held the bowl gently, and then as I sat there, I could swear that I felt the bowl beginning to move gently in my hands, as if it were being turned by someone. I did not want to open my eyes and break my concentration, but finally I felt as if I had no choice. Shakkai must have come back into the house. So I opened my eyes and looked down into the bowl. I blinked, because I could see only a very bright light, as if it were emanating from behind one of the tiny stones. As I looked more carefully, the rough little stone that was sitting there in the sand looked for all the world like Mount Fuji. I stared and stared at the light, wondering if I had been meditating too long. Perhaps I had gotten too tired. But again the bowl started to jiggle and dance in my hands. I couldn't imagine what was happening, but a tiny voice inside my head kept saying, *Look into the light, look into the light, never take your eyes away from the light.*

So I stared into this little pinpoint of light. Could this be a *kami* spirit playing games with me? And as I stared, the most astounding thing happened. At first I thought I saw a child curled up in a fetal position at the base of the stone, a tiny, tiny being. As I watched with fascination, my eyes growing wider and wider at the miracle occurring before me, I saw this little fetal being begin to uncurl, and before I knew it, sitting there on one of the little edges of the stone as if it were a plateau or a ledge on the side of a mountain, was the Old One. She was laughing at me.

"You see. I am even smaller than your thumb."

I looked at my thumb quickly and then at her. Yes, she was about a quarter the size of my thumb.

"What are you doing in my dancing bowl?" I asked stupidly. I could think of nothing else to say.

Again she laughed. "I am here to help you. You are having trouble with learning about the miniature world. You are having trouble imagining that this little stone could actually be Mount Fuji, or Mount Ontake. I want you to see that the world in miniature is, indeed, the world of power, so open your eyes, O Kiku. Wake up to what is real, to what is true."

"But I am trying, Old One. I am truly trying."

Suddenly there was a small movement on the other side of the bowl where the little pond was supposed to be. Ducks were swimming on the pond. I thought I must be going mad. I looked more carefully, and yes, little ducks were swimming in the bowl, and the Old One came down from the mountain and walked over to the shore of the pond and sat there on her heels, looking out across the water. Abruptly I realized that I was inside the bowl myself, inside this tiny world of miniature beauty and power. It no longer mattered that somehow I was also still holding the bowl. It was as if one lifetime or one vision of reality had been superimposed on another vision of reality. But it no longer mattered. My mind no longer mattered. All that I cared about was the warm feeling of expansion in my heart, and I sat on my heels next to the Old One, and watched the ducks with her.

"You are having trouble with your breathing, but breath is spirit, and breath is the source of life," she said. "I will help you."

She reached out her hand, and a beautiful mallard duck, with its metallic green head and shiny brown feathers, swam toward us and, with its long yellow bill, ate some crumbs from the Old One's fingers. Then, taking a feather that was floating on the surface of the pond, the Old One stroked the duck's head and back with it. It seemed to enjoy this immensely.

The Old One said, "Duck, give me some down so that I may do my teaching." And the duck, craning its neck and pecking its chest, pulled out a tiny piece of fluff from underneath its sleek and burnished feathers. Holding the down in its bill, the duck reached toward the Old One.

Gently she took the fluff from its bill, then turned to me and said, "Now close your eyes, little one." I did so, sitting in my traditional lotus position. She said, "No, sit on your heels as you did before. That is a good position for a woman." I did so. "Concentrate your breath between your breasts. Place this fluff just below your nose. When you inhale and exhale, you should not disturb the fluff; it should not move. Breathe as if you have become the earth, as if you were carrying the womb of the earth within yourself. You are the ultimate woman. You are the magnificence of the feminine, represented now, here, in this miniature world. Rejoice that you have been able to share this tiny world with me, for your life will be changed forever by the wisdom that comes through your breath."

And she placed the tiny bit of down on my upper lip, just below my nose.

"Now breathe, my child. You are going to learn to control your breath. You are going to breathe in now through your nose, concentrating on that breath between your breasts, and count your heartbeats. Count as many as you can, and one day you may be able to get up to a hundred, even a hundred twenty. Then, when you let out the air through your mouth, be very quiet and gentle. Let the passage of the air be silent, so that I cannot hear it, so that you cannot hear it, so that the little piece of fluff does not move. Breathe in, hold the breath between your breasts, and then, as you let the breath out, feel the energy moving out into your breasts and into your nipples. Hold your power, your goddess power, within that area, and feel the presence of the Goddess of the Sun."

I practiced with the Old One until I became tired. Everything went black, and I awoke the next morning on my futon. I desperately wanted to tell Shakkai about my experience with the Holy One in the bowl, but when I went to her, I could see in her eyes that she knew, and it was best not to speak of it.

Things went more easily now with the dancing bowl. Each time I would go into my garden, even though it might be raining a little, or cold and windy, I thought it a joy to exercise those rational muscles I have that take me into the world and out of the world as well. When I would return to the house, Shakkai would always have added something new to the dancing bowl. It was always a feat for me and a struggle to find that tiny pebble, something, that she had added in my absence and expected me to find.

This work went on for days. In the meantime I had chosen my gourd, my beautiful gourd, and I would sleep with it every night. She said that taking it into the Dreamtime with me would help it to become my own, to bond with it.

This teaching lasted for some time. Weeks went by. Shakkai's wounds healed, and everyone left us pretty much alone. I think that within the air, there was the presence of sacred teaching, and even Kat-san only came by a couple of times. He was expressed in my sacred *hu*. I knew he had to be a part of anything that I would ever create, because he was a part of me and I was a part of him.

21

Hidden Truth

◆

Walking in the sky, you climb to the gateway of heaven.

— LAO-TZU,

TAO TE CHING

◆

One morning, when Shakkai and I were taking a walk in the bamboo forest, I asked her about Master Hara.

"What has happened to him?" I asked. "Is he going to absolve himself in some way from your anger?"

Shakkai smiled as if she were smiling at an inner secret. She shook her head. The red tie around her hair, which was pulled on top of her head in a bun, swung back and forth like the comb on a rooster's head. She laughed, almost to herself, as she knelt and picked a tiny flower, yellow like a buttercup. She held it under my chin.

"Ah," she said, "you reflect the light of the sun very well."

"Shakkai, what has happened to the tea master? What has happened to Master Hara?" I repeated, wondering why she was evading my question.

"Master Hara-san has gone on a journey."

"He has? Why have you not told me this before?"

"Because I just learned yesterday that Hara-san has gone back to China to study with his old master, who has called him. I am sure he heard what happened. Hara-san has lost his way, and it is a good sign that he returns to his master. Remember, O Kiku, inside each of us is a mirror of flowers. There is an eternal fire that is the sacred life force that burns within each of us. Although it is hard to understand with the rational mind, even our enemies are part of us, and we mirror each other's imperfections as well as our brilliance. It was a hard lesson for him, but he needed to learn it. It was coming for a very long time. Never fear. Who would have thought that the tea master would have brought you and Kat-san together in such a meaningful way."

"The tea master!" I said. "I don't like him. He wants to kill you. He tried to steal your sacred *hu*. How can you say the tea master brought us together? We just did the only thing possible. As your apprentice, I had to return the *hu* to you."

"Don't you understand?" Shakkai said, picking up a flat stone and rubbing it between her fingers. "Don't you understand that the tea master stole the sacred *hu,* my *hu,* the empowerment of woman, so that he could embody the female principle within his own being? We have talked of this, but you don't see the whole story. Hara-san was very ignorant in something that he did, and I want you to learn this lesson very well." Shakkai closed her eyes, as if to tune herself to her own thoughts, and went on. "You understand that Kat-san knew he had to trick the tea master, that in some way he had to lead Hara-san's mind into making a mistake, and that is exactly what he did. When Kat-san took you with him, he told you about the *kami* spirits, and how, if they were to sit on the sacred *hu,* the *hu* would appear to have been stolen."

"Yes," I said.

"But you see, that was a trick. If Hara-san had been thinking, if he had been less attached to his need for the female aspect of his being, he would have known that he was being tricked, but what happened was that he lost his center. He lost himself, and in that way, Kat-san killed him without ever even seeing him. Do you understand?"

I thought for a long time and then started to laugh, thinking of Hara-san racing through the forest. "Yes, I do understand," I said, beginning to feel the constellation of her words in the center of me. It made sense, and there was an opening in my heart as I sat there with my teacher.

"Hara-san became hysterical. He thought the *hu* had been stolen from him, when actually it was just sitting there on his altar. Had he been aware, he would have seen the *kami* spirits, but instead, he went running from his house, allowing you to return the *hu* to me. Then, in his stupidity, he came back to my house. He tried to dishonor me. He dishonored himself. He lost his power and moved out of his center by attacking and trying to control the situation. I defeated him by using his own energy, so he defeated himself. I was just there directing the flow of power.

"You see, O Kiku, that is what people don't understand about love. When you want to control another person, you do not love

that person. Not only do you not love them, but you become incapable of loving, because controlling is a restriction, a constriction.
Loving is an opening and a letting go. When you let go to the
magic that is around you and allow yourself to be open to love,
then ecstasy is possible, because then you step into the world of
the unknown, where there is no control. Then you step into the
void where magic lives, where power lives. You become a true
warrior of spirit. That also is what Kat-san needs to learn. When
he accomplishes this, he will be unbeatable as a samurai."

Shakkai reached out and touched my hand and held it for several minutes.

"You see, my child, we are bright lights as teachers. Everything
is drawn to that light."

I remembered suddenly the teachings of the Old One, and I
looked at Shakkai for several minutes and finally said, "Did you
know about the Queen Mother of the West, the Old Holy One,
who visits me?"

Shakkai smiled and nodded her head.

"Did you know that she taught me about being hidden?"

Again, Shakkai nodded. "Yes, the teaching is very important,
and it should set your heart at ease about what we are doing
here."

"Yes, O-Sensei, sometimes I yearn for a beautiful restaurant
overlooking the bay. Sometimes I yearn for clothes and the noise of
the city and the excitement of urban life. I miss getting on a plane
and flying to other parts of the world. But it's only for a moment,
because I move into the vastness of my interior universe. I remember the teachings you have given me, and I understand, now, the
power of smallness, of moving inside, into the miniature garden.

"Hara-san has to relearn all of this. He was looking outside
himself. In fact, I saw that in him always. It is the one thing the tea
never taught him. He did not understand that power is within,
within the inner silence. He was always grabbing it from somewhere outside, from his gifts, from his students, from women.
Finally, now, I think he will learn his lesson. It is good, because in
spite of himself, he has great ability."

We walked on, the bamboo high above us, touching overhead in
a green cathedral of light and gentle sound.

* * *

On our return from our walk, we sat outside in the garden beneath numerous cherry trees bursting with pink blossoms. The trees had been planted close together, so Shakkai sat with her back against one and I with my back against another, facing each other, both of us looking out toward the reflection pond.

"O Kiku, you never told me what happened in your life that finally enabled you to come to me as a student," the old woman asked.

"Oh, Sensei, it took me so long to find my way to you. I spent so many years in reaction to everything—to my family, to my husband, to all of the things I've told you about. But in that process of going through life—academic learning, trying to live in the society of Japan—there was always an emptiness, a place within me that I could not fill, no matter what I did, no matter where I traveled. I always thought of you. I would hear about you. You were a legend in your own time. You were always there, somehow, Shakkai. I always felt your presence. I remembered your face when I was a child, and I remember my parents were shocked when you left all of us, when you disappeared into the mountains. It was unfathomable to me, mostly because it was unfathomable to my family. They could not imagine why you would do such a thing."

"Yes, O Kiku, I can imagine the stir it caused, and isn't it odd, because your family has the spirit in their way. They have been strong Shinto people for centuries, so it should have been understandable to them. It was a mystery to me the way people reacted."

"But, Sensei, it was because they missed you, because they could control you no longer. You were gone from them, and even though you weren't a member of our immediate family, you were a great teacher and a profound influence on everyone. It left a great hole in all of our lives. So, as I moved through my younger life, I always questioned your motives in my mind, hoping that someday I would have the answer to why you left. And then it happened to me. I woke up one morning and looked out at my beautiful garden at our home outside of Kyoto, and I knew that there was so much more in life to learn, and that somehow I had to search out the reason I was alive. I knew I had to understand my spirit in a different way. I knew there was only one person who could help me, and that was you. So I went in search of you, and that's what brought me here. It was really very simple. Even though everyone told me you had died, I knew better."

"You know, you could find me only because I wanted you to. If I had not been calling you as well, you would have walked down the path outside the compound and seen only an open field." The old woman laughed gaily and pinched my cheek. "See how lucky you are?"

I looked down at the ground, feeling very fortunate indeed, and saw that many of the cherry blossom petals had settled around me like a pink aura of moist light blanketing the earth.

"Oh, look," Shakkai said, pointing up to the tree above me. I looked and saw several blossoms that a yellow bird had dislodged with its tiny beak come floating down. "Those are *wabi,*" Shakkai said, smiling. "*Wabi* is explained many ways, by many people. To me it means a gift. At this moment it is the gift of the cherry tree to life, to the spirit on the wind. It is the giving of the masculine soul to the female acceptance of earth."

Suddenly a gust of wind carried the blossoms away from us, and they landed softly on the surface of the pond, making tiny ripples, concentric circles moving out toward the shore. "That is *sabe,*" Shakkai said. "*Sabe,* to me, means the settling of the male principle into the female womb. It is the receiving of the reflective light that could only manifest the Great Spirit, the Tao of life, into reality."

"The ripples seem to shimmer endlessly," I said, amazed at how far the ripples went across the water.

"Yes, O Kiku, just as your own existence in the world, your goodness and your ability to search out the truth, your curiosity for the mysteries of life affect everyone around you, the cherry blossoms settling on the surface of the water affect the pond in every aspect. We think that if we initiate an action, a movement, a design in Tokyo, it probably won't affect anyone anywhere else. But somewhere in Chicago, somewhere in Paris, it is felt in some way. Energy goes out from us we know not where."

"What about the tea master?" I asked. "What are his ripples like in the world?"

"Ah, but his blossoms fall to the earth and there are no ripples.

He does not know about *wabi* and *sabe*. He does not understand that when you put something out into the world, it must be received for the impact, for the lesson to be learned. That is why he tried to steal the sacred *hu*. He thought that taking the *hu*—the embodiment of power, of female receptivity, an actual womb of life—would be enough to make him complete. He felt that he could actually steal something and claim it as his own, and that then it would function for him. But you see, in the world of power, you can only force certain things. You can take power as women on this earth have had to do for thousands of years. Nobody gives it to them. But that is different from what the tea master endeavored to do. Without doing his homework, without making himself open like a field, like a fertile womb receptive to seed, he expected the *hu* to find a home within him, but there was no place for that *hu* to live, because he is an ignorant man. Any of your sacred objects are given life by your own spirit. With all his acumen and abilities and power, he still is an ignorant man."

"Do you mean, Sensei, that ignorance comes from a lack of totality, a lack of balance?"

"Yes, O Kiku, this is true. You see, people think they are sacred, and yet they will fight to the death for their beliefs against someone who believes differently. Isn't that humorous?"

But she was not laughing. She touched the wound on her arm that had bled so profusely the night of her fight with Hara-san.

"Did you mean to kill Hara-san?" I asked my teacher.

"Oh no, that would be a loss of a good enemy." She smiled at me.

"There's that phrase again," I said. "I don't understand it still. I don't understand all the tension, and why you would permit it into your life."

Shakkai opened up her hands as a cherry blossom floated down to the lined surface of the palm of her hand. She stroked the tiny petal with her fingers and said nothing for a long time. Then she turned to me, but didn't look at me directly. Instead she looked past me to the sacred mountain of her dreams and asked me to close my eyes, and I did so.

"Now take a deep breath," she said. "Watch your breath moving in and out as you breathe, and move yourself into your place of power." After several minutes of this, she asked me to describe my spirit, who I thought I was in the world.

"Well, I am a woman of Japan and I have a physical body, and inside the physical body I have a spirit."

"Describe your spirit," Shakkai said.

After several minutes of contemplating the question, I said that I felt a hollowness, an emptiness inside me that was filled with golden light. "I feel an expansion of my heart," I said. "I feel this light glowing intensely within me."

"And is that place inside you like a cocoon?" she asked.

"Yes, you could call it that. It feels as if there were a soft, protective cocoon around this light that protects it and contains it in some way."

"And where are you?" she asked.

"I am in the center . . . I am that light," I finally said. "I don't know where I am. Perhaps I am nowhere. Perhaps I am just that light. That's what it feels like to me."

"Ah," Shakkai said. "Yes. Now I want you to just sit in that light, in that state of perfection, in that tranquil place, as the cherry tree lives in this garden, beautiful and serene and simple, and yet radiantly beautiful. Sit within that light."

I felt the gentle warm wind on my face. It settled me into a trancelike state for what seemed like a very long time. Finally, as if from far away, I heard the voice of Shakkai.

"And where is the Tao?" she asked. "Where is the Great Spirit?"

I thought for several minutes, then said, "All around me."

"And what does that spirit look like?"

"It looks like light," I finally said. "It *is* light."

"And is that light different from the light within you?" she asked.

"No, it is the same, but the intensity is different."

"Ah," Shakkai said, "but it is only different in intensity because your light is a tiny bit smaller. But it is the same color, and emits the same flaming heat, does it not?"

"Yes, Sensei, it has the same feeling, and it feels so wonderful."

"And," Shakkai said, "think about the other people in the world. Think of your mother, think of Kat-san, think of even the tea master. Whatever you do in the world, whatever your body does, whatever your emotions in the west or your mind in the east or your spirit in the north or your physicality and substance do in the south, whatever that happens to be—a reaction or an action—you are still pure light in the center. Tell me, O Kiku, does all the activity of life matter, really? And is that light affected by all that activity?"

I thought for a while and realized something for the first time. "No, Sensei, no. Nothing has changed. In fact, I feel like the center of a typhoon, the center of a storm—it all whirls around me, but the light stays the same."

"And all the people in the world are just like that, aren't they?" she asked.

"Yes," I said. "I see that now. For the first time I see it—even my father, even the tea master—they are all the same. We are all of the same light."

"Yes," Shakkai said. "The first lesson of power is that we are all alone. We think we are our bodies. We think we are our belief structures, our minds, our egos. We think we are what we do in the world, but that is an illusion. So the last lesson of power is that we are really all one. Whatever we're doing out there is part of our learning process. But inside us is this magnificent light. It is the reflection of the sacred Tao. That is the same essence of the mountain, the sacred mountain, that lives within us and within which we live."

I sat a long time thinking about this, and for a moment the demon of anger tried to rise up within me as I remembered my father and what he had done to Kat-san, and of Hara-san and what he had tried to do to Shakkai. Relaxing and taking a deep breath, I said to my teacher, "Is it all just a big game, Sensei?"

"Not exactly," Shakkai said. "And yet it is truly so. It is a great game and a dangerous one and a fatal one, is it not?" I nodded my head in agreement. "It is a game that is painful for all of us. It is not easy to be human, and we have all chosen this game so that we may learn, so that we may grow into varying stages of enlightenment."

"But what does that mean, Sensei? What does it really mean to be enlightened?"

"I like to describe it like this," she said. "Think of the light within you. Think of the radiance that you are, that we all are, and think of death, when your body lies down and goes back into the earth, into the sacred mountain. What is left?"

"The light?" I replied.

"Yes, the light. It is never-ending, and it goes back to its source. That light is purely of the sacredness of life, and it goes back to God, it goes back to the Tao. It is the Tao. It is the Great Spirit. You are the Great Spirit. And that's really all there is."

She stood and held out her hand for me. I opened my eyes. I was now covered with tiny white and pink blossoms. Shakkai laughed as she gathered them in the palm of her hand to take them into the house and place them in a bowl of water where they would float, touching one another and creating patterns.

"Thank you, Sensei," I said, clasping my hands together and bowing my head to her. "I feel better now. I understand more."

22

The Absolute Control Stone

◆

*As long as the mind has not
reached supreme quiet,
it cannot act.*

— THE SECRET OF
THE GOLDEN FLOWER

◆

Outside Shakkai's beautiful garden was a flat area she had designated for me to build my own personal nature shrine, my miniature of the universe in garden form. I had been working in my garden since daybreak, clearing away the ground carefully, trying to contour the land so that when I placed my stones and rocks, they would represent mountains. When I put in my small reflection pond, it would be a replica of a wilderness place around Mount Koyo where I had gone often on pilgrimage. I wanted it to represent that area and yet still have a piece of my own soul within it. Shakkai joined me as the sun came up over the mountains. We sat together in the dirt, and I explained to her what I was doing.

"It is going to be very beautiful," Shakkai said. "It is a very difficult thing to do. A true master of the garden works a lifetime to develop the ability. How you place each stone is essential, just as it is in the dancing bowl. It must come from a place of truth within yourself—each steppingstone, each plant that is placed into the earth. One of the most important things is to remember that this work is really about truth, is it not?"

"Yes, O-Sensei, I believe it is," I answered.

"When you speak of truth . . . " Shakkai swung her arms around in a circular motion to take in the expanse of nature that surrounded us. "When you speak of the beauties of wisdom and knowledge, it is very difficult to contain that knowledge within the confines of a word or two, or a sentence, because each word, each innuendo of sound, means something different to each person who speaks it and who hears it. We are talking about communication, in a sense, with the Tao, with our creator. To manifest a truth into the world is sometimes better done through art. You can express through art the subtleties of form and color and brushstroke. A stone placed a certain way in a garden stimulates a sense of knowing that is indescribable, that is beyond the spoken word. It is like poetry. The real truth of poetry is between the words, between the lines. Do you understand?"

I nodded in agreement, my eyes watching my teacher as she spoke. She seemed to move into a place of power within herself when she spoke in this way to me, as if she were living in a mysterious center that no one else could ever touch. Her eyes began to look inward, and her physical form seemed to recede slightly. I sat very still in her presence, my heart open and loving her so much for sharing her knowledge with me. I wanted to please her with all my heart.

She smiled briefly, as if she heard my feelings. "Your garden, O Kiku, is an art form like a painting. It will express so much more than your words could ever express. One of the most sacred aspects of your sacred garden is a certain stone that has a Buddhist-like name, the Absolute Control Stone. Its purpose in your garden is to be a guardian. When that Control Stone is set properly, it will bring good fortune. If it is in the wrong place in your garden, it will not bring good luck to you. A Control Stone that is set properly, like the Fulfillment Stone, helps your prayers to be answered. It helps keep out darkness and evil from your garden. It controls the area and makes it powerful for you and helps you to manifest your dreams into being."

"What kind of stone is it, Sensei?"

"Come," she said. "I will show you my Control Stone. Perhaps in seeing the rock that I chose and how it is placed will answer your question." We left my patch of land and walked through the moon gate into her garden.

"This is the Reverence Rock." Shakkai touched the stone with the tips of her outstretched fingers. I had become familiar with its placement in the garden, because it was from there that I first observed her work of art. "It is from this position that you observe the rest of my garden. You begin from here to pray with the garden and let it teach you its wisdom."

We knelt on the ground and bowed to the power of her garden with full respect, touching our foreheads to the ground. Then, in a quiet state, I opened my eyes and began to observe her exquisite landscape, where the everyday stress of life was forgotten. Each rock, tree, and pond committed itself to a world of silence and inner freedom. The secludedly placed blooming irises and pink spring flowers lent a peaceful fragrance to the air. I looked carefully from one end of the garden to the other, and the deeper my eyes searched, the more tranquil I became.

Shakkai said to me, "Observe the feeling of the body of the garden, as if it were the body of your lover. Caress it with your eyes, with your sensibilities. Be aware of the balance that is created within it, and let that balance bring harmony to your soul."

I opened myself and allowed the spirit of the garden to enter me in a quiet way, as if I were meditating with Kat-san. As if it were his spirit, I let the spirit of the garden merge with mine. Presently, on the periphery of my vision, I had the sense of the *kami* spirits, the fairies of the garden, the guardians, floating near me. I moved into a timeless sense from another dimension and floated there for many long hours. It became clear to me that Shakkai's Control Stone was off to the left. It was in a place of power, perfectly balanced between the height of the rocks that represented her sacred mountain and the stones that encircled the pond. It represented to her, I felt, the steppingstones into the unconscious. When you moved near the pond and the pool, you felt the reflection of her emotional and subconscious mind as a woman, the great depths of feeling that brought such strength and power to her ceremony.

The Control Stone was white granite with mica in it that reflected tiny pieces of light from the sun, giving it a shimmering quality that made it look soft on the outside, like a cocoon of light that encircles the soul. But inside was a hard reality, a truth, like jade or a knowledge that has been striven for with tremendous difficulty and effort. The stone was obviously in control, and watched over the entire garden. It had the feeling of a sentinel, a guard, and I could sense the *kami* spirits surrounding it. They wanted me to come to the Control Stone and stroke it, to honor it with my presence.

I asked Shakkai, "May I go to the stone? I want to touch it." She nodded and let me go on my own.

I walked sunwise around the garden to approach it respectfully. As I came up to the stone, I felt my solar plexus warm with the sun. I felt the strength of her. She was female, and I was surprised at that. For some reason, I had felt that the Control Stone would probably be male. Then I remembered Shakkai's wonderful stories about the warrioresses and their power in the ancient legends and about the islands of Mu and the eternal life that was found there. I felt a real understanding of the Isles of the Immortals, and of the emperors who had sent their ships in search of them. It was the spirit that lived on forever in me. To me, the secrets of Mu and the islands that lived in the center of the sea would be obscured by fog and the sacred dream when you approached them, so that you would sail on by and miss them altogether, as I might have missed Shakkai's compound. I felt that same presence within this Absolute Control Stone. I felt that if you were not worthy, if your spirit were not pure, if you wanted to do evil or harm, this stone would be practically invisible to you. Somehow it would block your way by misting your vision so that you could not see properly. That was the way that it protected the garden.

I wondered about Master Hara. I wondered about the Control Stone and how it was affected by him and his darkness, and how he had pitted himself against us to build his own power. As I thought of these things, I felt as if the stone were speaking to me, as if a light went on in my head. I sat with the stone and looked out across the garden from its viewpoint, and I saw how impeccably placed it was. There was not a corner of the garden that this stone could not see. Even though it was not at the highest point, it was at the best vantage point for seeing every corner of the garden, watchfully, without intruding on the space of the garden at the same time. In answer to my query about Master Hara, it was very clear that the stone was in control of the garden. The stone was controlled by Shakkai. She was very clearly the Empress of the Spirit Garden.

I reached out my hands and touched the surface of the stone. It felt almost like the skin of that tiny lizard, but it had a quality of aliveness. I could tell that it had been touched for years by other hands. I moved my hands around it. It was a large stone, large enough for me to lie down upon. Yet it had corners that had been rubbed away. I felt that it was not a river that had done so, or water, but human hands.

I turned, bowed to the stone, walked back to Shakkai, and sat with her at the Observation Stone. I told her my feelings, and she smiled at me.

"Yes, O Kiku, you have heard correctly. It is true. I am the mistress of this painting, but the Control Stone has its say. She is an old grandmother and she takes good care of us. She has warned me of Master Hara. She looks out for us. It is she who brought you out of the house early in the morning to find the lizard. She is the one who speaks to you. Listen to her. She will help you in finding your own Control Stone.

"Past the bamboo forest and across the falls where we sat that day listening to the river speak to us, there is an outcropping of granite where big boulders came off the mountainside many thousands of years ago. Those are the great control rocks, I believe, of this area. They are sacred, and they will speak to you. They are all of the same family as this stone. You will know when you see them. I am going to pack you a lunch, and I would like you now to go out and find your Control Stone. You have sat in your garden now for weeks, and you have felt the earth, and you know, even though you have not realized it consciously, what your Control Stone must be like and how big it should be. You know exactly where it needs to be in your garden. You know it in your heart, if you don't in your mind. Is that not so?"

I thought for several minutes, and I knew what she was saying. "Yes, Shakkai, I know exactly where it must be, and I am excited. This is the moment I have been waiting for."

"Come. Get Sami-san, and we will make you a good lunch. I want you to go alone this time and find your Control Stone. Take as long as you need."

As I set out on the trail through the bamboo forest where Kat-san and I had spent so many beautiful afternoons, I walked with a spring in my step, full of joy and purpose. I adjusted the small bag of offerings for the stones, including my sacred *gohei,* and secured it to my sash. In the sky above the towering bamboo, puffy white clouds were moving thousands of feet above me. The sky was like cobalt blue satin. I was seeing the stones on the path differently now than I ever had before, and I wondered if I would be attuned enough to pick out the stone that would serve me best. I thought of Kat-san and how much I loved and missed him, and I realized even more today than ever before that he was always with me. When he was doing his work and I was doing mine, it was as if we were side by side, rubbing shoulders as we walked along. I could hear his voice inside my heart, and I smiled, feeling the rhythm of his body next to mine.

As I left the bamboo forest behind, I could hear the waterfall in the distance. It was a calming sound to my spirit, and I drank it in welcomingly. Finally I came to the jumble of stones, like giant agates, at the base of the mountain. They were beautiful—some of them covered with moss and pine trees, juniper trees growing up among them. I walked through the forest of stones. It was almost as if I could hear their voices. They were a family, a very large family, some of them feminine, some of them very masculine and strong and craggy; some were grandparents; some were very old. Then there were the younger ones, which almost reached out to me. The *kami* spirits were everywhere, and they wanted to play. Once in a while they would roll a stone in my direction and scare me out of my wits, and I would jump from one side to another.

I found a large flat rock overlooking the valley and the lake far below, and sat there in the sun, watching the clouds above me leaving pools of light and dark all around me. I ate my lunch and let myself become totally immersed in the language of the rocks. I closed my eyes and meditated for a very long time. Then I felt a desire to stand up and turn around to all of the four directions and give gratitude for their power and their help. I heard hawks in flight high above me, calling to each other, floating on the air currents. I looked up and saw their shiny wings catching the reflections of the sun, making them look deep reddish brown in color.

Then there came to me a very slight, subtle sound, like wind whistling through the high pine trees in the forest. I stopped a moment, wondering if I was imagining it. It came again, from off to my left. I jumped off the stone and walked around one boulder after another, and then I saw her—a beautiful granite stone, settled in the center of a circle of much larger stones. She was as tall as I was, as I walked up to her. I sat on my heels, and kneeling there, I honored her presence. I knew beyond a shadow of a doubt that she was, indeed, my Control Stone. I stayed with her all afternoon, until the sun was very low in the sky. I touched her all over, running my hands over her beautiful white body, tiny pieces of mica sparkling in the sunlight. Ah, yes, she was not a daughter to Shakkai's stone, but a sister, a true sister—a much younger one, but a sister nevertheless. I wondered how in the world we were going to get this stone back to my garden, then I noticed that there was an opening in the rocks through which the stone could be dragged without any problem. At least it would not have to be lifted over other boulders. I sat there and knew that eventually I would hear her voice very clearly, that she was the guardian stone for me, without question.

I reached into my bag and left offerings of lavender flowers and herbal incense to her, and I asked the *kami* spirits to watch over her until I returned. I planted my wand, with its *gohei*, a folded-paper representation of lightning, attached to the top, into the ground next to my stone, so that the spirit lightning could conduct the God-spirit into my rock. I walked down the mountain through the bamboo forest. The wind had come up and the bamboo was making its beautiful hollow wooden song, clacking together with a mysterious rhythm that excited my heart. I ran down the path toward Shakkai's house. I couldn't wait to tell her that I had found my stone.

As Shakkai and I ate the dinner that Sami-san had cooked for us, I told her about my journey and about the stone. Shakkai was very pleased.

"It is very rare for an apprentice to find her Control Stone so quickly. Sometimes it takes years for that stone to present itself to you. It is a great sign for you that the spirits of the garden are with you and helping you. I am so pleased," she said. "Now that you have found your Control Stone, I have a gift for you. It is just outside."

We walked out of the house, down a few steps toward the garden, and I saw an object in the twilight shadows sitting there under a tree. It was a square stone with a bowllike indentation carved out of the top, ready to receive a simple bamboo trough for spring water to flow through. She took me over to it and I realized that it was my well, the well that provides a place of nourishment and cleansing where you can dip into the water with a bamboo scoop, sip of its contents, and rinse out your mouth. The rest of the water is run over your hands for a symbolic purification. It was perfect for me, and exactly the shape I would have made, were I to make a well of my own.

"Oh, Shakkai, it is so perfect and special. Thank you so much."

I placed my hands on the curved, rounded stone. It felt warm and strong. It still held the energy of the sun in the encroaching darkness. I gave Shakkai a hug with tears in my eyes, I was so excited.

"I don't know where I am going to put the well yet," I told her.

"Of course you don't," she answered. "That will come. We will place it near the garden and let them get acquainted. In the meantime, Sami-san will go in a sacred way to retrieve your Control Stone. I will send him with some helpers. It will not take long to bring it to the garden. Tomorrow we will do this, if that pleases you."

"Shakkai, I am so excited, I can hardly wait."

"We will sleep now," she said. "Tomorrow is going to be a very long day."

The next morning I was up before the sun, doing my *kinchen* meditation before the altar. Thoughts of my garden filled my mind and my heart. I was outside on the ground in my garden as the sun came up, walking from one end to another, sitting in one place and another, making sure exactly where I wanted my Control Stone to be. I realized that the Control Stone should really be set after much of the other foliage and many of the stones had been placed. I had yet to gather them, and I knew it was going to take quite a while. So I thought, Well, I will start. Perhaps the first placement will not be right and it will have to be moved again and again, but at least I will begin; I will start.

I didn't know if that was the way it was supposed to be done, so when Shakkai joined me, I spoke with her about this, and she began to explain to me the traditional way to set up a garden. She explained that my Control Stone had to be here for me to be able to place the other stones in my mind. I needed to feel her presence, so, shortly after sunrise, we all went with Sami-san and the helpers he had called to join us. Sometimes the old ways are simplest and best for moving stones, Shakkai had said. The helper friends of Sami-san had brought an ox they called Suki with a cart, and together we went to the rock. Moving it was not as difficult as I had imagined. With the use of long levers, they placed the stone on the cart, and shortly after noon we returned with my Control Stone.

We placed it on the ground where I had meditated. I beamed with delight as I saw it sitting there, imagining the rest of the trees and plants and the other stones in relation to it. I sat there with my teacher for many hours, as we planned my garden. She taught me much about form and color and what it meant in relation to my own spirit. I felt that I had accomplished so much, because as I designed my garden, I realized I was designing, in a sense, aspects of my own spirit. I was manifesting who I was in physical form, and as that manifestation occurred, I began to grow with it spiritually. I began to be more whole. There was a new totality that I felt, a receptivity to the essence of things. An ability was being born, a more aggressive ability that I could see was part of my male shield. I was being enabled to express in rock and sand and water and trees a picture of who I was and my own personal truth. The reality began to dawn on me, and it was a very beautiful truth. It was beyond description. The garden said so much more than I could ever say about the magnificent goddess spirit that was blessing us in our every move.

23

The Holy One in the Gourd

♦

The mind is the ruler of the body,
while the spirit is the treasure
of the mind.

— HUAI-NAN-TZU

♦

One morning very early I went outside as I had been instructed to do, and sat on the sweet clover area of the sacred garden. I sat in a lotus position underneath an acacia tree, meditating for some time. The pond was in front of me and my eyes were closed. As I moved my consciousness out of my meditation, I heard a tiny stone strike the surface of the water, and opened my eyes to see rivulets of turquoise blue water moving toward me. I looked around, wondering if Shakkai had come to join me, but no one was there. Again, a tiny stone hit the surface of the water, and then I heard a giggle above me. I turned and looked up into the branches of the acacia tree, and sitting there was the Old One.

"Are you awake?" the old woman asked me as she looked down through the branches, a wide, toothless grin on her face. Her mad gray hair stuck out in all directions, and the look of a wizard, of a wild one, was in her eyes.

"Of course I'm awake," I answered. "But what are you doing in my garden? I didn't hear you approach."

"What you mean to say is that you extended me no invitation to be in your sacred tree, but if you look carefully, you will see that actually I am a part of the tree, so you, in fact, invited me after all."

I turned around to watch the old one carefully as her gnarled fingers began to twist and turn together in a movement of prayer. Then she took hold of one hand with the other and began to pull her arm and twist it, as if she were twisting loose bark on a branch around and around.

"Be careful!" I yelled. "You're going to hurt yourself. Be careful, old woman."

But she ignored me, and lay down along the branch that she was on and began to twist around it like a snake. I watched her in awe as she began to stretch along the branches of the tree. Even her brown kimono top and dark pants began to blend into the tan color of the bark. Her legs and feet slowly appeared to become gnarled like old branches on the sacred trees that stood among the stones. The dwarf juniper trees were placed in the rocks to look like the cliffs of Mount Ontake.

"Stop, stop, Old One! You are frightening me." I clutched my stomach and sat down onto the ground again. What she was doing was so unbelievable. I shook my head to see if I was sleeping; perhaps I was dreaming, but the warmth of the sun was bursting through the clouds above and drenched us in a pool of yellow light.

Softly she began to contract her body back around the branches from whence she had come. Very slowly, over five or ten minutes, she collected herself together to the old woman once again.

I took a deep breath and sat down in a patch of sweet clover beneath the trees. "Come, Holy One, come sit with me and teach me," I said, tears running down my cheeks.

Slowly the Old One smiled at me. "Ah," she said, "you have been talking to someone. Now you know who I am." She laughed wildly, her hair catching the leaves, some of them staying in their new nest, as she bounced down the trunk of the tree and landed squarely on the ground like a clown. She sat down on a rounded stone next to me, and it was only then that I noticed that she had a walking stick with her, about seven feet long. She held it in her right hand, her fingers almost indistinguishable from the gnarled staff. I looked carefully at the staff and at the gourd tied near the top of the knobby stick. I counted the nodes on the gourd. There were nine. She watched me as I perused her staff.

"It is very beautiful," I said finally. "Do the nine nodes signify the apertures of the female being?"

I was so intense and serious that, again, the old wise one threw her head back and laughed. Then, with the end of her staff, she poked me in the stomach quite hard.

"Stop," I said. "That hurts."

"Ah, you have good willpower," she said, poking me again in my shaman center. "Would you like to touch my staff?"

"Yes, I would."

I took the staff gingerly between my fingers. It was light and beautifully polished. I ran my hands up and down the knots. It was so powerful it almost vibrated in my hands. Then I touched the gourd tied to the end.

"What is in this, Holy One?"

"I have drawn pictures of the five sacred mountains that live within the gourd, and there are sacred, magical herbs. If ever you should fall ill, they will be yours."

"Thank you. I honor you and your presence."

"It's about time," she said, laughing again uproariously, putting me quite in awe. I had never seen such a being as she. She never ceased to surprise and frighten me with her uncollected manner. My fingers stayed around the gourd as I laid the stick down next to me.

"You're learning about the sacred *hu*," she said. Her eyes widened like moons, and again she laughed.

I couldn't help liking her. "Yes," I said, "I am constructing and learning about the universe in a miniature way."

"Do you understand your teaching?" she asked rather gruffly.

"It is difficult for me."

"I would like to talk about the gourd. A long time ago," she said, "I had a great master." She pulled a leaf from her hair. "A long time ago I learned how to live forever. The ancient Taoist masters talked about the Isles of the Immortals. I can teach you how to travel there, as my master taught me. My teacher became no bigger than your thumb."

She held up a gnarled thumb and twisted it into the opening of her gourd.

"Your gourd is like a gateway into the womb of the universe. And I will show you how to go there tonight. And I believe that O-Sensei, your great teacher, has promised to teach you something very special. I'm going to teach you how to go into the gourd world you have created and take part in the magic and beauty that live there. Did you think there was nothing more to learn, that all there was was the construction of the gourd garden? Do you think that's all that matters?"

"Well, I don't know."

"You have much to learn, my child. Tonight, when the moon is full, come into the garden. Bring your gourd and incense and a lamp. I will join you in a great ceremony, because you are not long for this world."

I looked at her curiously, wondering what she meant. She kept staring into my eyes. I could not take my eyes away from hers. As I looked at her eyes, they began to change. They looked like cat's eyes, and I kept looking and looking. Slowly the yellow eyes that drew me so compulsively turned very dark, like deep black pools, but not pools of danger, like the eyes of Master Hara. They were simply unfathomable depths, and I felt that I could fall into them and be lost. I had the feeling that there was no one there, and I blinked my eyes, and it was true. The old woman and her staff were gone. I sat there for some time, wondering about the experience. I absolutely did not know whether the old woman was real or not.

That night, when the moon was full, Shakkai situated herself in front of her altar and her *hu,* and then as always she meditated all night on the full moon. She would sit there in contemplation and pure joy, completely gone from this world. Once in a while I would put a shawl around her shoulders, because she would be very cold to the touch, but she did not feel me, nor was she aware of my presence.

Shakkai looked at me just before she sat before her altar, and she said, "Here. Your sacred *hu* is ready."

She took sacred white silken cloth, folded it over and over around the *hu,* and then handed me the gourd I had worked on so carefully.

She said simply, "You know what to do now. You are a real woman."

I looked at her questioningly, not knowing what she wanted me to do. I did not know quite how or where to sit, but finally I found a spot by the pond and got comfortable. The moon was bright and cast long, quavering shadows as the trees bent to the wind. I lit my lamp and incense and meditated a long time; it seemed like half the night. Then, presently, I heard a voice, far away, like the sound of wind in the high pine trees, and it said, "I am the Queen Mother of the West, Queen Mother of the West. Look toward Mount Fuji." As I did so, I saw the old woman, standing there with her staff, but she was no longer of human height. She was tiny, and the mountain looked enormous. I thought perhaps my eyes were playing tricks on me. I blinked furiously, then stood up. And then she disappeared. I heard her voice calling me to follow her. I began walking down the trail behind the mountain. Then I saw her. She came around to my Control Stone and waited for me. I walked to her, frightened, my heart pounding. Why was I so frightened? And in answer to my question I sat down with this holy mother of light.

She said, "I come to your ceremony to enliven your tree of life. I come to you from the Isles of the Immortals to teach you about eternity."

She reached out her hands and touched my sacred *hu*. Taking it, she held it to her heart, and then to her forehead.

"Ah, yes," she said, "little one of light. You shine brightly," she smiled. She held the *hu* in front of her and said, "Do you know why we teach you about miniature gardens?"

I thought carefully and said, "It is a temple, because it is a place where I can contract the world into its essence of beauty."

"Yes, because when we are of the world, we are prey to anyone who sees us. Everyone wants the great people, the masters, the great minds of our time. They move into the world and they are destroyed. People want what they have, because they shine so brightly everyone is attracted to them and can see them. Hidden in the mountains are beautiful ones and sacred ones, but because they do not hide well enough, they are hunted and destroyed. Jade is hidden within a rock. It is not enough that its beauty be left there. The rock must be smashed and the jade revealed and polished. This is not because we want to harm the rock, but because we want the jade for its beauty and value. The great deer, the beautiful deer, do not hide well enough, and the hunters find them and kill them, because of their beauty and their flesh. The bears that hibernate are hidden in the *yin* caves of the mountains. If they do not hide well enough, they will be shot and taken for their pelts, for their power. So I say to you, the better you hide, the better you will be protected. If you hide behind the mountain screens, you will not be seen. You will not be killed. The sacred *hu* will hide you. That is why, when there is great wisdom in the world, its beauty shines and everybody sees it, and then the world will take it for their own use. So the great sisterhoods and brotherhoods recall the knowledge and the wisdom. They reveal this knowledge and wisdom through the rocks, trees, and sacred springs, and perhaps through a gnarled and crippled old woman.

"Who would want me?" she asked as she pulled her hair up straight and curled it around a craggy finger. "Who, indeed, would want me? I am nothing. I am useless, and therefore I am saved. I am not beautiful, and no one sees my shining, except for you and very few others. So I hide in the trees. I am tree woman. I am Holy Mother. I am the Queen Mother of the Heavens, perhaps. Perhaps I'm just an acacia tree. It doesn't matter."

As she said this, she began to turn again in the branches of the tree, as she had earlier that day. She stretched her neck like a swan, and breathed deeply.

"You see," she said, "when you lengthen the trunk of a tree and twist it and make it gnarled, like the sacred bonsai, it lengthens the channel for the sap, so it lives much longer than a normal tree. I do this with my arms, with my twisted arms, and it gives me longer life so that I may teach the young ones coming up, the ones in search of wisdom and knowledge. And like a chameleon, I can hide anywhere. I can turn into a rock or a tree. I am a shape-shifter. I can become the size of a thumb and move into your gourd with you."

"I don't know how to do that," I said.

"I will teach you," the old woman said. She placed her hand on my power center. "Now, breathe. Close your eyes and breathe. Imagine that you are very, very tiny, O Kiku."

It was the first time she had used my name. I jumped up on hearing it. I opened my eyes momentarily and she smiled at me, that toothless grin.

"Close your eyes. Breathe deeply."

This time she reached out and pushed down on my shoulders. And a strange thing began to happen. I felt compacted. I felt different. I felt concentrated in some way and much stronger.

"Keep your eyes closed. Never compare yourself to any other living thing," she kept saying. "Dream. Dream yourself. Dream, dream. Hold my hand." She took my hand and pulled me gently, instructing me not to open my eyes. She led me forward, and I felt as if I were surely imagining things. She told me then, as she helped me sit down, to look up and see the moon. I opened my eyes and the moon was very bright. Sitting next to us was an incense burner and a lamp. She instructed me to watch the smoke moving around the stones. The landscape was different, and I realized that we were sitting at the foot of the sacred mountain, Ontake, that I love so much, one of my sacred mountains. It had been an inspiration to me throughout my life, and I watched the smoke shape messages for me. The messages essentially said that I had done the right thing in containing my life and in protecting myself from my family and from the society that I lived in. It was appropriate for this time in my evolution. But I needed to collect myself. Because of the stress of other lifetimes, I needed peace in this one. I needed the tranquillity of building a garden and understanding the world in miniature, that it was a gateway, simply a gateway into a much larger world, into a much larger meaning, so profound that my heart opened and nearly burst with the joy of it. Tears filled my eyes. I took a deep breath and contemplated the smoke, its tendrils moving along the rocks and juniper trees and obscuring the mountain view for a moment. The depth of smoke, dark purple and gray, filled me with a sense of peace and serenity.

Slowly the night passed, and I felt a closeness to this old woman, as if I had known her for all time, this strange clown of a woman who tickled and opened my heart and my mind. And as dawn came, the first moment of light peeking over the mountain, the old woman took her finger and wiped the dew from a leaf and placed it on her eyelids. She indicated for me to do the same. I reached out and touched the dew on the plants, the beautiful purple irises that bloomed around the pond. I dripped the dew on my eyelids, and as I did so, I closed my eyes and went into a deep sleep.

When I awoke, I knew not how long it had been, but the sun was up and I was sitting beneath the twisted juniper tree by my Control Stone, and I was alone. The sacred *hu* was on a white cloth before me. The old hag, the Holy Mother, the Wise One, was no longer with me, but I felt that she was near. And then it occurred to me. I was amazed at what had just happened. I had spent the night inside my sacred *hu,* in deep meditation, in a world of such peace and tranquillity that I was at a loss to explain it.

I went to Shakkai to talk about the sacred *hu.* I found her having tea. "I want to speak of the old Holy One who has visited me," I said.

Shakkai placed her finger over her lips, shaking her head. "You keep the holy ones inside you. To speak of them is to lose them," she said. "It is enough that you have spent the night in meditation and that she has honored you with her presence."

"But I spent the night in my sacred *hu,*" I said. I couldn't help blurting it out.

"Yes, yes, I understand," she exclaimed with great happiness. She clapped her hands and bowed to me. "Have some tea," she said. "It is good. We will talk now."

·24·

The Breath of Nature

There is no thing; whom else do you seek?

— ANCESTOR OF LU

Shakkai woke me early and took me outside to a high point of land over my garden, so I could watch the sun rise with her. We meditated for a short time, and then she asked me to watch the light as it moved across my garden area. She told me to be very alert and aware.

"I want you to look at the configuration of the hills around my house," Shakkai said. "I want you to notice that it resembles an animal. Can you tell which one it is?"

It took me some time to understand exactly what Shakkai was getting at. I walked around from one area at the top of the hill we were on to another, looking at the ridges of land and the hills surrounding her house. I realized finally that there were two legs to my left, like arms reaching out from a central ridge that came down from the sacred mountain. There were another two legs that reached out before the ridge dwindled away into a kind of taillike structure down toward a lake. Along these ridges coming down from the higher mountain was a surging stream that moved in a zigzag line through precipitous cliffs and enormous boulders. Then there was a meadow and a stand of trees and bamboo. It was very craggy, rough terrain.

Finally it came to me. I whirled around, and looking at Shakkai with my eyes filled with excitement, I said, "It's a dragon, isn't it? It's as if your house were right at the midsection of the dragon, which, I guess you would say, is a little lower than where his heart might be."

Shakkai clapped her hands and smiled, her teeth glistening white, perfectly straight. She was obviously pleased. Then, holding my hand, she led me down off the mountain into my garden. She told me to walk around the garden four times, carefully and quietly, placing my feet noiselessly from one steppingstone to another.

I had worked very hard placing the stones so that one could comfortably walk in serpentine patterns through my garden. Then we sat at the Absolute Control Stone.

"Take a deep breath," she said, "and close your eyes, O Kiku. I want you to feel the breeze that is coming up from the south and imagine that we are, in fact, living on the back of a dragon, as if the earth were the skin of the mighty dragon. See if you can sense the breath of nature that surrounds us. The dragon is the power of nature's spirit. And sleeping nearby is a white tiger, a friend to the dragon. The dragon is not practical. The tiger grounds the energy of the great dragon, and if the land is in proper configuration, you will sense a great vortex of power around you. It will come to you, actually, as the breath of nature itself. Take some time, O Kiku, and sense what you have created. Sense how you have, purely through the magic of your intuition, placed your garden."

At this point Shakkai walked with gentle steps, her hands folded and her eyes cast down and inward in a pose of meditation. She moved away from my circle of land and back to the moon gate that led into her own garden.

As I sat by my Control Stone, her power and courage moving through me, I listened to the birds in the trees, and felt the gentle wind caressing my cheeks. I flattened my palms against the earth and felt her life beneath me. Presently I became aware of the force of the dragon. I had not felt this being before, because I had not known of its existence. Now I realized that I had, indeed, felt this vortex of energy, and it was that power that had led me to make my garden in this location. I was excited. I realized that the Tao had moved through me and led me, as surely as Shakkai had led me by the hand. I wanted to dance, to move with the energy flows that I was feeling. I stood up and lifted my arms away from my body, slightly bending my knees, and I began to move quietly and gently, as my eyes closed. I moved *ch'i* up from my center of power into this new world of energy that I was discovering. The breath of nature became clear to me—as clear as my own process of breathing. I sat down, finally, my eyes wide with the wonder of it all, and thought about my life previous to working with Shakkai. I thought about how much I had missed in my early days.

I felt a warmth from behind me. Slowly I turned to find Kat-san

sitting in a lotus position a few yards away, in respect for my soli-
tude. I smiled at him. I was so happy to see him. In the last few
months I had learned to be in the presence of Kat-san and speak
not at all. Communion between us was so deep and profound that
words seemed to lessen our understanding.

Kat-san walked to me and handed me a beautiful pink lotus
blossom. "For you," he said. "I offer you this flower from the
dark soul and the murky beginnings of my early life, so that you
may know all that I am."

I smiled as I took my favorite of flowers, thinking of the mud at
the bottom of the pond, the extraordinary depth from which this
flower had been given birth. I thought of my own beginnings, the
loneliness and difficulties of my early life.

"Your trust is my greatest gift," I said to him, bowing.

Kat-san sat with me for a long time. I had been working on my
garden endlessly. I had not had much time for anything else,
except for my moments with Kat-san. It was as if we had been
together a lifetime. The experience of molding and building my
tiny shrine of trees and flowers and reflection ponds and stones
was the deepest experience I had known on the physical plane.
Even to begin my garden, I had had to dig away in places of darkness within my own soul. I had extraordinary respect for the masters of this art. I realized the meditation and care that it took to
place one stone in such a way that it could bring enlightenment to
even the sorriest of souls.

"What power there is on this path," I said quietly to Kat-san.

"Your garden is breathtaking," he answered, his eyes glowing
with respect as he put his arm around me and supported my shoulders. "My garden was full of craggy, jagged rocks and stones that
represented the difficult road toward one's illumination."

For all the world, sitting here at my Observation Rock, the tiny
garden looked like the high mountains around Mount Koyo, and
the beautiful mirrored pond seemed large enough for the greatest
sailing vessels to cross. I knew I had succeeded, at least in some
measure, at my new-found art of the *shakkai,* the captured landscape.

Comparison of Realities

◆

Having drunk the wine of longevity,
you wander free; who can know you?

— ANCESTOR OF LU

◆

After waking in the Dreamlodge, we had gone to Agnes's cabin, where I lay down and fell into a deep, dreamless sleep. The next morning I awoke and peeked out from under the covers like a mouse looking out of its hole, searching every corner of the room for impending danger. I wanted to crawl back under the covers and go to sleep. I often exaggerate my feelings to myself. I felt a lack of courage, a sense of sadness nearing depression. Agnes was sitting at the wooden table in the center of the room, doing beadwork. I wondered how long she had been up, but said nothing as I crawled sleepily out of bed and went to the window. Pulling the curtains aside, I looked up at the sky, to the heavy, dark clouds that loomed on the horizon.

"My most unfavorite weather," I muttered to myself.

There was a flat gray light to the dawn. Looking at the trees and rock formations outside the cabin, everything looked dusty and forlorn. I heaved a sigh and turned around to look at Agnes. Deep lines, like waves, traversed her forehead as she concentrated on the tiny patterns of red and white beads that she was diligently working on.

"Oh, God," I sighed.

"You called?" Agnes laughed. "Well, the morning came, peeked in the window, and went away in tears with that welcome," she said.

"Agnes, sometimes I get so tired of myself, of my own pain, of my own struggle."

Sitting down heavily in the chair, I reached out and ran my fingers over some of the beadwork Agnes had completed. It was perfect—a beautiful rendition of the morning star in bright blue, white, and yellow beads. The beads were representative of a forgotten time, or at least I felt so this morning, and it made me sad.

"Other people seem to be so much smarter than I am," I moaned. "They accomplish so much more with what they have than I do."

"Who are these people?" Agnes asked, not looking up from her work.

"Oh, I don't know," I answered. "Just everybody."

Reaching out to the basket of fruit on the table, she took an orange and set it in front of me.

"Little Wolf, what is that?"

"An orange," I answered.

Agnes nodded and then reached over to the basket and plucked out an apple and set it in front of me.

"Now, what is this?"

"Well, it's an apple, Agnes, of course."

"How do these two fruits compare to each other? Lift them up. Hold them, one in each hand. Tell me how you compare them."

I picked up the orange in my left hand and the apple in my right, and said, "Well, you really can't compare this orange to this apple. You can talk about how different they are, but you can't compare them, really, because they're different. It's just simply known that they're different. So why would someone even want to compare one to the other?"

"Exactly," Agnes said.

She reached over and took a banana I had brought her from the trading store and set it on the table in front of me, and then she took a walnut and set it next to the banana.

"Now," she said, "how do these two items compare?"

I was getting exasperated. I lifted the banana in one hand and the walnut in the other, and I said, "Agnes, you can't compare these two things. They're different. Why would anybody do that? They're completely different. They're two different beings in the world."

"That's right," Agnes said. "Get it?" she asked.

"Get what?" I said.

Then Agnes took some grapes and set them in front of me and a papaya that I had brought her. "Now," she said, "how do these compare?"

I said, "Agnes, how can you compare? They're two different

things. You can't compare two things that are as different as they are. I guess you can say that they're both fruit."

"Well, that's something," Agnes said.

"Agnes, what are you getting at?"

"I know it's a little early in the morning, Lynn, but I am trying to teach you something."

"Could you be a little more clear?"

"I am being perfectly clear," Agnes said. "What I am trying to tell you is that you cannot compare yourself to any other human being on this earth. There will never be another person just like you. Thank the Great Spirit," she said under her breath.

"What?" I asked.

"Never mind." She laughed and patted my arm. "There will never be another human being like me. I am the only one that will have my traits, the structure of my body, my heart and my mind, and my shadow being. My etheric field is purely mine. My spirit shield, the soul that animates this body, is completely mine and individually mine. So, Little Wolf, how can you compare Lynn to Agnes?"

She picked up the orange in one hand and the apple in the other. Holding up her left hand with the orange, she said, "Lynn, this is you. You're an orange, and I am over here, an apple. I am Agnes. We cannot be compared to each other, because we are so vastly different."

"But we are both human. We are both part of this dream," I said.

"Yes, and this apple and this orange are both fruits, and part of this dream, but you still cannot compare them, because they manifest differently on this earth, as do each of us."

I thought for a long time about my friends, about people who I thought had done so much better in the world than I had, who had expressed themselves better, with more clarity. And I thought of people who had not done so well, who had missed the many chances that had come their way, and I started to feel better. I started to get a glimmer of understanding about what Agnes was saying. What she was saying was very simple, and yet it was very complicated in its essence.

I looked at Agnes, who had put down her beadwork and sat

back in her chair. Her face looked very dark in the shadows of the cabin. A ray of sunlight was peeking through the clouds, as I could see through the window, past the curtains that were blowing in the gentle breeze through the partially open sash. The light illuminated the left side of Agnes's face, leaving the right side in darkness. The illuminated side looked very young. She looked like a girl; the play of light erased her wrinkles and lines. The other side of her face looked like that of an ancient grandmother—furrowed lines, deep crevices around her mouth and across her forehead, smile lines etched on either side of her eyes.

"You are a great magician," I said to her as my spirits lifted even more, and I realized how simply she had seduced me out of my depression. I smiled at her, feeling great love at that moment for my teacher.

"Pulling you out of depression makes me a great magician?" she smiled at me.

This morning that was quite a feat. I did not feel well.

"Do you understand why your mood has changed?"

I thought for several minutes. "I am not sure, Agnes. It had something to do with getting my mind to think about something in a new way."

"That's right, my daughter. I taught you something new, and that is the trail out of depression. When you work with people who are troubled, teach them something new. Not only does it bring them out of a destructive mood, but it centers them. It changes them, like poetry, like a beautiful work of art. When a shaman works with you, he or she works on the tapestry of your life, helping you tie new knots, bring in new colors to your design, and when that happens, your heart opens and all of life becomes possible again. So many times we have worked with White Star Woman, the goddess from the Pleiades. Do you remember long ago when Ruby and I were working with you with the Mother Rattle? We had moved you into a visualization with White Star Woman, and she appeared to you. Do you remember what she held in her hand?"

I thought for several minutes, and then it came to me. I looked at the apple I was holding in my hand, and held it out to Agnes. "She was holding an apple. I remember I thought that was oddly synchronistic with Adam and Eve and the Garden of Eden, because White Star Woman has given me power and strength and knowledge."

"Haven't you ever wondered why she was holding the apple?"

"I did at the time, Agnes, but I guess I forgot to ask you about it."

Agnes squinted her eyes at me and took the apple out of my hand. She went to the sink, and taking a Buck knife, she came back to the table and cut the apple laterally. Two pieces fell away from the knife blade, sitting in front of us on the table.

"What do you see?" she asked.

I looked at the inside of the apple and saw that the configuration of the seeds made a five-pointed star.

"There are women of power, ancient women, who would have called this a pentagram, if you remember the Woman of Wyrrd," Agnes pointed out.

"Yes, that's true." I looked again at the apple and the perfection of its design.

She said, "Now look at the center, the very, very center of the apple where the life of that apple has come from, as life comes from your navel."

I looked at the center. There were seeds that held the genetics of the apple, and then there was nothing. The very center was a tiny, star-shaped hole through which I could see the table. I said, "But there's nothing there. There's only space."

Agnes smiled at me. She said, "Exactly. Everything eventually comes from nothing." Holding out her arms to take in the room, she said, "Our universe is magnificent in its manifestations of power, but when you go to the center, when you go to the beginning of things, you move, not out into the world for your instruction, but to the interior world, the universe that lives within. It is from the essence of that universe that all life is born, as this apple tells you so clearly, so simply. The genetics of this apple are born from space. When you got up this morning, you felt an emptiness. Instead of allowing that emptiness to be the void that it truly is, the void that you carry as woman, you forgot that the origin of power is within that void. Sometimes you are frightened by that void, and instead you experience the abyss. We become terrified and we move out of our center into the world, trying to regain our equilibrium. And that is our tragedy," Agnes said. "There are so few teachers in the world today. There are so few societies that will allow a Crazy Horse, a Buddha, a Christ even to exist. They are destroyed before they are only a few years old. Today, to be a holy man or a holy woman, one has to hide and protect one's knowledge for the few that seek it, so that it is not destroyed or misused. We are all equal in the gift called life. We are not all equal in what we achieve with our gifts. Some people put very much more effort into their enlightenment than others.

"If, when you got up this morning, instead of being self-indulgent, you had gone outside and placed your hands on the earth, your back against a tree, and smelled the grasses in the air and the new flowers of spring, you would have experienced the emptiness that is indeed the fullness within you. When you turned to me to help you and I taught you something new, you felt better, but I will not always be here, so these are things that you need to learn. These are things that you need to teach your apprentices. Teach them about the apple. Teach them about White Star Woman and the Pleiades. Teach them about the sacredness of the stars and the emptiness that animates them."

26

Life-and-Death Stone

♦

All life is of cosmic origin!

— ANCIENT TEUTONIC SAYING,
EIGHT THOUSAND YEARS OLD

♦

One morning I walked out of Shakkai's house at dawn to find, much to my amazement, that something was missing. The very old bamboo wall that had defined the southernmost edge of Shakkai's garden had been taken down. I couldn't imagine how it could have been torn down in the night without my hearing it. Or had it been missing during the previous days and I had just not noticed? In its place was the tall stand of young bamboo that had always been there, but now the barrier was removed between my garden and Shakkai's. I ran to my garden, then to hers. I could not see into one garden from the other, except for a momentary glint of light reflected from the pond, or a glimpse of the mountains in the center of her garden when the bamboo would move in the wind. I was fascinated by this event.

The sound of Shakkai's flute floated toward me on the still morning currents of air. I looked toward a rock that was partially up the side of the mountain in the center of her garden. She called it, with a certain sense of humor, her Life-and-Death Stone. I walked toward her, listening to the somewhat mournful melody that she was playing. The tones were deep and elongated, suddenly turning to a more fanciful composition as she turned to face me. Shakkai played her bamboo flute beautifully. She told me she had never learned from a teacher, but had seen a flute lying in the grass one day as she was walking through a forest, and had picked it up. It had obviously been lying there for a long time, because a tangle of grass had grown around it. She told me she had very gently separated the blades of grass and the weeds and picked the flute up. Holding it in her hands and brushing the dust and the dirt from its surface, she had felt an immediate kinship with it. It was obviously very old, and she lifted it to her lips. It was the very first time she had ever held a bamboo flute. She held it out to the right side of her face, and blowing gently into the mouthpiece, she began to play as if she always played it. It had been a profound moment in her life. Tears of joy had washed her cheeks as she told me the story. Now she played her bamboo flute almost every day. She said that it helped her etheric body to fly.

Shakkai set her flute down on its red silk case and motioned for me to join her. Sitting together on the Life-and-Death Stone, facing out to the south, we looked out past the bamboo curtain that separated her garden from mine. The morning sunlight slanted across the mirrorlike surface of the pond. I could see the orange-and-white carp below the surface creating ripples on the water with their expectant mouths as they looked for breakfast. Great white clouds billowed in the sky above, in the fast-moving air currents at higher altitude.

"So our gardens are no longer separated by a wall," I said, my face beaming with delight.

Shakkai nodded, observing my smile and my happiness. Her own face echoed my delight as she reached out and touched my shoulder with affection.

"It's like life and death," she said gently.

"What do you mean?" I asked.

Shakkai took two plum blossoms out of my hair where I had placed them, and set them on the stone that we were sitting on. Then, making a knife out of the palm of her hand and her fingers, she placed her hand vertically between the two blossoms.

"There is a barrier," she said, "an invincible barrier between the physical world and the next world that we are born into at death. Look at my hand," she instructed. "My hand could be that barrier. If you were the blossom here"—she pointed with her finger— "you could not look through my hand to the blossom over there. The blossoms are equally beautiful. Life is beautiful in so many aspects, and death is merely a passageway to the next state of beauty, another blossom, another flowering. We have only three dimensions in this physical world that we call life," she said. "When we move on to the other side, we have more to experience. We have a fourth hoop of power. We are moving into four dimensions. Our awareness, our vision, our ability to perceive truth and God, the sacred Tao, is expanded beyond your imagination."

"Is it like what they say heaven is?" I asked.

"No," Shakkai answered. "It is not heaven. To many it will seem like heaven, because the slowness and the density of physical existence is removed in so many ways."

"Shakkai, explain that to me. I don't understand. Can you give me an example?"

Shakkai was still sitting with her hand between the two flowers. She lifted it away and indicated for me to look toward the bamboo that grew between our respective gardens. "When we look through the bamboo now from my garden," she said, "we get a glimpse, an impression when the wind is right, when the light is just so, of something beautiful on the other side. Do we not?"

"Yes," I answered.

"When you are working with me, when you are disciplining your mind and moving into a heightened state of consciousness, as you do when we meditate and when you work in your garden and you are extending your heart and your spirit into the world, you get a glimpse of the other side. Do you know that?" she asked.

"I know that I am moved, and more than just in my consciousness. I know that something actually *happens* to my physical body, but I've never been able to describe it."

"Let me explain," Shakkai said.

Now she drew a small outline of a human body in a little patch of sand that had gathered in a crevice in the stone.

She said, "This is you. This is you in your physical life. Now, when you move deeply into trance, into your work in the Dreamtime, the Dreamtime of the Tao, of sacred life, you will find yourself experiencing a kind of sleepiness, a kind of dizziness. Is that not so, my daughter?"

"Sometimes I get a little disoriented."

"What is happening is this." And she drew a shadow, another outline, of the physical form off to the left of the figure she had first drawn in the sand. "You see, what happens is the etheric body begins to shift, begins to move out of the physical body. That's what happens when you sleep. That's what allows you to sleep. You move out a long way, sometimes, in your etheric body. Your etheric body, remember, has many qualities, just like this flower."

She lifted up the plum flower and held it up to the morning light. It was moist and pink and delicately beautiful.

"This flower has many aspects. It has petals, and it has a center that holds the pollen. It has leaves and a stem, but when you look at it, you talk about this as a flower. You perceive it as a flower in its totality. There is another side, another hoop of power that you move into in death, and we talk about that as the other side, the other world. However you term it, it has many aspects, just as your etheric body has many aspects and different colors at different times. You spend a great deal of your life in higher learning. In this process you grow, you become lighter. Sometimes, O Kiku, you appear almost transparent, and that is because you are melting, in a way, with your etheric body. You see, your etheric body holds your mind, your thought processes. Your identity as a personality, as a being on this earth, is held in the etheric body. When the etheric body is absent, the physical body feels nothing. It has no emotions or personality or actual identity. It is like a suit of clothes. It is like a dress. It is like this kimono I put on this morning. When it is old, when it is worn out, it is discarded."

"Do you mean to say, Shakkai, that when I move through death and into the next life, it will simply be like putting on another set of clothes?"

"It is similar to that," Shakkai said. "When my master died, or passed over, she asked me if I wanted to join with her and come with her. She held out her hand to me. She said that she could teach me to transform with her, that we could move past several of the dimensions on the other side together, that we had done so much work together and found such a clarity that we were able to go much further than many other people who just simply died and went to the next dimension. Each dimension is a schoolhouse. Each dimension is part of our process of illumination and evolvement.

"Consider my garden for a moment, O Kiku. It is a garden of silence and serenity. It is the spirit of the Tao manifested in the physical in this plane. Your garden is beautiful in very different ways from mine. It is craggy in the mountains. It reflects the difficulties and turmoil and energy that are needed to find enlightenment in this lifetime. It is like the next dimension, because in the next dimension, whatever you *think* becomes manifest instantly. It is very, very different from the physical world we know here, where we have an idea and then try to move the physical mass with great difficulty. The next dimension is very hard for those who have not done much spiritual work in the physical realm, because they will have no map to follow. The beauty of the plum blossom and the lotus will be falling into the desert for them. There will be no reflection pond, no serenity, no flowing rivers of transformation. They will find it hard, but their lessons will eventually be learned.

"Your garden is like the next dimension. It represents to me death in the best sense of the word. It represents transformation. That is why I took down the barrier, because, truly, the barrier between life and death is only terrifying if we think it to be. Where were you before you were born?"

"I'm not sure," I answered.

Shakkai picked up the flute and began to play a haunting melody. I closed my eyes and dreamed of other worlds.

The next thing I knew, I was back in Manitoba. It was night, and I was in the ice-cold stream, screaming my head off at Agnes and Ruby to stop trying to drown me.

"Damn it, Ruby, you're trying to kill me!" I yelled, as she shoved my head down again under water.

Finally they wrapped me in a Pendleton blanket and let me sit on the shore.

"It is about life and death," I said, glowering at her.

"*This* is about life and death," Ruby said to me, pinching my cheek.

"Ow," I said. "Stop it. We were talking about my etheric body. It was so interesting and peaceful, so wonderful, so different from being here," I said.

"Yeah, well, it's a good thing your etheric body is connected with a real tough cord. That's all I can say," Ruby said.

"What do you mean?" I asked.

"I mean you are not listening, Little Wolf. You go off into the Dreamtime, into the future mysteries, Great Spirit knows where, and that cord follows you, connecting you to this body. If you don't pay attention to me, one of these days you might be in trouble, real trouble," she said, tapping me on the top of my head.

"But that cord cannot break," I said.

"Well, let's just put it this way. I wouldn't defy Mother Nature. You are no match for her. Remember that."

"But this is *all* part of Mother Nature, isn't it?" I swept my arms out in a circle.

"Well, you could say that, but I think we are playing with the rules a bit, don't you? I mean, it's not every day that someone moves into the radiance of a future lifetime and walks down the trail in a faraway place out of time and space," Ruby said, lifting her hands to the night sky.

She sat in silhouette, dark against the striations of pink, orange, and flashes of yellow light in the spectacular aurora borealis. The sky was turgid with pulsating light behind her. It was as if the Sky Fathers were in the midst of a great celebration. I felt very small before the wonder of it. For a moment I remembered Shakkai and the rising golden sun of the morning. I could almost hear the lilting quality of her flute music and the sound of the wind in the bamboo of the garden.

I stared at Ruby. For a moment her skin became very dark. It was as if her mind had turned inward to some secret place where her imagination lived. She was sitting very straight, her arms folded in front of her. Her eyes were intense and angry as they looked at me with great ferocity. Her expression frightened me. She looked like an old tintype photograph I had seen of her grandfather. It was taken at a trial where their Native American nation had been removed from their lands, a tragic moment in history that should never have happened. It was one of the few photographs that Ruby kept in her medicine bag.

I felt suddenly suspended in time, my mind moving from the ancient history of Ruby's ancestors to sweeping images of Shakkai, encompassing all the history in between. I felt overcome with a deep, primal sadness for the ignorance that humans seem to be possessed of. And what good is our effort? "What am I doing?" I whispered.

Ruby, clucking her tongue and shaking her head as if I had spoken aloud, answered me. "Through all the veils of ignorance, the truth and goodness of life and nature will survive," Ruby said. "With each act of power that you perform, the light on earth is increased a tiny, tiny bit. It is like looking to the bamboo and see-ing the morning light reflecting off the pond. It brings you closer to home."

I stared at Ruby, wondering if I had mentioned the bamboo and the removal of the barrier between my garden and Shakkai's. I knew I had not spoken of my dreaming, so how did Ruby know?

27

Book of the Child

♦

Wherever I look,
cherry blossom, crimson leaves,
nowhere to be seen;
A rush-thatched hut by the cove
in the twilight of autumn.

— SHUKO

♦

It was a beautiful morning around Shakkai's house and garden. The little yellow birds were chirping passionately in the high juniper trees. A small tribe of brown-and-green-feathered ducks had come to visit the pond. Shakkai and I finished our meditation before dawn and left her compound early, walking through the bamboo forest and out into a meadow. Morning fog hung low over the grass. I could barely see the outline of the trees in the distance—they were Kabuki-like shadow dancers in the morning light.

Shakkai knelt in a patch of brown grass and placed the palm of her hand over the ground. She looked up at me sadly. "This grass should be green at this time of year."

"What has happened?" I asked.

"The weather is changing. There should be snow on the mountains. There is no snow. There is little rain. The water in the creek is low. The lakes are low. It is flat here in this meadow, but still the ground is responding. The grasses are dying. Great changes are happening around our Mother Earth. If we do not alter our ways very quickly, this great temple, the schoolhouse that we live in, will no longer support life."

She stood again, and we walked across the meadow. Shakkai looked like an ancient porcelain doll with her hair tied up in a knot and her antique red kimono trailing over the blue-green grasses. Every once in a while she would point out an herb, talking of its power and its essential value for life force, for healing.

"Sensei, there is something I have not completely understood in my work with you, and that is the healing properties of plants."

"When one is ill," Shakkai explained, "one's body vibration, the actual frequency of one's electromagnetic field, vibrates at a certain tone."

Shakkai was carrying her flute in her sleeve. Now she took it out, and lifting her elbows like a red bird preparing for flight, she played a sound, a long, vibrant, low-pitched tone.

"It is that tone, imagine for a moment, that a person with tuberculosis might have. He lives in that tone. It is a tone that he's not aware of. In the shaman world it's called an interior sound."

"Shakkai, I don't understand what you mean by an interior sound."

Shakkai thought for a long time, obviously deep in concentration. Then her eyes brightened. She looked at me as we continued to walk.

"O Kiku, when you feel love for Kat-san, something happens inside you. Perhaps you do not know it on a conscious level, but your cells begin to dance. They move in a rhythm. Love is a very healing energy, and there is a reason for that. It is healing, because love picks up on a higher vibration or tone and brings your inner ecology up into a level where wholeness is possible. When you are in love, you become receptive to another human being. You open yourself to a merging of personalities and spirits. For that to happen, your vibration must be much higher."

Twirling like a young girl, her kimono floating out around her like a red cloud, she blew a note on the flute, a high-pitched sound that echoed into the forest around us. Shakkai moved over to the right and picked up a tiny flower, blue in color, and held it up to me.

"This flower is butterfly clover, and it has the ability to change your perception of the world."

"You mean it's a hallucinogen?" I asked.

"No, if you ingest its essence, it changes your perception of the world by opening your heart. It has a very distinct effect on the cellular structure of the chest area of your body. If you were to ingest this in the proper way, it would give you the effect that love gives you. What do you think would happen to your body then?" she asked.

I thought for a while and held the flower that she handed to me. I closed my eyes and tried to sense the healing of the flower. Finally I looked at her and said, "Perhaps it has the same tone that you were speaking of in a love situation."

"That is correct. In other words, if you can find truly deep feelings in your life, your creativity is expanded. If you find relationships in your environment that open your heart, you can recreate those feelings once you know the trail. Once you know the trail, you can find herbs that can marry you, that can give you a quality of life that is very different from what you ordinarily experience."

"Is that where homeopathy and flower essences come from? Is that the origin of the idea of healing with such elements?" I asked.

"Yes, it is. It has to do with the frequency in your body. It is really very simple, but because it is something you cannot really test and see with the physical eye and with consciousness, with the rational faculties, scientists have ignored this science for centuries and centuries. Shamans around the world for all time have known these secrets to be true and have healed with them consistently, using them throughout the ages.

"Now, O Kiku, you have an expanded aura. Your heart is very open in a state of love, not only for me, but for Kat-san. Because of this, your innocence is very beautiful and you have been able to do many things very quickly. It is love that has helped you, and through love you become one with the Tao. The spirit of the Tao is moving through you with great beauty. Now I want to teach you something. I want to teach you how to stay in the frequency of love, even if Kat-san were no longer in your life, even if you had to move back to Kyoto or Tokyo, to go back into the world as a businesswoman, and I was no longer with you."

"But, O-Sensei, you would always be with me. If you were not with me physically, you would be in my heart."

"Yes, and that is what I mean, daughter. To maintain that frequency on a physical level, I am going to show you a field of flowers."

We walked through the forest and down into a small hollow nestled into a ravine in the mountains. The hollow was carpeted with wildflowers such as I had never seen. They were almost neon-like in their brightness. I followed my teacher down a narrow path that had not been walked on in some time, until we came to a meadow. Little patches of grass and clumps of weeds grew amid the stones that marked the way. She took me to a patch of blue flowers with yellow centers. Very carefully we walked through the flowers so as not to disturb the tiny plants. Finally we came to a clearing in the ground with some flat stones. She placed a woven straw mat there, and we sat amid the flowers and meditated for a very long time. She asked me to quiet the inner voice in my head and move my concentration into my heart. I expanded my heart until I thought it would burst. Then she asked me to lie down in the flowers with her. As it happened, I fell asleep in the sun, feeling the warmth on my belly and in my heart.

A very strange thing happened, because of Shakkai and my dreaming. I did not remember, of course, that I was already in a dream. So when I slept in the field, the fullness of my heart opened and with my vulnerability at its highest peak, I dreamed I was back with my teachers in Manitoba. I dreamed of being with Agnes and Ruby. We were doing a ceremony with some of the elders from the Sisterhood of the Shields, and they presented me with a great book in this dream. It was the Book of the Child, which I had seen only once before in my life, in the Himalayas of Tibet. Standing next to this book was Windhorse, my spirit husband. Windhorse had been with me since my journey in Nepal, and he was my spirit husband who guided me in my life back in Los Angeles. I dreamed of the Book of the Child and I wrote in that book of my life with Shakkai. I wrote many chapters, and we did ceremonies late into the night. They told me of life and death and how the order of the universe would be for me. Many of the things they told me, they asked me not to write about. One day, perhaps, I would be able to tell of these things. They gave me new symbols, alchemical symbols, for bringing illumination to the spirit. They talked about the Great Spirit. They talked about the angels, and they told me to keep helping the animals on Mother Earth. They said that we owed a great debt to the animal kingdom, and that if we stopped killing the animals, perhaps we would then learn to stop killing each other.

When I awoke from the dream, I found Shakkai sitting next to me. Her eyes were closed, and for a moment I didn't recognize her. For a moment she looked like Ruby, deeply lined and dark, her brown skin glowing in the evening mist. I had passed the day in a dream, and I remembered Lynn in Los Angeles, and I remembered Lynn in Manitoba, and Agnes and Ruby.

I reached out my hand to Shakkai, needing desperately to hear her voice. She took my hand and said, "It is all right. Everything is as it should be, O Kiku. Do not fear the visions that you see, for your heart is open and your path is one of heart, not of darkness."

Then she opened her eyes and smiled at me. I was terribly confused and shocked at what I had seen. I told her of my dreaming. She listened, her expression remote, as if she were deep inside herself in meditation, although her eyes were open. I could not fathom the depth of her spirit.

Then she returned to me and looked into my eyes and said, "We will talk of your confusion after you have had a chance to digest your dreaming. When you travel the other dimensions of life, remember that there is truly only one life, and that one life encompasses all of eternity. What you are living now, O Kiku, is a dream from another lifetime, and that other lifetime is a dream from the sacred Tao. The Great Spirit moves through you and through all of life. We are connected as we will always be."

Then, very carefully, she reached out. On her hands and knees, she was looking through the tiny blue plants until she found what she was looking for.

"These are mature, ripe plants," she told me, and prayed over the plants before she actually took them, giving thanks for their life force and their giveaway. Collecting the plants in a tiny sack she carried in the sleeve of her kimono, she said, "These are plants for you. They are sacred to you because they help you in the Dreamtime, but they will only help you in your dreaming when your heart is full, like the moon, so, when you use these plants, be sure that it is not a new moon. That is the way in the dreaming of this particular species of plant. When a plant knows you well, it can give you everything. When you take its essence and bring it down to its primal origins, you can take that plant and it will heal you. It will heal you of your pain. You carry much pain, O Kiku, from the conditioning of this lifetime and others. It's in your cells, and that pain is like the pain of all human beings moving toward enlightenment. It is through this pain that we grow.

"Now you, my daughter, pick the last plant. Hold it in your hands. Feel the heat and the cold of the plants in the palm of your hands. Find a plant that is warm, that is calling out to you, because it wants to become a part of you. In taking the plant, you help it to move on to a higher state of being. You are that plant's hope of transformation, so do not think that you are killing the plant. You are only giving it transformation and new life, just as it is giving the same to you. That is what a sacred giveaway is all about."

Shakkai sat back on her heels. She held her head high, her hair tied up in the familiar knot on top of her head, bright red silk streamers coming from the tie. She took out her flute and began to play a beautiful, haunting tune. When she was through, I had found my plant, and I presented it to her. She nodded and smiled and opened the bag so I could put it in there with the other plants.

"How do you feel?" she asked.

"I feel good," I answered. "I am happy."

Rolling thunder interrupted the silence of the evening. I looked up to see great blue-black stormclouds gathering above, around a full moon.

"Quickly," she said, "we must hurry before the rain comes."

Shakkai walked ahead of me, carrying her bag of plants over her shoulder. A pungent aroma of earth and grasses filled my nostrils as the first drops of rain dappled the path ahead.

28

Goddess of the Sun

♦

Brambles should be cut away,
Removing even the sprouts.
Within essences there naturally blooms
A beautiful lotus blossom.
One day there will suddenly appear
An image of light;
When you know that,
You yourself are it.

— SUN BU-ER,
CLEAR AND CALM FREE WOMAN,
1124 C.E.

♦

It was late in the afternoon. I found myself walking with my teacher down a village road in northern Honshu, the largest island of Japan. The sky was orange, gold, and yellow. The mountains and the trees were silhouetted against the glow like an ink drawing by Basho, the branches etched into the red of the sunset like the masterful calligraphy of the highest master. The wooded mountains on either side were interspersed with clouds of pink and white cherry blossoms. Occasionally we would walk through a small forest of cherry trees, the blossoms meeting overhead in canopies of brilliant color. We were on our way to one of the most sacred shrines of the Shinto world, a shrine I had visited every year as a child with my family. Thousands of people trekked down this village road every year to pray and to ask the spirit of God into their beings for communion and reverence and thanksgiving. I had not been to this shrine in a long time, and I welcomed the experience once again.

As we came closer to the temple, I could see the temple outbuildings—simple wood structures, unpainted, with deeply thatched roofs and gracefully curved eaves. Giant pine trees reached above us, forming a natural gate to the heavens. The surrounding grounds were plateaus of perfectly cared for gardens.

When finally we reached the Amaterasu Omikami Temple itself, erected to the Goddess of the Sun, we waited as pilgrims, one after another, took off their robes, laid down their staffs, and, clapping their hands as they knelt, lay down on the ground in front of the sacred white veil that hung from the lintel of the gateway. No one could see past this curtain, except for the emperor and the highest of the priests. We would never set foot through that threshold in this lifetime. It was interesting to me that there were no icons, and I realized it more as an adult now, coming to this great shrine, than I ever had before. There were no gods or goddesses enthroned in gold, but simply a curtain, a veil, that to me represented the spirit and face of God. I clapped my hands and held my *gohei,* the paper lightning antenna that brought down the spirit of God. I knelt and then lay on the ground in front of the temple with great thanksgiving in my heart for the simplicity of this religion. It seemed so right to prostrate myself in awe and worship of the curtain that separates us from our own enlightenment. So I prayed that that veil might be torn away for me, that I might be able to part that curtain in this lifetime and allow the brilliance of God to dwell within me. When I was finished, I clapped my hands to let the spirit of God know that I was now finished and that it could leave me and go to the next pilgrim on his way.

Shakkai and I walked down a less trodden path leading into a forested area.

"Where are we going, O-Sensei?" I asked.

"Just follow me," she said. "I have something very interesting to show you."

I followed her through the dense forest until we came to a clearing with a smaller shrine, a temple also made of unpainted wood, with stairs leading to the entrance, and a thatched roof. And we again prostrated ourselves, clapping before we prayed to bring in the spirit. "This is a temple erected to the goddess Aramitama Nomiya. This is called the Temple of the Rough August Soul. What that means is that she is the dark side of the Goddess of the Sun. It is said in legend that, centuries ago, there was an empress who came to worship the Goddess of the Sun, and she was possessed by her dark side. It was then that they erected the temple in her honor."

I asked, "What do you mean, 'in her honor'? The dark side of the goddess must be like the devil."

"That is correct. Often the Shinto people see the devil as a fox. In their being, the fox is the fool's side of the gods. Very seldom do they erect a temple to honor the opposite side of the goddess. So there must be a reason for this, and this is the real reason why I brought you here. I want you to sit and listen to your heart, because I know you have been concerned about Master Hara and all that has occurred. I want you to think about him and realize that, long ago, spirit possession permeated almost every area of the Shinto religion. Today that has been almost forgotten. When we call in the spirit of God, in a sense we are possessed by that spirit. It is not unlike the cults that used to abound in this tradition. So think well, my child, about this."

I sat for a long time, looking again at the golden sky and the long sunset that we had enjoyed, and I wondered about all that Shakkai had told me. Then suddenly there was a burst of light in my heart. I could feel a glow emanating from my chest, and something occurred to me for the first time. I had gotten an inkling of it before, but never like this, and I looked at Shakkai and said, "Aha."

Shakkai looked back at me and said, "Aha!" and laughed. We laughed together, and she slapped me on the back. "Now tell me," she said.

"Now I understand. Now I really see it," I said. "It is so often in life that we learn from the opposite side of the goddess or the god. It is that dark side which possesses us, in a sense. That's our failing. That's our weakness. And it is from that side that we learn. It is from that side that we receive the teachings that bring us to our wholeness. I understand, truly. I don't know that I can actually put it into words, but suddenly I no longer hate Master Hara for what he did to you. I understand from the depths of my soul, and I feel great compassion for him and the pain that he must live with every day of his life. O-Sensei, what will ultimately happen to Master Hara? It is not that I feel sorry for him. Don't misunderstand me, but I am really curious."

"As I said, he has gone back to China, to his masters, and I think he has had a very deep lesson, and I pray for him," Shakkai said. She held her *gohei* to her heart and to her forehead, to her third eye. "I pray that he will come back to us whole once again, though it may not be in this lifetime."

"Taoists do not believe in many lifetimes, do they?" I asked.

"I believe that each lifetime is another reflection in the great mirror of the sacred Tao, that other lifetimes are contained within this lifetime, and that this lifetime is contained within other lifetimes, that there is no difference, and there is no time. There is only our perception of this dream that we call reality. So, yes and no to your question. I feel that we are never born and that we never die. To be caught within the imprisonment of a specific faith or belief structure—Shintoism, Buddhism, whatever—is a frightening idea to me, because it leaves no room for something new, for something bright and polished and foreign, within which the mysteries of life may be contained, and yet I have reverence for many aspects of different faiths.

"I hope that you will witness your feelings of anger toward Hara-san and others who come your way. Perhaps your father will now take a different position in your heart. It is not that I am asking you to give away your anger in life. It is important to feel every emotion, but to be consumed by that emotion would be a tragedy."

Shakkai got up from the ground, held my hand for a moment, and smiled at me in that wonderful way of hers. The sky was almost dark. There was a chill in the air, and the last glow of the sun reflected in her eyes, giving her the appearance of a giant primal feline ready to pounce. For a moment I was taken aback. Then my teacher softened her eyes, knowing that in some way we had understood something new between us. We moved on down the path on our journey home.

29

Isles of the Immortals

Before our body existed,
One energy was already there.

— SUN BU-ER

This time, when I moved out of my Dreamlodge and into the dream with Shakkai in her compound, we were sitting by the pond in my part of the sacred garden. I looked around at the trees that had grown. Everything looked as if several years had passed. I realized, as I looked at my own hands and at Shakkai's face, that many, many years had passed. There was a different timbre in my voice, and I could sense a degree of serenity in my spirit that I had not experienced as a younger O Kiku. But there was also a sadness in this meeting.

"I cannot imagine my life without you," I said to O-Sensei.

The old woman looked at me with a smile, and then she stood up carefully, but with the agility of someone many years her junior. Taking her flute out from her sleeve, she played a haunting melody that seemed to catch in the wind and float around us, leaving me with a feeling of joy and brightness. Then, placing the flute on the cloth in front of me that was spread for lunch and tea, she said, "Music is like life. The song that you just heard was here for a moment, and now it is gone somewhere else. It has moved away for someone else to enjoy. Our life force moves through us like this melody."

She sat down across from me and looked in my eyes for a long time. There was a communication far beyond words, which would only restrict her meaning. Picking up a stick, she felt its smoothness with her fingers and then gave it to me, saying, "Hold this stick for a time, while we speak."

I held the twig, feeling its roughness and the smoothness of its bark, as she continued.

"We can never imagine losing the people that we love most, because it is so mysterious. Most people build a home and function within society, and then their downfall is that they identify with that family or that job they have created. Most people, O Kiku, think that they are the job that they do. Don't you?"

I thought for a moment and said, "Yes, it is true, Sensei. I think of myself as an apprentice. I think of myself even as a woman. Perhaps, considering what you're saying, even that is too tenuous."

She smiled and sat back on her heels and looked up. The blue of the sky reflected in her eyes with such a depth that it matched the pond that shimmered peacefully next to us. I looked at her beautiful face as the sunlight played across the furrows at the corners of her eyes and across her forehead. Gray tendrils of hair came down around her face, and the wind caught them and moved them like the sweet grasses in the meadow. I loved this woman so, I could not bear the thought of our not being together for all time. Finally I expressed this sense of longing to her.

"I cannot understand, or really even forgive, life for being set up the way it is," I finally said. "This circle of regeneration, of death and rebirth, with all that we have done together, Shakkai, with all that I know in my heart to be true about eternity, I still want to make this life more permanent. I still seek a home, a temple, in which we can always worship together and feel the presence of the sacred Tao."

"But don't you see, my child?" Shakkai said, reaching out and brushing the tears from my cheeks. "The sacred Tao is already within you. You do not want to stay in school forever. You need to move on, and the more you try to make this life a fixture, something you can hang on to, the more it will disappoint you. There is no way to make anything in this life substantial enough to depend upon. It simply is not the nature of this life, and you are fooling yourself if you think otherwise. The only permanence in this life is your sacred witness, that place of power and emptiness within you which watches the unfolding of time forever. That place of witnessing, in truth, is all that any of us have. And the wisdom that you bring to that watching, to that place of power, is the imprint that is left on your spirit shield, and it shows that you have lived the goodness of your heart.

"Now take that stick I gave you a moment ago and write your name in the water of the pond."

I leaned over, pressing the grass beneath the palm of my hand, feeling the earth, a little damp and very fertile between my fingers. It gave me a sense of strength. Taking the stick, I started to write my name, and as I did, little rivulets of water were formed that caught the reflection of the sun and the sky, and even, for a moment, the cone of Mount Fuji. Almost instantly those rivulets were gone. I kept writing and I kept writing. Then I sat back and thought for some time. Shakkai simply watched me, her eyes remote again in that place of mystery.

"And what is that to you?" she finally said, indicating the pond.

"Writing my name in the water is like my life, isn't it, Sensei? It is written for a moment, catching the light of the sun and the essence of the earth, and then it is gone, as if it were never there."

"Oh no," Shakkai added, "that is not quite the way it is, because you were never born and you never die. Your name is written from one lifetime to another. And each time it is written in the pond, a different light is reflected. It could never be the same again."

"I feel, inside me, something that wants to hang on," I said. "No matter what I know, no matter what I do, I don't want to let go of you, and I don't want to let go of Kat-san. It is too hard for me. I feel like a wanderer in the forest. I have no place to rest, no temple within my own soul."

Shakkai looked at me for a long time, waiting. Then she took a ruby ring off her finger and placed it on mine. "It was my mother's," she said. "I have worn it always. You are truly my daughter now."

I held the ring and her hand to my heart. I felt so much love for my teacher. And then something happened. My heart began to open, and as it did, Shakkai rose and came behind me and again placed the palm of her hand over my heart. Gently she told me to close my eyes. As I did so, I went into a deep trance, with Shakkai holding me. My heart opened until I thought I would burst. My mind was filled with a golden light like the sun. I took a deep breath, and a serenity came upon me as if in the stillness I had frozen my spirit, and all that I had been saying seemed to run like water down through my body and out through my feet into the earth. I saw the face of power, as if for a moment my eyes opened up and saw the truth of what is, that we are all part of each other, that we are, indeed, all one, that there is no death, that it is the mind and the desire and the yearning for wholeness that keeps us from being whole. In that moment of such profound sadness a moment ago, it was as if I let go, finally, because the pain was so deep. I just simply let go. And I realized that to control life is to lose life, that in fact, all that I had thought to be true in the physical world was part of an illusion, a sacred dream, through which we learn.

Still sitting in this trance of extreme grace, I heard the voice of Kat-san from far away. My intent followed the sound of his voice. In the dream he took my hand and asked me to come sit with him in my most sacred part of the garden. There was a loud cracking sound at the back of my neck, and a pulling sensation in my solar plexus. I was moving out of my body in the practice of *hsien*, the art of lifting the astral body out of the physical body. I walked forward, leaving my physical being behind with Shakkai, and I followed Kat-san, my hand in his, my heart full of love. I knew that I had stepped into a third hoop of power, as if what I had been was over now. I had finally found the sacred key to the gateway, to the next level of my understanding. I realized, as I went the short distance with Kat-san, that I no longer had that endless fear of letting go, of losing someone. I suddenly was no longer afraid of ending my life, of experiencing death. The terror of the unknown that had haunted me through so much of my experience was gone. I knew Kat-san was leading me to a ceremony that would celebrate these realizations in such a way that my spirit shield would be imprinted with this wisdom for all time. I knew that Kat-san was my spirit husband incarnate, and that this day would only bring us to the end of one dream of our many dreams together.

I turned to find the Holy One sitting next to me. Her arm was around my shoulders, balancing me. She looked into my eyes with the wildness of her stare and laughed uproariously at the confusion on my face. Then a great silence permeated every cell of my body, and I knew that there was no more to say, that she had given me the supreme gift—the gift of vision, the gift of understanding. I looked around for Kat-san. He had gone to sit respectfully some distance away in meditation below my Absolute Control Stone. I felt a tremendous need to share my thoughts with him. Presently he crossed the garden, carefully, each step silent and carefully placed, until he reached my side. I turned to introduce him to the Holy One, but she was gone. For a moment there was a gripping sensation in my heart, and I realized that I would never again see her in this lifetime, that she had come to teach me, and that was over now. I asked him to be silent for a moment, and out of my *hu* I took sacred herbs and held them up to the sky, to the sun, to my sacred mountain. Letting the herbs drift in the wind from my fingers, I thanked the sacred Tao and the Goddess Mother for allowing me this time with the Holy One, that she had taught me well. I thanked her spirit from the bottom of my heart.

Then I turned to Kat-san, who was sitting quietly by my side. He took my hand.

"For true love to live between a man and a woman, or any two people, you must die into the other," he said. "O Kiku, think deeply. Move your mind into a more placid place. Think carefully about a vision you had last night in your sleep."

When I did this, an image floated to the surface, like a tiny piece of seaweed from the bottom of the ocean. I realized that last night in my sleep I had had a sense that Kat-san had shifted into a feminine being for just a moment, that he had moved into the feminine shield that he was learning to carry so well in the world. I realized that he had appeared to be androgynous for one split second before I lost the vision.

"You see, O Kiku, we are not separated, not even by our sexuality. Remember, as I have told you and your teachers have said so many times, the first lesson of power is that we are all separate. We are isolated from each other in this sacred dream called life, and then, in a moment of your sleeping last night, enlightenment appeared to you like a death, which in fact it is. It is a death to the way that you have always envisioned the world. People experience that death differently. Some go crazy for a while. Some become filled with unnamed fears and move through the ancient Bardos, the plateaus of judgment after death, one by one in a waking state. They go through the terrors of their past and present lives, not understanding that the energy is simply clearing, making wholeness possible. You see, you were given the gift of vision very quickly. The veils were torn away. Through your ability to visualize so clearly, what you imagine is real, and you have learned that well. Always remember the last lesson of power is that we are all part of each other, and there is no separation between you and a horse or a dog or a stone or me, that we are part of the same life force, and all mirrors of each other's different aspects."

I fully unwrapped my sacred *hu* and showed it to Kat-san. We shared the great intimacy of our experiences together. I had left herbs in a tiny pouch inside the *hu,* and just like the Holy One, I had drawn pictures of the sacred mountains and the valley I had gone to as a child that had been a womb of innocence for me. I gave him these pictures and the herbs, saying, "These are for you. They are for your healing, if ever you become ill. These are pictures for your spirit, and when you are lonely and we are apart, take out the pictures and go, and I will surely meet you there."

We sat together for a long time contemplating the sweet voices of nature. Then I knew it was time. I opened my eyes as Kat-san rose to his feet. For several minutes I contemplated a lotus blossom resting peacefully on the surface of the pond. Then all I could hear was the sound of wind at high speed. The whistle was so piercing and intense that it hurt my ears. I saw nothing but the white flower. Kat-san stood before me, standing in his position of power, his sword raised to strike, but I did not see it move. My eyes fixed on the lotus blossom; I saw it move imperceptibly into the air and then settle back down onto its stalk. It was cleanly severed. I had not blinked. I had not seen the blade move through the air, it had been so swift. The samurai's movements had been impeccable, faster than a cobra's strike. The cool morning glow of the sun shone down through the branches of the bamboo trees that surrounded the pond next to us. The snow-covered cone of Mount Fuji glistened in poised reflection and power. I knew that all existence was perfect, that this lifetime was about to end, like the life of the lotus blossom. The flowering of my youth was gone, but the fragrance of my life force continued. Soon I would be like that magnificent flower, my head severed from my body and yet still resting on the stalk as if nothing had happened, as if everything was as it had been.

I looked toward Kat-san, knowing that our hearts beat as one.

There was no space between us. There was no difference, man or woman. It did not matter that no one understood that. The mysteries that we had shared together were ours alone. I was holding my sacred *hu,* my gourd that represented the *shakkai,* the captured landscape of our lives together. Too tiny was the garden to step into with anything but our spirit feet, and we would walk there for all time, knowing the blending of our souls and the history of our work together on this earth.

There were no words between Kat-san and me. We knelt facing each other on the tatami mat spread with sacred white silken cloth. I placed the *hu* between us. We had created a magic that would live on beyond our years. I bowed before my samurai and he raised his sword. I looked again at the lotus blossom shimmering in the sunlight. It was still moist with the morning dew, each droplet reflecting a tiny picture of our sacred mountain, just as every one of us reflects the light of the Great Spirit. In moments I would be like the lotus blossom, forever gone to this reality and yet reflecting its magical light into the universe. The last thing I heard was the swish of the blade. It sounded like the freedom of the wind that I so dearly loved. How fitting that it was my last awareness. Our sacrifice was the offering of life to the highest dream.

I was at sea. Again I heard the sound of wind rushing by my ears, but it was constant. Then I looked up and the garden and Kat-san were gone. I realized that I was on a ship. Above me were white sails straining against the blustering winds. There were many people in the boat around me, but I did not recognize them, nor did I really focus on their faces. Off in the distance was a vision so wonderful that I could not tear my eyes away. I was not frightened. I felt that an inner truth was leading me toward a destination, and I saw ahead of me three islands lifting their craggy mountains and dense green foliage above the clouds and the morning mist. They sparkled like crystal in the sunlight, as if they were encrusted with fine and sacred jewels.

As the ship sailed closer, I remembered, far back in my mind, my teacher's voice, and I heard her speaking to me about the Isles of the Immortals. It was then that I realized I had passed into another dimension, that I had died to the reality I had always known. I looked down at my body. It seemed unimportant now. There was only a shadow there. I didn't look too closely. My eyes were drawn back to the islands toward which we were sailing.

Shakkai's voice in my head was sweet and gentle. "The Isles of the Immortals," she said, "are the islands of eternity. Smallness is power, because in smallness we condense and contain the vastness of the universe within a single seed, and from that seed is born all of life. It is in your smallness that you have been able to go through the tiny neck of your sacred hu, your beautiful gourd, into the garden of the immortals where all life is possible. You are never born and you never die. It is on these islands that you will live forever. It is love that has brought you here. It is your love for me, for Kat-san, for the sacred Tao, and your love for all of mankind and the earth and the universe and all that lives. It is the teachings of the path of heart, the expansion of your soul with goodness and joy, that have brought you here, to this sacred sea. When most travelers approach the Isles of the Immortals, the fog descends and the clouds obscure the island mountains from view, and the ships pass without so much as a hint of where they really are.

"For centuries the great shoguns and the great emperors and empresses have sent ships out to sea. Legends have been told to them about eternal life, but they did not understand that when you go outside yourself, when you search outside of your own sacred circle, the islands will always be obscured from sight. It is when you move to the interior world, to the sacred gardens and shakkais within each of us that then you may chart a sure course across the sea. When you look through the fog this time, you will see the mountains gleaming in the dawn's glow. When you move inside, into the tiny atom of your power, you will find a strength like no other. It is then, when you set sail across the sea, that you will find eternal life."

As I looked out across the bow of the ship and heard again the wind in the sails like music on the horizon, I saw that soon we would be beaching the boat on the sacred islands. But just before we reached the sand, I felt a dimness to my eyes and a sinking, and

I knew with a profound sadness that I was not yet to set foot on the Isles of the Immortals, that it was a glimpse of truth given me by my teachers so that I could then relate the story to others. I knew beyond doubt that there is hope and a meaning in this life, that for all the tragedy and pain in our struggle toward enlightenment, there is a great design, that there is an art to this sacred painting, and that we are all lending it our color and inspiration.

·30·

The Sisterhood of the Shields

♦

The task is the door.
When the task returns to One,
the One is ever present.

— SUN BU-ER

♦

The next thing I knew, I was looking up at the sky in Manitoba from the bottom of the now-familiar creekbed. Icy water was flowing over me, and I was struggling to the surface with hands holding my shoulders down. I thought surely I would drown. I was gasping for air and screaming at the top of my lungs for them to let go of me. Every bone in my body ached. Every muscle screamed for relaxation, as Agnes and Ruby once again dragged me out of the creek and wrapped me in a Hudson Bay blanket. I sat down in the sand and glared at my teachers.

"But I had almost reached the shore," I whispered.

"The what?" Ruby asked, hands on her hips, shaking her head at me.

"The shore of the Isles of the Immortals. How could you have thrown me in the creek and awakened me so rudely?"

I was furious. I looked at Agnes, who was sitting next to me on her heels, not unlike Shakkai. The thought of Shakkai brought tears to my eyes. I looked at Agnes and Ruby, and I knew that I would not be traveling back to see Shakkai, perhaps ever again. Agnes came and put her arms around my shoulders and held me for a moment.

Then, sitting down brusquely in front of me, Ruby took my head in her hands and forced me to look into her eyes. "You were gone too long, Little Wolf. You frightened us nearly to death. That must never, ever happen again. You went almost too far this time. If you had set foot on the Isles of the Immortals, that would have been the end of it, that would have torn it. That would have been all she wrote," Ruby said, almost yelling at me, slapping her knees for emphasis. Then she got up and paced back and forth furiously. I had seldom seen her so angry. I pulled the blanket around my shoulders and simply sat there. There were so many images in my mind that I was having an extraordinarily difficult time remembering who and where I was.

Finally, Agnes asked me to look at her. She looked into my eyes for a long time, felt my muscles, and poked me all over my body.

"What are you doing, Agnes? Stop it," I said.

"I am just testing you to make sure you are really here, that you have come back to us whole."

Ruby guffawed at that statement. Then, sitting down again in front of me, Ruby said, "Now come. Your circle is waiting for you."

"What do you mean, Ruby?"

"In your absence," she said, "the Sisterhood of the Shields has gathered to welcome you home."

I stood up, and in the distance I could see smoke curling up through the branches in the high pines near the cabin. A dense fog had gathered in the valley, and as I strained my eyes, looking through the tendrils of fog that swirled in and out around the stream and the poplar trees, I could see, in the distance, tripods and shields with their symbols, feathers, and brilliant colors shining with a dazzling presence around the sacred fire. I could see, walking toward me, my sisters, my teachers. Twin Dreamers was moving down the trail with Zoila and She Who Walks with the Wind. I had not known of this gathering. It had been several years since our entire circle had met in ceremony. I was so profoundly excited to see them that I was speechless. Tears of joy ran down my cheeks, and I realized with a deep expansion of my heart and spirit the incredible experience that I had just lived through.

For a moment there was a movement in a tree down the trail and off to the left. For a moment I thought I caught sight of the Old Holy One in the tree, her wild hair catching the leaves and her marvelous, toothless grin imitating me in a gentle laugh. I stood up, searching the branches through the mist, but I guess I was wrong, because there was only the shadow of a hawk circling high above, her shadow fashioning spirals over the ground where we stood.

I took a deep breath of northern air, the scent of sweetgrass and pine pungent in my nostrils. I took Ruby's hand as Agnes reached out and took my other hand. They led me down the trail toward the Sisterhood of the Shields.

Then Ruby stopped and turned to look at me. She said, "You have danced with the Wheel of the Ancestors. And you have danced with the Wheel of Karma. Your cup is full now. Come. The Sisters wait to hear of your story and your dreaming. Then your cup will be empty once again. Your next teacher awaits you. It is time, now, to go back to your self-shield in the center of all these teachings, to the Wheel of Dreams, where you will begin to understand the third hoop of power and how all of these life paintings fit together into one great sand painting called your life. You are awake now. Come. We will all feast together and do ceremony."

ing and pull another hand," Aldib said as he drew the spear toward the spearhead of the Shield.

"Then Rand stopped and stared. He had to look at top, she said. "You have danced with the Wheel of the Ages once. And you have danced with the Wheel of fortune. You can't can now. Come, the sister will go free of your lands, and your liberation too. They will supple once again. Your axes as they are to you too. It flows that came back to your old shield might wake of all that reaches, to the Wheel of Destiny here you will keep or could send the third body of power, and how afraid these life sentence. All together and one once more pointing, pulled your way beauti-ful to now. Come. We will all start raging and do it anyway."

For the last ten years, I've been describing my learning and my path. It has been a joy to do this. In continuing my journey, I would be grateful if you would share your insights with me.

Please write me at:

Lynn Andrews
2934 1/2 Beverly Glen Circle
Box 378
Los Angeles, CA 90077
800-726-0082

Please send me your name and address so I can share any new information with you.

In Spirit,

Lynn V. Andrews